Lucifer's Flood

and the

Little Season

Lucifer's Flood

and the

Little Season

Allan Cornford

Table of Contents

Preface

The primordial world referred to in the Bible as "the world that then was", perished by water, and this by the Word of God. A deluge of cataclysmic proportions, which is sometimes referred to as Lucifer's Flood. By the same Word, this present world which began with Adam, will finally end, along with the heavens and the earth, in a cataclysm of fire. This will occur at some point after the end of the 'Little Season', a time of great Satanic deception, such as humanity has never experienced before. Hence the reason for the title of this book; 'Lucifer's Flood and the Little Season'.

Differing Views

The thousand-year reign of Jesus, also known as the millennial kingdom, is a period of time between the great tribulation and the little season, when Jesus will reign over all the earth. The purpose of the thousand-year reign is to allow for the fulfilment of the promises God made with Israel, Jesus, the Gentiles, and the very creation. For the entire one thousand years, Satan remains bound within the bottomless pit.

Revelation 20:3. And cast him [Satan] into the bottomless pit, and shut him up, and set a seal upon him, that he should deceive the nations *no more, till* the *thousand years* should be fulfilled: *and after that* he must be loosed a *little season*.

Revelation 20:7. And when the *thousand years* are expired, Satan shall be loosed out of his prison,

Full, or Hyper-Preterism would have us believe, that ALL end times Bible prophecy has been fulfilled, including the final war of Gog and Magog, and the Great White Throne Judgement. God's forever plan is now, and society and the world in general, continues its decline into a cess-pit of immorality and criminality without punishment. Our hope is in death, followed by entry into New Jerusalem, in the new heavens and the new earth.

Futurism would have us believe, that come 70AD, Jesus Christ had only fulfilled half of the prophecies that he had previously made during his ministry years. He will come back when society and the world in general, is perverted and wicked enough, to rapture the Christians, and to judge everyone else, for killing him and all the prophets and saints.

A-millennialism would have us believe that the kingdom of God is here, and will keep getting better and better.

Post-millennialism would tell us that the millennium has passed, but the kingdom of God remains forever.

Little Season post-millennialism, believes that the millennium has passed, and the kingdom of God reigns, but Satan, the prince of the power of the air, and the god of this world, or age, is deceiving the nations into thinking that he rules. Which in one sense he does of course, but *only* under the authority of our sovereign God. For Satan effectively works for Jesus Christ, and he knows it.

People fall into three categories: Those who actively serve Satan, those who actively serve Jesus Christ, and those who are still trying to find meaning in life, and remain largely ignorant of the spiritual battles constantly raging around them. This third group need to wake up before it's too late.

Introduction

In my previous book, "Tartarian Reign? Or Millennial Kingdom?", we explored how throughout our lives, we have been deceived over pretty much everything. Such would include how the better part of one thousand years of world history has been falsified, distorted, and kept hidden from the historical time-line. And how there's a strong possibility that we, and the few generations before us, have all been born into the time period, warned of in Revelation 20:3, and referred to as the 'Little Season'. An open-ended time-period of great deception, leading up to the final battle on earth, against Jesus Christ.

Such a notion would fly straight in the face of what is generally taught by the mainstream denominations, and by far the majority of the evangelical churches. Yet it is worth noting that no church or denomination, and no theologian or individual, has a one hundred percent monopoly on the interpretation of Scripture.

Including myself of course. For the very best I can offer, is to share my understanding of the Scriptures. And whilst I can never profess to have got everything right, not by any stretch of the imagination, my intention is to concentrate on certain subject matters, which generally speaking, are avoided like the plague by the majority of churches; mainstream or otherwise.

Having said that, let me be very clear, this is not intended to be a scholarly work, for I am not a Bible scholar. I just praise God that he doesn't require one to have a Master's Degree in Theology, before he sheds light upon his word. Do you feel like a king? Neither do I. But nevertheless;

It is the glory of God to conceal a thing: but the honour of kings *is* to search out a matter. *(Proverbs 25:2.)*

A Firm Foundation

Back in 2010, I spoke to fifty different church ministers or their secretaries, in my home county of Sussex in the UK, This was a complete cross-section of denominational and non-denominational churches, with the exception of the *Gospel Standard Strict Baptists*, who use the *AKJV*, and the *Roman Catholic* Churches who tend to use the *New American Bible* or the *New Jerusalem Bible.*

Out of the fifty, there was **not** one who still used the AKJV. Forty-one used the *NIV* as their main Bible of choice, although some said they would also consider using other modern versions including the *Message*. None though had given much thought about using the AKJV, apart from one *Anglican* minister, who took a reading from it during the Sunday morning service, for the sake of his elderly congregation. The rest of the time he used the *New International Version*. I spoke to three ministers who used the *New King James Version* as their Bible of choice, whilst the remainder of the fifty I contacted, used either the *Revised Standard Version* or the *English Standard Version.*

I was quite surprised at the findings, but have since heard of a Minister from Lincolnshire who done similar research back in 2004, and was only aware of three other churches in the entire county still regularly using the *AKJV.*

When asked why they chose not to use the *AKJV*, the church leaders I spoke to, all gave a fairly standard response, which went along the lines of; 'Well, we know it was once used by every church in the land, but it's out-dated, hard to understand, and is full of thees thys and thous.' 'Okay' I thought, that's true enough, but why didn't the modern translations just replace these words with you and yours etc. and modernize the verb endings? For by now I had discovered with certain words altered or omitted, deeper truths could no longer be found in most of these modern versions. Furthermore there were instances of grammatical differences in more recent translations and versions, which completely changed the emphasis of a particular verse or entire passage.

There are certain words in the KJV, that act as signposts, if you like. A signpost directs you somewhere, and without that signpost, you often don't realize there is somewhere else to go. The word *replenish* being a classic example. For there are certain teachings contained within the KJV, which have been systematically removed from nigh on all other versions of the Bible. Why? To keep us ignorant about a former age which existed between the first two verses of the Book of Genesis maybe? An age, aeon, or world, that was completely wiped out, and leaving the earth barren and lifeless?

Here then is a question. There are two men, each with a different version of the Bible in their hand, and they both make the same statement. 'I have in my hand the word of God, which is the final authority on all matters of truth.' If both versions 99 percent of the time teach exactly the same thing, but the other 1 percent of the time have slightly different teachings, then which man is right? It certainly can't be both of them, for when it comes to the final authority of God in a matter, there can be no room for error.

Am I saying that I think the translators of the AKJV were divinely inspired? No, or at least, not in the sense that those who penned the original scriptures were. But I do believe that certain specific words and the precise use of grammar, came by way of informed choice, rather than a case of holy guesswork on the part of the translators. For the Author's signature is all over the AKJV, which when seen, is undeniable evidence of supernatural intervention.

The Jesuits know this *now*, and knew it back then, in 1605, when they plotted, but failed, to assassinate King James, in order to prevent him from financing the the 54 men separated into 6 groups in 3 different locations, from rendering the Word of God (accepted as inspired texts) into English.

The AKJV has, and will in the future take the brunt of criticism as being a Masonic Bible, the private work of King James I, having been altered by Francis Bacon's (nome de plume of Sir Matthew Tobie) Rosicrucian 'Knights of the Golden Helmet', or a document written in King's English. This is a bold-faced lie; for it is the *only* Authorized Word of God in the English language.

Authorized King James Bible

Nobody, not even God, can have more than one testament. Both the Old and the New testaments, testify of one person. Jesus.

John 5:39. Search the scriptures; for in them ye think ye have eternal life: and they are they which *testify* of me.

There is a very real sense by which, it's not possible to separate the Word=God *(John 1:1)* which became flesh, from the word, as it is written. It could even be said, that the Bible is God in written form. For whilst it is at the name of Jesus, that every knee shall bow, God is so protective of his truth, he has magnified his word above *all* his name. Furthermore his words are purified *seven* times. The number seven in Scripture, being the great spiritual number of perfection and completeness.

Psalms 138:2. I will worship toward thy holy temple, and praise thy name for thy lovingkindness and for thy truth: for thou hast magnified thy word *above all* thy name.

Psalms 12:6. The words of the LORD are pure words: as silver tried in a furnace of earth, purified *seven* times.

Proceeded by the Tyndale Bible, the Matthew Bible, the Coverdale Bible, the Great Bible, the Geneva Bible and the Bishop's Bible, in 1611, the King James Version became the *seventh* purified word of God, and the only Authorized Bible in the English language.

The original bible was divided into 49 books, rather than 66. This does not affect the accuracy of the texts in the KJV; Seven is the great spiritual number of Divine Perfection. 7X7 has a Divine Stamp whereas 66 (11X6) is the Stamp of Man. Study and or Margin Notes are *all* the work of man. The KJV is not a new Bible, it is the inerrant Word of God delivered via the Holy Ghost, and the Father, the Word, and the Holy Ghost are one. *(1 John 5.)*

Heptadic Design

Dr Ivan Panin proved beyond a shadow of a doubt, that the KJV adheres to the Heptadic Structure of 7, impossible for the writers from Genesis to Revelation to duplicate. This Heptadic design is, if you like, God's Self-authenticating Signature.

After graduating from Harvard in 1882, the Russian-born agnostic, Ivan Panin, converted to Christianity. He made a discovery in 1890 that showed a phenomenal mathematical design underlying both the Greek text of the New Testament and the Hebrew text of the Old Testament.

Writes Pastor Bob in *'The Inspired Word of God', par*t 4;

> From that point on, Ivan Panin devoted over 50 years of his life to exploring the numerical structure of the Scriptures; he generated over 42,000 pages of detailed hand-penned pages of analysis notes.
>
> This discovery became known as the "Heptadic Structure" of the Bible. The recurrence of the number "seven" - or exact multiples of seven - is found throughout the KJV Bible. Some examples of this feature are the Sabbath on the seventh day; the seven years of plenty, and the seven years of famine in Egypt, the seven priests and seven trumpets marching around Jericho and the Sabbath Year of the land. All are well-known patterns of the number "seven" found in the Scriptures. Don't forget the "seven" years it took Solomon to build the Temple or the narrative in 2nd Kings, chapter 5 where Elisha sent a messenger to tell Naaman to wash in the river Jordan "seven" times. The book of Revelation is filled with surface patterns of "sevens".
>
> To the general population, and even the Christian community, these patterns appear as some sort of a senseless riddle or strange joke. However, there is a much deeper meaning to the number "seven" as Ivan Panin discovered. There are amazing numerical properties hidden within the Biblical texts-both the Old Testament Hebrew and the New Testament Greek of the Textus-Receptus manuscripts - that not only demonstrate an intricacy of design but also testifies to the authorship of a "supernatural" origin!

Nuggets of Truth

The word "man", is a generic term, which is even applied to Lucifer, and the angels at times. Yet the word "mankind" is only ever used of man created in the image and the likeness of God, and only appears *six* times throughout the Scriptures. Because man was created on the sixth day, hence the number 6 in the Bible, is representative of human weakness, sin, and the devil, and has its fulfilment in the number 666.

The words in italics in the King James Bible (the pronoun "he" for example) are words that were added by the translators, purely for grammatical reasons. The number 7 in the Bible is considered to be the spiritual number of perfection and completeness.

When God first spoke to Moses from the midst of a burning bush, he declared his name as I AM.

Exodus 3:14. And God said unto Moses, I AM THAT I AM: and he said, Thus shalt thou say unto the children of Israel, I AM hath sent me unto you.

On *seven* occasions in the Gospel of John the words "I am he" are spoken by Jesus. Without exception the pronoun "he" appears each time in italics for grammatical reasons. For example;

John 13:19. Now I tell you before it come, that, when it is come to pass, ye may believe that I am [he.]

I've heard some say that the italicized words should be removed from the KJB because they did not appear in the original Hebrew or Greek Text. Okay, so let's give it a try. Hence on the 7 occasions in the original Greek Text Jesus declares himself as I AM. (God in the Flesh).

On the evening of his arrest, a band of armed men led by Judas along with officers from the chief priests and Pharisees approached Jesus in the garden of Gethsemane.

We're looking for Jesus of Nazareth, they said, to which Jesus replied I AM.

John 18:6. As soon then as he had said unto them, I am [*he*], they went backward, and fell to the ground.

The entire band of officers and temple guards were bowled over backwards by the power of the words *I* AM.

And no, one has no need whatsoever to be a Greek scholar to grasp hold of this astounding Truth.

One Lord

The AKJV, which is its own interpreter, clearly teaches that Jesus, being one with the Father, is God. Who is the one Lord? For the scriptures tell us that the one Lord is our God. Yet the same scriptures tell us that Jesus is the Lord of all.

Deuteronomy 6:4. Hear, O Israel: The LORD our God *is* one LORD:

Mark 12:29. And Jesus answered him, The first of all the commandments is, Hear, O Israel; The Lord our God is one Lord:

Acts 10:36. The word which God sent unto the children of Israel, preaching peace by Jesus Christ: (he is Lord of all:)

Ephesians 4:5. One Lord, one faith, one baptism,

Philippians 2:11. And *that* every tongue should confess that Jesus Christ *is* Lord, to the glory of God the Father.

So, I ask again; who is the one Lord? For it cannot be Jesus **unless** he is God. Certain names, including Lord, are capitalized in the KJV for a reason, because LORD is a SPIRITUAL designation of JESUS, and the covenant name of God is JEHOVAH *(Exodus 6:3)* JAH *(Psalms 68:4),* JESUS *(Matthew 1:25.)*

Jesus, the Word made flesh, the Creator of all things, didn't evolve, or grow up from childhood to **become** Christ the Lord. He was Christ the Lord on the very day of his birth.

Luke 2:11. For unto you is born this day in the city of David a Saviour, **which is** Christ the Lord.

YHWH (Yahweh/Yeshua) has no reference at all in the KJV, nor in the original inspired texts. YHWH is equivalent with the Canaanite god El, (Saturn) and the Edo-mite national god Qos, and was later introduced into Scripture by the Masoretes ("Jewish" Scribes) and the Masoretic Texts dating from 1008AD.

There is 1 Bible aka the Word of God, 100% accurate and dependable; you can trust your soul with it. New Bible versions were born with Zionism in the 1880's and are drastically altered, or include footnotes to fit the agenda unfolding right now. There is no future 7 year tribulation; no new dispensation for Israel, no pre-tribulation rapture and no Hollywood-style aliens; don't be fooled. Jesuits invented these false doctrines just as they did Coronavirus.

World

The world, aeon, or the age in which we live, is shrouded by an intricate web of deceit, one which can never be fully unravelled by man, and it is not my intention to try and do so. Rather, to encourage the reader not to be satisfied with superficial answers, for the word of God, can withstand the most thorough of investigations, and God's Word and God's world, will *never* contradict one another.

Although we tend to use the terms "the earth" and "the world" interchangeably, this is not so with the King James Bible. They are two entirely different words, with two entirely different meanings, and one is *never* used as a substitute for the other, nor vice versa.

The *earth* always refers to the stationary, relatively flat, and circular plane that we live ON. Whereas the *world* is always a time-related word, which generally refers to the inhabitants, along with the environment and the social system, of the age that we live IN. But it can also refer to "the world to come", *(Matthew 12:32),* or even to the previous aeon, known as "the world that then was". *(2 Peter 3:6.)*

Luke 18:30. Who shall not receive manifold more in this **present** time, and in **the world to come** life everlasting.

Throughout the Bible, the emphasis is upon the *world* of mankind, those who dwell upon the *earth*, rather than the earth itself. The difference however between the earth and the world, becomes far more apparent in the New Testament.

Because God so loved the *world*, he gave his only begotten Son, and via the portal of a virgin womb, a child with no human father entered this *world* as Christ the Lord. *(Luke 2:11).* The light of the *world*. *(John 9:5).* A Saviour, foreordained before the *world* had even begun *(1 Peter 1:20),* to take away the sin of the *world*. Jesus defeated the god of this *world*, yet claimed himself to be *not* of this *world*. I could go on, but I'm sure you get my drift.

This failure to differentiate between the creation of the earth and the foundation (conception) of the world, has caused some creation ministries to teach that the *earth* itself is only 6,000 years old. This is not the case, but rather a teaching based upon a misunderstanding of certain terms used in Scripture. It is the world or age we inhabit which is a little under 6,000 years old.

For this reason, the creation of the earth, and the foundation of the world mean two entirely things. Two entirely different events in fact, and each separated by an untold period of time. Yet once again this Biblical truth is rarely, if ever, taught in church. It is a truth gleaned from studying the Bible, and reasoning from the Scriptures.

Foundation of the World

The word "foundation" appears 27 times in the New Testament, 10 of which are used in the term, "foundation of the world". The Greek word used in the New Testament for a literal solid foundation is *themelioo* as seen in;*Luke 6:48.* 'He is like a man which built an house, and digged deep, and laid the *foundation* on a rock'.[.......]

H*emelioo* means a literal solid foundation, whereas the meaning of the Greek word *katabole* is a deposition, or figuratively a *conception*, and is translated elsewhere in reference to Abram's wife Sara, as "to *conceive seed*". *(Hebrews 11:11)*. On each of the further 10 occasions where *katabole* is translated from the Greek text it is *always* found in the term, 'Foundation of the World'. The literal meaning of which would be, "the conception of the present world, aeon or age".

So as can be seen, although *katabole* and *themelioo* can both be translated as 'foundation' each has an entirely different meaning. Hence, because the words 'earth' and 'world' also have two different meanings, the *creation* of the *earth* and the *foundation* of the *world* are two entirely different events. Along with the heavens, the earth was created by God, in the *beginning*, whereas the foundation of this world, aeon, or age, occurred a little over 6,000 years ago, with the creation of Adam, or modern-day man, made in the image and likeness of God.

In the Book of Hebrews, we read that God made the *worlds (Hebrews 1:2)* and how by the word of God, the *worlds* were *framed*. *(Hebrews 11:3)*. It's very true that all things, both in the heaven and the earth, both the seen and the unseen, were created by God. *(Colossians 1:16)*. The term God 'Framed the Worlds' however, does not mean that he created the celestial orbs.

Worlds is translated from the Greek aion, and *Strongs New Testament Greek Dictionary* defines Aion as an Age (past, present or future). The Greek word translated as 'framed' is *Katartizo*, which means to repair or adjust, to fit, frame, mend or restore.

From a literal interpretation, we can now correctly understand that the worlds, or Ages, were Repaired or Restored by the Word of God.

Hebrews 11:3. Through faith we understand that the **worlds** were **framed** by the word of God, so that things which are seen were not made of things which do appear.

The point being, the Bible records three individual aeons or worlds, each one succeeding the other. The previous world utterly perished. This present world will end dramatically when the heavens dissolve and the elements melt. *(2 Peter 3:10-12.)* The world to come to be inherited by those who receive eternal life.

One way of understanding the 'world' which I've personally found to be helpful, is to imagine it as an incredibly long and permanently sealed cylinder, with one single entry point at one end, and one single exit point at the other. With no say in the matter, a series of physical contractions literally force each of us into the cylinder via the portal of the womb. When mother's waters break, it ensures that all who arrive in the world do so born of water, and although born innocent, all are destined to sin and to die. Any who rely on inherited religious tradition, and claim we 'choose' to sin have missed the point.

All men have an appointment with death, for none are righteous, all have sinned, and the soul that sins shall die. *(Ezekiel 18:20).* We all knowingly do wrong at times, but is sin really a personal choice? Or is it a person's destiny? An estimated 121 Billion souls have lived in this world since Adam, and 121 Billion have, or will die. Not sure about you, but to sin and die sounds pretty much like man's destiny to me. The big question is why?

Man cannot change his own destiny. But Jesus who takes away the sin of the world, and defeated death on man's behalf, certainly can.

For men of one blood and all nations, are here in this 'cylinder' as a result of a previous judgement. *(Psalm 82:1-7).* Yet men of one blood and all nations enter this world with a God-given birthright and purpose. Namely, to seek after and to find the Lord. *(Acts 17:27).* Jesus Christ died for the sins of *this* world alone. Not for the sins of 'the world that then was', nor those in the world to come.

All are subject to death even within the womb, hence already short of God's glory. For he is Life and life Everlasting. No man by natural birth (of water) is born as 'a son of God,' nor is he born into the 'kingdom of God'. We are born flesh and blood, and as such, cannot inherit the kingdom of God. *(1 Corinthians 15:50)*. All born of water are 'sons of men' and arrive in the image and likeness of a 'fallen' human father *(Genesis 5:3)*. While Jesus 'lights' every man born into the world *(John 1:9)*, all are delivered into a kingdom, and held captive by the power of darkness. *(Colossians 1:13)*. In a spiritual sense none are born as a child of the day, but born as a child of the night. *(1 Thessalonians 5:5)*.

Though it may seem rather harsh, all are born subject to the god of this world who holds the power of death. In other words, this world or age that we inhabit could be described as a terminal prison, a death-camp, and humanity are its prisoners. Although constantly faced with choices, we have no other choice but to be carried by time as we pass through the cylinder, until finally we arrive at the exit.

With no say in the matter, all leave the cylinder via the portal of death, beyond which lies the judgement. *(Hebrews 9:27)*. Regardless of social status, race or religion, all men are united in one thing. All will die for all have sinned, and all come short of God's Glory. *(Romans 3:23)*.

Ever wondered why Jesus insisted "Ye MUST be born again?" Not of water (the womb) and delivered IN to the world once more, but be born of the Spirit of God, and delivered OUT of the world.

John 3:5. Jesus answered, Verily, verily, I say unto thee, ***Except*** a man be born of water ***and*** of the Spirit, he ***cannot*** enter into the kingdom of God.

John 3:7. Marvel not that I said unto thee, Ye ***must*** be born again.

No man by supernatural birth ('Born of the Spirit') is delivered out of this world as a son of man or a child of the night, but as a son of God, and a child of the light. *(1 Thessalonians 5:5)*.

No longer subject to the god of this world, the power of darkness and death, but to God the Father of Lights, who is life and life everlasting. Our mortal body will still age and die of course, but our spirit remains secure in Jesus, and an immortal and glorious resurrection body awaits us. *(1 Corinthians 15:52)*.

The irony is, none can 'choose' to be born again, any more than we chose to be born in the first place. But we do have the freedom to seek after the Truth, and to believe that Jesus Christ died for our sins, that he was buried, and rose back to life on the third day according to the scriptures. *(1 Corinthians 15:3-4.)* And to repent.

In fact, since the time when Jesus fulfilled ***ALL*** righteousness, the ***only*** commandment that God has for all of mankind, is to repent. And having done so, God's only commandment for mankind is to believe.

The rest is down to God, for the moment a man truly repents and believes with both heart and mind, the truth of the gospel, he is instantaneously born of the Spirit, and empowered by Jesus Christ to become a son of God. For try as he might, no man can attain the degree of righteousness, required by our most holy God. But that which is impossible for man to achieve, is possible for God. For the righteousness of God is by faith of [in] Jesus Christ. *(Romans 3:22.)*

John 3:16. For God so loved the world, that he gave his only begotten Son, that whosoever believeth in him should not perish, but have everlasting life.

2 Corinthians 5:21. For he hath made [Jesus] *to be* sin for us, who knew no sin; that we might be made the righteousness of God in him.

Romans 9:31. But Israel, which followed after the law of righteousness, hath not attained to the law of righteousness.

Acts 17:30. And the times of this ignorance God winked at; but ***now*** commandeth ***all*** men every where to repent:

1 John 5:3. For this is the love of God, that we keep his commandments: and his commandments are not grievous.

1 John 3:23. And this is his commandment, That we should believe on the name of his Son Jesus Christ, and love one another, as he gave us commandment.

John 1:12. But as many as received him, to them gave he power to become the sons of God, *even* to them that believe on his name:

Yet this wonderful news is only made possible, because God had ordained, and chosen us in Christ, ***before*** he had even created mankind, or ***prior*** to the foundation of the world.

Ephesians 1:4. According as he hath chosen us in him before the foundation of the world, that we should be holy and without blame before him in love:

1 Peter 1:20. Who verily was foreordained before the foundation of the world, but was manifest in these last times for you.

Many might say; "but I played my own part, for it was I who chose to believe in Christ." In one sense you're right, for we all made a choice. But it's not possible to truly believe in Jesus, and what he has accomplished for the likes of you and I, without the faith to do so. And faith is a gift from God, which comes by hearing his word. For in the truest sense, it is you and I who were chosen by Christ. Not the other way round.

John 15:16. Ye have *not* chosen me, but I have chosen *you*, and ordained you, that ye should go and bring forth fruit, and *that* your fruit should remain: that whatsoever ye shall ask of the Father in my name, he may give it you.

Ephesians 2:8. For by grace are ye saved through *faith*; and that *not* of yourselves: *it is* the *gift* of God:

*Romans 10:17.*So then faith *cometh* by hearing, and hearing by the word of God.

Ye are gods

Many will argue how Jesus cannot possibly be God. For God is not a man, they say. In one sense of course, they are absolutely right. Yet the scriptures clearly inform us, that the Word, who was with God and **who was** God in the beginning *(John 1:1)* became flesh and dwelt amongst men. *(John 1:14.)* In other words, as a man, Jesus was the Word=God incarnate.

Let me be absolutely clear, for incarnation and reincarnation are 2 entirely different terms with 2 entirely different meanings, and only the former is a Biblical truth. The doctrine of incarnation is central to the Christian faith, for not only is man a fallen creature, who enters this world born of water (the womb) but is also born subject to death. Desperately in need of a Saviour, man himself is also an incarnate being. For it is Written!

"I have said, Ye *are* gods; and all of you *are* children of the most High". *(Psalms 82:6.)*

Confirmed by Jesus himself, who quoting from Psalms 82, said;"Is it not written in your law, I said, Ye are gods?" *(John 10:34.)*

When taken literally, the scriptures inform us that we all pre-existed as gods, and were born into this physical world as the result of a former judgement. The sentence being, Ye shall fall and die.

For way back in the depths of time, the children of the most High, referred to as "the gods", were summoned to attend an ancient heavenly courtroom. Here, judgement was duly executed by the most Righteous Judge, the most High, the God of gods; and sentence was passed.

Judgement for what exactly, we are not told. Nevertheless, it would seem that the sins committed by the gods, were severe enough to warrant the death sentence. It would also seem however, that because the gods are immortal, for the death sentence to be carried out, they first had to become mortal, otherwise known as incarnate beings. Hence, the gods were ordained to fall like one of the princes, and to die like a man.

Psalms 82:6-7. I have said, Ye *are* gods; and all of you *are* children of the most High. But ye shall die like men, and fall like one of the princes.

In *John 10:31* Jesus claimed that he and the Father are ***one***. The Jews ***rightly*** understood what Jesus was actually saying, but they refused to believe him. Hence they set out to stone him for blasphemy;

"because that thou, being a man, makest thyself God." *(John 10:33.)*

Instead of correcting them or even denying he was making himself God, Jesus quoted directly from *Psalms 82*. "Is it not written in your law, I said, Ye are gods?" *(John 10:34.)*

So what do you do with a statement like that? Did Jesus mean exactly what he said? How can men be gods? Remember, Jesus never took the words of scripture out of context. And the entire context of Psalm 82 is one of Divine Judgement upon the gods. Jesus continued his discourse with;

John 10:35-36. If he called them gods, unto whom the word of God came, and the scripture cannot be broken; Say ye of him, whom the Father hath sanctified, and sent into the world, Thou blasphemest; because I said, I am the Son of God?

What Jesus was effectively saying is; "Why castigate me for claiming to be God incarnate, when your own scriptures declare you are all gods incarnate."

The gods, who are immortal, were once judged and sentenced to fall, and thus to become mortal men and die. A 'religious' mind may find this hard to process, but there's a world of difference between religion and Truth. The Scripture is clear that the congregation wherein God stood, and those upon whom he passed judgement, were not an assembly of mighty humans, magistrates or otherwise, but an assembly of mighty gods.

Psalms 82:1. God standeth in the congregation of the mighty; he judgeth among the gods.

Psalms 82:7. But ye shall die like men, and fall like one of the princes.

Created in the likeness and the image of God, but made a little lower than the angels, Adam became the first man in this present world, to fall like one of the princes. Having been murdered by his own brother, Abel was the first in this world, to die like a man.

Like all men since Adam, Jesus too entered this world via the portal of the womb, hence born of water. Not as a mere god in the flesh, nor as a babe sired by a man, but born of a virgin, as Christ the Lord, the only begotten Son of God, the Word made flesh, or God in the flesh. The only person throughout all of time and history, who has entered this world via the portal of the womb, who was **not** born subject to death.

For Jesus-the Word, is God incarnate (in the flesh), the everlasting Father in spirit, and the Holy Ghost. *(1 John 5:7.)* The beginning and the ending, the Almighty *(Revelation 1:8)* the King of kings and the Lord of lords.*(Revelation 17:14.)*

Dare I say, that the mercy of God, *which endureth forever,* extends way back to the very beginning? Back to the age of the gods, and **prior** to the creation of Adam? Back to the aeon recorded in scripture as *the world that then was,* that existed in the heavens **of old**, and which was wiped out by deluge, maybe? *(2 Peter 3:4-6.)* In an ancient heavenly courtroom during an age **prior** to the world of flesh and blood, where there was zero remission for sin?

Hebrews 9:22. And almost ALL things are by the law purged with blood; and without shedding of blood is no remission.

Matthew 26:28. For this is my blood of the new testament, which is shed for many for the remission of sins.

For having made peace with mankind through his shed blood, not only was God in Christ, reconciling the world of mankind (gods in the flesh) unto himself, but his sacrificial blood was sufficient to reconcile **all things** unto himself. Whether they be things in earth, or things in heaven.

2 Corinthians 5:19. To wit, that God was in Christ, reconciling the world unto himself.[..........]

Colossians 1:20. And, having made peace through the blood of his cross, by him to reconcile **all** things unto himself; by him, I say, whether they be things in earth, or things in heaven.

Food for Thought.

Just as the angels are immortal, so too is the spirit of man. But none are eternal, as God is eternal, for each had a beginning. *Ecclesiastes 12:7* makes the clear and unambiguous statement that whilst the body returns to the dust, the **spirit** shall return unto God who gave it. Even though Adam received his spirit and the breath of life from God to become a living soul, his physical host body was made from pre-existing material.

Genesis 2:7. And the LORD God formed man of the dust of the ground, and breathed into his nostrils the breath of life; and man became a living soul.

It's estimated that the number of atoms in the average adult human body is 7 followed by a staggering 27 zeros! Another way of saying this is "seven billion billion" .

According to Dalton's Atomic Theory, Atoms cannot be created (except by God) and cannot be destroyed. The law of 'Conservation of Energy' states that energy is not created or destroyed, it just changes forms.

As our body develops and grows, it is not by creating new atoms, but by drawing pre-existing atoms in the form of energy, from our surroundings, from the food which we eat, to the very air that we breathe. When we die, our physical body returns to the dust, but just like the human spirit, the atoms themselves cannot be destroyed.

Maybe you and I are 40-50 years old, but the atoms of which we consist, are infinitesimally older, because they were created by God in the *beginning*. The very notion that we consist of atoms which originated perhaps hundreds of thousands of years ago, is hard to get one's head around, but it's apparently true.

So, what of our God-given spirit? The true person, the inner man, contained within the physical host body. When was that created? When did God create all things, both the visible and the invisible? In the *beginning*!

There is a sense of ancientness about us, that at times, and like the briefest flash in the dark, we may be dimly aware of, but tend to dismiss the notion immediately. Who has never asked the question; who am I? Why am I here? Who has never pondered on that fleeting moment of Déjà vu? The strange phenomenon of having the strong sensation that an event or experience currently being experienced has already been experienced in the past.

Is it just possible that life in this world and the death which awaits all, must be experienced, due to who we once were in a bygone age? An age known in Scripture as 'the world that then was'.

If we did pre-exist and have no recollection of it, could this dark world we inhabit be the land of forgetfulness?

Psalms 88:12. Shall thy wonders be known in the dark? and thy righteousness in the land of forgetfulness?

My personal understanding is as follows. Simply put, and in a nutshell, at their creation, the children of the most high (the gods or sons of God) were perfect, but something occurred for which they were judged. No atonement for sin was available in the previous world, and gods and angels cannot die. To die as a man, one must be born as a man.

In this present world, God's will is that no man born of water should perish, and all have the opportunity to seek after the Saviour, repent, and *believe* in the only name given under heaven by which man can be saved, and become born again, or born of the Spirit of God.

God sent his only-begotten Son to die for sin committed in THIS world alone. *(John 1:29)*. To those who find and receive him, Jesus gives the power to become sons of God. Is the Father waiting expectantly for his prodigal sons to return home? Are we returning to a Father we have previously known and loved?

Methinks we are not going to a new country, where we have never been before. We return like a traveller, back from a foreign country to be with the Father, in the home and the place where we belong.

Is Jesus restoring the fallen sons of God, to the original and perfect state? For the moment we can only ponder and wonder about such things, but the time will come when we will know for certain.

1 Corinthians 13:12. For now we see through a glass, darkly; but then face to face: now I know in part; but then shall I know even as also I am known.

Adam

Genesis 1:26-27. And God said, Let us make man in our image, after our likeness. So God created man in his own image, in the image of God created he him; male and female created he them.

Genesis 2:17. But of the tree of the knowledge of good and evil, thou shalt not eat of it: for in the day that thou eatest thereof thou shalt ***surely die***.

Genesis 3:4. And the serpent said unto the woman, Ye shall ***not surely die:***
….

Genesis 5:5. And all the days that Adam lived were nine hundred and thirty years: ***and he died.***

Adam was at once extremely intelligent, and blessed with the gift of tongues'. For he could converse with his Maker immediately, and named all of the animals and birds. It could rightly be said that he was the first 'king of the earth', for he was given full dominion over it.*(Genesis 1:26)*. But who exactly was Adam? For apart from Jesus the Christ, Adam is the ***only*** individual in the entire Bible to be personally named as being a 'son of God'.

Luke 3:38. Which was the son of Enos, which was the son of Seth, which was the son of ***Adam***, which was the ***son*** of ***God***.

In the Old Testament, the term 'Son of God' (singular) is used exclusively of the manifest person of Christ *(Daniel 3:25)* and 'sons of God' (plural) used exclusively of angelic beings. *(Genesis 6:2. Job 1:6)*. Because Jesus is the ONLY Begotten Son of God, or the only son ever to be ***born*** of God, then reason demands that Adam and the celestial beings were the sons of God via direct ***creation***. Not one single angel was ever begotten, for all were created. *(Hebrews 1:5)*.

Adam was totally unique, for he was the only person in the entire history of this world, to have been a direct creation of God. Adam's offspring included, the rest of us have arrived here via ***procreation***. Hence where mortal man is concerned, Adam is the only person named in the entire Bible, as being a 'son of God'.

Adam alone was directly created in the image and likeness of God, and the original 'image' is long gone. By natural birth not one of us has been born as a son of God, but as a son or daughter of man. Neither are we born by natural birth into the kingdom of God, but into a kingdom of spiritual darkness. A world (age) of which Satan is god. *(2 Corinthians 4:4).*

Adam's own offspring included, all of mankind have arrived in this world via procreation, and born of water (the womb) in the image and likeness of their fallen human father.

Genesis 5:3. And Adam lived an hundred and thirty years, and begat a son in *his own* likeness, *after his* image; and called his name Seth.

Jesus Christ of course, is also unique, yet unlike each individual angel and Adam, he wasn't created, but was begotten of God. Hence over the entire history of the Cosmos, Jesus is the ONLY Son ever to be begotten, or born of God. He was named JESUS by an angel whilst in his mother's womb, and was conceived of the Holy Ghost. *(Matthew 1:20-21).* He was the Saviour from the moment of conception, for he was Christ the Lord on the day of His birth. *(Luke 2:11).* No man was involved in his arrival, for he entered the world via the portal of the womb of a virgin. Though born of water, God was his Father, not his Creator.

Jesus came to this death-ridden world, NOT in the likeness and image of God. But as the image of God *(2 Corinthians 4:4)* and in the likeness of man. *(Philippians 2:7).*

ADAM; by direct creation in the image and likeness of God. Hence a 'son of God'.

ALL OTHERS: Via procreation, born in the image and likeness of a human father. Hence a 'son of man'.

JESUS CHRIST: Born of a virgin (without procreation) both in the image of God, and the likeness of man. Hence, because Mary his mother was of the lineage of Adam via Seth to Noah to King David, Jesus the 'last Adam', was both 'son of man/David', and Son of God.

Temple and Light

1 Corinthians 3:16. Know ye not that ye are the temple of God, and that the Spirit of God dwelleth in you?

Since the resurrection of Jesus, this verse applies only to those born of water AND of the Spirit. Yet Adam's created body was designed as a temple, and he was indwelt not only by his own spirit, but also by the Spirit of God. It could perhaps be said that as a man, he was an expression of the glory of God, and with full dominion over the earth.

But from the moment he disobeyed God, he became 'empty' of God, for he died that day in the spiritual sense and in the physical sense became subject to death. The temple was defiled and the Spirit of God departed, leaving Adam physically alive, but spiritually dead. Part of him 'died' on that fateful day, just as God had warned, and although he continued to live for many hundred years, physical death ever awaited him.

Genesis 5:5. And all the days that Adam lived were nine hundred and thirty years: and he died.

As the last Adam *(1 Corinthians 15:45)* Jesus came to restore what the first Adam lost. On one occasion, to give them a glimpse of his glory, who he truly was, and of things yet to come, Jesus took three of his disciples aside, and transformed himself before their very eyes, to appear as a figure of light.

Matthew 17:2. And was transfigured before them: and his face did shine as the sun, and his raiment was white as the light.

God is the Father of lights *(James 1:17)*, and believers in Christ are described as lights in a spiritual sense. But Scripture also informs us that at the resurrection, our lowly bodies which are currently subject to death, will be changed in an instant to become immortal and just like His glorious body. *(1 Philippians 3:21).*

1 Thessalonians 5:5. Ye are all the children of light, and the children of the day: we are not of the night, nor of darkness.

1 Corinthians 15:52. In a moment, in the twinkling of an eye, at the last trump: for the trumpet shall sound, and the dead shall be raised incorruptible, and we shall be changed.

Flesh and Bone

After Jesus had risen from the dead and first appeared to his disciples, they were scared half-witless, thinking they'd seen a ghost or a spirit. By showing them his wounds, Jesus assured his friends that not only was he very much alive, but unlike a spirit, his body was comprised of *flesh* and *bone*. Yet he was able to travel effortlessly and appear and disappear at will. He could go unrecognised yet could also eat and drink and sit with his disciples and talk. Although his resurrection body appeared to be natural or physical, in truth it was supernatural, a spiritual body consisting of flesh and bone, but no longer bound by the physical laws.

Luke 24:39. Behold my hands and my feet, that it is I myself: handle me, and see; for a spirit hath not *flesh* and *bones*, as ye see me have.

Ephesians 5:30. For we are members of his body, of his flesh, and of his bones.

There is a natural body, and there is a spiritual (not spirit) body. *(1 Corinthians 15:44)*. Jesus' claim to be flesh and bone is as simple as it is profound. Simple, because his flesh and bone body was now bloodless. Profound, for his blood had been shed to atone for the sins of mankind, and because Scripture cannot be broken, even Jesus could not inherit the kingdom of God as flesh and blood. *(1 Corinthians 15:50)*.

Jesus, the last Adam, was put to death whilst in his natural body of flesh and blood, but was raised from the dead as a spiritual body of flesh and bone (of which we are members). The first Adam who had once declared to be flesh and bone (a spiritual body), died spiritually and became a natural body of flesh and blood.

Genesis 2:23. This is now *bone* of my bones, and *flesh* of my flesh: she shall be called Woman, because she was taken out of Man.

God's expectation of Adam as a husband was the same then as it is now; that he love his wife to the extent that he would willingly lay down his own life for her sake.

Ephesians 5:25. Husbands, love your wives, even as Christ also loved the church, and gave himself for it;

Jesus died for the sake of his bride! And husbands are asked to love their wives in like manner. When reasoning from the Scriptures, it is my firm conviction, that Adam and Eve as a direct creation of God, and made in his image and likeness, were supernatural beings of light. For the light of Christ flowed from the heart of the temple within, and coursed through the body of flesh and bone. From the moment they disobeyed God and became subject to death, the Spirit of God departed, and the light instantly turned into blood. Remember, God can change the body in a moment, in the twinkling of an eye. *(1 Corinthians 15:52)*.

It's often been said that whereas Eve was deceived into partaking of 'the fruit', Adam was not deceived, but had been given the choice, but I strongly suspect it wasn't that cut and dried. After all said and done, being fully aware of the consequence, why would Adam wilfully choose to disobey God? Yes, I'm sure he was presented with a choice, but I suspect the choice he made was born out of love, and made under sudden and extremely difficult circumstances, rather than a premeditated deliberate act of disobedience to God.

Remember, the serpent/Satan was more subtle, crafty, cunning, than any beast of the field, and certainly more than a match for an innocent woman. He knew that the onus was upon man, and right from the outset, his sights were set upon Adam.

But he spotted the weakness of a tender heart, and therefore used Eve in order to get to his prey. When toying with Eve, Satan not only accused God of being a liar, but also of putting a restraint upon her. The enemy blatantly twisted things around. 'You will not die', he said, 'but will be enlightened with knowledge and hence become as the gods. And you really think God doesn't know this'?

Genesis 3:4-5. And the serpent said unto the woman, Ye shall *not* surely die: For God doth know that in the day ye eat thereof, then your eyes shall be opened, and ye shall be as gods, knowing good and evil.

Adam did not choose as such to disobey God, but his wife had become mortal. What might he have witnessed? A totally distraught, inconsolable wretch, standing weeping and naked before him? As her husband, what should he do? Remain immortal? Or be united with his wife? Adam most likely, stepped from immortality into mortality and 'died' for the sake of his Bride!

It could even be said that 'the lights went out', and this sudden transformation from a being of light to a mortal, exposed their nakedness and caused their shame. As flesh and blood, and empty of God, our original parents were cast out from the garden of Eden, and permanently excluded from the kingdom of God.

1 Corinthians 15:50. Now this I say, brethren, that flesh and blood *cannot* inherit the kingdom of God;.[..............]

Genesis 3:7. And the eyes of them both were opened, and they knew that they were naked; and they sewed fig leaves together, and made themselves aprons.

Genesis 3:24. So [God] drove out the man; and he placed at the east of the garden of Eden Cherubims, and a flaming sword which turned every way, to keep the way of the tree of life.

The deception instigated by Satan, not only caused the downfall of

Adam, but introduced sin and death to all of mankind. By default, the god who held the power of death, had set himself up as the 'god of this world'.

The Serpent entered the Garden via the Tree of Knowledge of Good and Evil. (Gnosticism). The scriptures indicate this occurred on the very same day Adam and Eve were created. God created man in his own image on the Sixth day, placed him in the Garden of Eden, gave him a wife to cherish, and effectively told Adam and Eve to do what husbands and wives do naturally. Make love often, have many children, and restore the earth to its former fullness. *(Genesis 1:28).*

This did not happen immediately, for their first union as husband and wife did not take place until after they were banished from the Garden. Cain and Abel were not conceived in an earthly paradise, but in the cruel and fallen world beyond Eden. *(Genesis 4:1).* Every indication points to Adam and Eve being cast out around sunset on the very day they were created. Their time in the garden was extremely short-lived indeed.

The popular Serpent-seed doctrine by the way, where Satan had sex with Eve and became Cain's literal father, is occult myth. Whilst it's as good as certain that Cain and Abel were twins, Adam alone was the father of both. Eve was not impregnated by both her husband as well as the serpent, which produced twins, each with a different father.

The serpent-seed doctrine is partly based on the assumption that the garden which God planted eastward in Eden, for the benefit of Adam, is one and the same as Eden, the garden *of* God. For the trees which grew in the latter, are identified as being personal entities. Based on this wrong assumption, adherents of the serpent-seed doctrine, believe that Adam and Eve were just two of many humans on earth at the time. For there were other "trees" in the garden of Eden, which they wrongly assume to be other persons. They also believe the word "eat" to have a sexual implication.

Having been commanded not to eat [have a sexual relationship] with the fruit of the tree of knowledge of good and evil, are we then to believe that God gave Adam and Eve the freedom to eat [have a sexual relationship with] the other "trees" [persons] in the garden?

Genesis 2:16. And the LORD God commanded the man, saying, Of every tree of the garden thou mayest freely eat:

Further more, whilst she had been deceived, if Eve's transgression was by indulging in a sexual union with the serpent, what exactly was Adam's transgression? Did he too commit a sexual act with the serpent? Or was it a threesome, so to speak? Personally, I don't think any more needs to be said, because it doesn't bear thinking about.

Some folk who hold with the serpent-seed doctrine, also believe in an eighth day creation. They claim that mankind in general were created by God in his own image and likeness on the sixth day, whilst Adam and Eve were a separate creation. For they would produce a godly bloodline, sometimes referred to as "the scarlet thread", which ultimately would be inherited by Mary, the mother of Jesus. In other words, there were two different races, one of which would eventually produce the Saviour, on behalf of those created on the sixth day. To support this belief, they argue that when Cain arrived in the land of Nod, the land was already inhabited, because he found a wife there, and started his own family.

A close reading of scripture however, indicates that when travelling to Nod, Cain wasn't alone, but was accompanied by his wife, and having settled elsewhere, she became pregnant. His wife being one of his un-named sisters. Because both sons were working at the time, it's safe to assume that when Cain killed his brother, they were at least in their late teens, or even young adulthood. In which case, after 20 years or so, it's also safe to assume that by now they had a fair number of sisters.

Genesis 4:16-17. And Cain went out from the presence of the LORD, and dwelt in the land of Nod, on the east of Eden. And Cain knew his wife; and she conceived, and bare Enoch: and he builded a city, and called the name of the city, after the name of his son, Enoch.

Genesis 5:4.   And the days of Adam after he had begotten Seth were eight hundred years: and he begat sons and *daughters*:

Replenish

Many have argued that because in the original Hebrew text, the word *maw-lay'* means to fill, the King James Bible translators made a big mistake when using the word replenish at Genesis 1:28. Tis true, Strongs Hebrew Dictionary does indeed give the primary meaning of *maw-lay'* as fill. But it's equally true that replenish is given as a secondary meaning. And no, one has no need to be a Hebrew scholar to figure it out, because Strongs is written in English.

Genesis 1:28. And God blessed them, and God said unto them, Be fruitful, and multiply, and *replenish* the earth, and *subdue* it: [......]

Everyone knows that the prefix re- means to repeat something, and the first known use of the word "plenish" was in 1513, according to Merriam-Webster, who define the word plenish as;early Scots *plenyss* "to fill up, stock, furnish," borrowed from Anglo-French *plenis-,* stem of *plenir* "to fill, occupy.

If one's theology dictates that in no way whatsoever, was the earth inhabited prior to Adam and Eve, then the word *replenish* becomes a major stumbling-block. For the word replenish can only mean fill, in the sense of restoring a vessel to its original fulness. It can *never* mean to fill a vessel for the *first* time. The AKJV is one of only a few Bible versions to use the word replenish, and upon further investigation, it contains an incredible teaching about the history of the earth, which is virtually missing from most all other versions of Scripture. For whilst sin and death entered this *present world* through Adam's disobedience to God, a record of death and mass destruction of life, already existed beneath Adam's feet, in the form of the geological and fossil record.

For by way of reason, if God told Adam and Eve to be fruitful and multiply, in order to restore the earth to its former fullness, it can only mean *one* thing. Just as the earth was inhabited prior to the flood of Noah, when God used the selfsame words, somebody or something, had inhabited the earth *prior* to the creation of modern-day man, and *before* the six days of Genesis.

Genesis 1:28. And God blessed them (Adam and Eve) and God said unto them, Be fruitful, and multiply, and *replenish* the earth, and subdue it...........

Genesis 9:1. And God blessed Noah and his sons, and said unto them, Be fruitful, and multiply, and *replenish* the earth.

By the grace of God, eight souls were saved from the flood in Noah's day. But had there already been a far earlier flood, one of such catastrophic proportions, from which no life whatsoever was spared? A deluge on the scale of an Extinction Level Event? Sometimes referred to as Lucifer's Flood? And for good reason, because he was the one charged with turning the [primordial] world into a wilderness, and destroying its infrastructure.

Hard to believe? Then let's go on a journey through the Scriptures, and check things out for ourselves. But before we start, a question.

Genesis 1:1. In the beginning God created the heaven and the earth.

John 1:1. In the beginning was the Word, and the Word was with God, and the Word was God.

Which is the first verse of the Bible? For chronologically speaking, without John 1:1, there would be no Genesis 1:1. Time as we know and measure it today, began *not* in the beginning, as per the first verse of Genesis, but in verse *three*, at the start of the *first* day, when God said "Let there be Light". Prior to the the first day, all was in pitch darkness, and the earth, described as being "without form and void", is submerged beneath the face of the deep. For God didn't command the dry land to appear from the waters until the third day.

Genesis 1:3-5. And God said, Let there be light: and there was light. [..........] And the evening and the morning were the *first* day.

Genesis 1:9-10. And God said, Let the *waters* under the heaven be gathered together unto *one* place, and let the dry *land appear*: and it was so. And God called the dry *land Earth*; and the gathering together of the waters called he *Seas*: and God saw that *it was* good..[..........] And the evening and the morning were the *third day. (Gen 1:13.)*

The Fall of Lucifer

Masons call Lucifer the 'Grand Architect of the Universe' (GAOU); Science calls Lucifer the 'Graviton' or 'Dark Matter'; Muslims call Lucifer 'Allah'; New Agers call Lucifer 'The One'; Twelvers like Mahmoud Ahmadinejad call Lucifer 'al-Mahdi'; Hindus call Lucifer 'Krishna' and Mormons call Lucifer Jesus' brother.

The question has often been asked as to whether Satan and Lucifer are both one and the same person? Although there is no actual verse that states Satan to be Lucifer, nor that a third of the angels followed him in his rebellion against God, when reasoning from Scripture it leads us to those conclusions. Both Jesus in Luke 10:18, and John in Revelation 9:1 allude to Isaiah 14:12, connecting the fall of the one mentioned there with the fall of Satan.

Luke 10:18. And he [Jesus] said unto them, I beheld Satan as lightning fall from heaven.

Isaiah 14:12. How art thou fallen from heaven, O *Lucifer*, son of the morning! *how* art thou cut down to the ground, which didst weaken the nations!

This verse has caused much controversy over the years, because the word 'Lucifer' is not in the original Hebrew text. The Hebrew word is helel (or heylel), from the root, hâlâl, meaning to shine or 'bear light.' The similarity between hâlâl and the Arabic 'hilal', meaning crescent moon, is quite striking. And in a Sovereign God kind of way, it's no coincidence that the root word hâlâl is an anagram of allah.

Rather than translate *helel* directly from the Hebrew, the KJB translators adopted Lucifer as a proper name. Lucifer is actually a Latin word, an adjective which appears in the Vulgate, or Latin translation of the Bible.

Isaiah 14:12. Quomodo cecidisti de cælo *Lucifera*, qui mane oriebaris?

As an adjective, lucifer means 'light-bringing' or 'light-bearer' and whilst used as an epithet of Venus, it was often applied to the moon. Diana for example, the Roman goddess of the moon, was also known as Diana *Lucifera*. The Greek equivalent to Lucifer is eosphorus, and appears as such in the Greek text. Therefore, in the English version of the Septuagint (Greek Old Testament) eosphorus has been correctly translated as Lucifer.

Yet although the three major versions, the Septuagint, the Vulgate, and the Authorized King James Bible are all in agreement, virtually all of the modern versions have since removed the name Lucifer altogether, and now read 'How you have fallen from heaven, morning star, son of dawn!' Or something very similar. Why? Because Witches, Warlocks and Lucifer worshippers just can't have people knowing that their god is none other than Satan.

Not only have modern translations concealed the fact that Lucifer and Satan are one and the same person, but once again have caused a degree of confusion. Because elsewhere in Scripture the term 'morning star' is used exclusively of the one who is the 'Light of the World', Jesus Christ. *(Revelation 22:16.)* He once came from heaven voluntarily, whilst Lucifer had once fallen. And yet most modern versions of the Bible use the term 'Morning star' or 'Day star' for both Jesus and Satan.

Wilderness

From the time of his creation until he became overtaken by pride and self-love, Lucifer the Anointed Cherub is described as perfect in both his appearance (beauty) and in his ways.

Ezekiel 28:12. Son of man, take up a lamentation upon the king of Tyrus, and say unto him, Thus saith the Lord GOD; Thou sealest up the sum, full of wisdom, and *perfect* in beauty.

Ezekiel 28:14. Thou [Lucifer] *art* the anointed cherub that covereth; and I have set thee *so*: thou wast upon the holy mountain of God; thou hast walked up and down in the midst of the *stones of fire.*

Ezekiel 28:15. Thou [Lucifer] wast *perfect* in thy ways from the day that thou wast created, *till* iniquity was found in thee.

At the time, Ezekiel was prophesying against the human king of Tyrus, but simultaneously addressed the ancient malevolent spirit person operating in the background. For no human being (king or otherwise) has ever walked amongst the stones of fire. Such a privilege is reserved for mighty angelic beings. How long Lucifer remained in this state of perfection is unknown, but it certainly didn't last, and due to his pride and rebellion against God, he eventually lost his privilege and authority, and was cast out as being profane from the mountain of God.

Taken from *Ezekiel 28:13-16.*

> Thou hast been in Eden the garden *of* God; every precious stone
> was thy covering [.......] Thou art the anointed cherub that
> covereth; and I have set thee so: thou wast upon the holy
> mountain of God; thou hast walked up and down in the midst of
> the stones of fire. Thou [wast] perfect in thy ways from the day
> that thou wast created, till iniquity was found in thee.
>
> By the multitude of thy merchandise they have filled the midst of
> thee with violence, and thou hast sinned: therefore I will cast thee
> as profane out of the mountain of God: and I will destroy thee, O
> covering cherub, from the midst of the stones of fire.

Isaiah once prophesied against the human king of Babylon, yet at the
same time he also addressed the ancient malevolent spirit person
operating from behind the scenes. Human kings don't fall from
heaven, but angelic beings do.

Taken from *Isaiah 14:12-17.*

> How art thou fallen from heaven, O Lucifer, son of the morning!
> how art thou *cut down to the ground*, which didst weaken the
> nations! For thou hast said in thine heart, I will *ascend* into
> heaven, I will exalt my *throne above* the stars of God: I will sit
> also upon the mount of the congregation, in the sides of the
> north: I will *ascend* above the heights of the clouds; I will be like
> the most High.
>
> Yet thou shalt be brought down to hell, to the sides of the pit.
> They that see thee shall narrowly look upon thee, [and] consider
> thee, [saying, Is] this the man that made the earth to tremble, that
> did shake kingdoms; [That] made *the world as a wilderness*, and
> *destroyed* the cities thereof; [that] opened not the house of his
> prisoners?

As far as we know from the Bible, Lucifer was the first created being
to pit his own will against the will of the Creator. A closer look at
Lucifer's statements of wilful intent, all suggest ascending
heavenward in the literal sense. Which would make the earth his
starting point, and in all likelihood, the earth was the location of
Lucifer's throne in the previous world, and the original kingdom of
heaven.

We know that Lucifer once had a throne, and most likely would have
been amongst those present, and joyful when witnessing God laying

down the foundations of the earth. *(Job 38:6-7.)* Yet he became the one responsible for making the world (that then was) a wilderness, and the destruction of the cities.

I have no idea what "the house of his prisoners" not being opened refers to, but it certainly suggests injustice, and some form of slavery. Whatever was going on at the time, it resulted in a water judgement of such intensity, that 'the world that then was' perished, and the earth became "without form and void, and submerged beneath the frozen surface of the great deep.

This had to have occurred during *the gap* between the first two verses of Genesis. For there is nowhere else in the Scriptures, where an event of such a catastrophic nature could possibly have taken place. Furthermore, when Lucifer (light-bearer) appeared as the serpent in the garden of Eden, as Satan (the adversary,) he was already a fallen being.

Whatever may have taken place, it's made clear that the actions of Lucifer were the result of a wilful abuse of the authority which he'd been given. It would seem that once that choice had been made, it could never be retracted, and would determine his ultimate destiny (the lake of fire) as well as that of the angels who chose to follow him. Note that whilst we're told the everlasting fire is 'prepared', there's no indication that it has yet been ignited.

Matthew 25:41. Then shall he say also unto them on the left hand, Depart from me, ye cursed, into everlasting fire, prepared for the devil and his angels:

Ancient Giant Trees

Geologists have organised the history of the Earth into a time-scale of which large expanses of time are called periods and smaller ones called epochs. On this chronological scale, each period is separated by a major geological or palaeontological event, such as the mass extinction of the dinosaurs, or the end of the ice-age.

However, a growing number of researchers are now looking at the earth and the cosmos from a different aspect to the one presented by mainstream science, and many have come to the conclusion that there's a hidden element to Earth's history which lies far beyond the repetitive cycles of natural disasters. This history they claim, is dark and macabre, for it reveals purposeful violence and destruction.

Is it possible, some researchers ask, that a highly advanced civilization once battled for dominance in the heavens above, and Earth has been caught in the crossfire?

With this great cosmic controversy in mind, William F. Dankenbring writes in 'Beyond Star Wars', (p.75).

> This "war in heaven" must have been catastrophic in nature. It must have been the greatest battle of all time! Armies of angels clashing with each other! The entire cosmos must have been shaken. The fantastic truth of what happened aeons ago makes the Star War movies pale into nothingness by comparison!

The Bible certainly speaks of a war fought between hosts of angels in heaven, but one that affected the entire cosmos? Surely not? Well, maybe it does, but in some aspects inherited theology has much to answer for, and when reading the Bible we have a tendency to overlook it. However, because God only informs us of certain things on a 'need to know' basis, the Bible presents us with a glimpse of a bigger picture, but one that gives little detail.

It is starting to come to light that a great deal of what we've been taught concerning the ancient history of Earth, is a case of Mistaken Identity. For much of geology is in fact, biology, i.e. the *petrified* remains of former gargantuan trees and other colossal life forms, being presented as geological features.

A common theme in folklore and mythology across the world is *petrification* where people are turned into stone. ***Petrified*** (wood) comes from the Latin root petro meaning 'rock' or 'stone'; literally *'**wood turned into stone'*** and is the name given to a special type of fossilized remains of terrestrial vegetation. Petrifaction of wood is the result of a tree or length of wood having ***transitioned to stone*** by a unique mineralization process that occurs in an oxygen-free environment underground when the wood becomes buried in water-saturated sediment, or volcanic ash. Unlike other organic and plant fossils, which are typically seen to be impressions or compressions, petrified wood is actually a three-dimensional, anatomical representation of the original organic material.

The Petrified Forest National Park in Arizona for example, is famous for its public display of petrified wood, claimed to be more than 200 million years old. At least nine species of fossilized trees, or wood turned to stone, have been identified; all of which are extinct.

The Patagonia region of South America has been called "the land where life has turned to stone" for it is home to an extraordinary concentration of eerie petrified forest. Littering the landscape in Chubut province, Southern Argentina, are strange stone monuments to life, that thrived it's claimed by evolutionists, up to 65 million years ago. Yet petrified forests are not unique to America, for they are located on every continent on earth as well as on numerous individual islands. The Greek island of Lesbos for example, where scientists have discovered vividly coloured fossilised trees, produced they claim, by successive volcanic eruptions circa 20 million years ago. Stretching across almost all of the Greek island's western peninsula, the petrified forest, a Unesco global geopark, is among the largest in the world.

To describe this phenomena as a forest however is somewhat misleading. For in most cases, the petrified wood on display to the public consists of little more than a collection of petrified logs, the majority of which appear to have been sawn or neatly broken and laying horizontal close together. Studying the images carefully, one gets the impression these petrified logs did not originate from the trunk of a tree that once grew locally, but rather, are the petrified branches of a former massive tree which were then sawn or broken into manageable sections and transported in from elsewhere. Found in northern Thailand, the longest petrified log measures 72.2 metres (237 feet) which suggests the original tree towered more than 100 metres (330 feet) skyward.

Silica plays an important part in the petrification of trees. Evolutionist theories say each molecule of the tree was replaced by a molecule of silica over millions of years, but where did the silica come from, and how would solid rock transfer it to the logs? Fallen trees usually start to rot within a few weeks on the forest floor, so what would force them into the state of rock or become petrified?

For them to become fossils, they must have been buried in silt very rapidly, and most likely flash frozen, and their chemical composition morphed into rock. Radio halos seem to indicate if not prove, that the logs were petrified very quickly, rather than over millions of years, and since some of them are oval, the logs must have been buried in sediment very rapidly as well.

A few years ago a Crimean man calling himself *Людин Руси*, posted a video on You-Tube titled *"There Are No Forests On Earth"*, which some may already be aware of. If not, you're quite likely to find the rest of this chapter somewhat hard to take in. For when presented with hard to digest information that challenges our world-view of reality, it calls for a total rewire of the mind, as in the way we think.

We've all seen forests, we all know exactly what they are, so how could anyone in their right mind claim there are no forests on earth? A very strange title indeed, yet a title that begins to make some sort of sense as one continues to watch it. For me personally, not only did I find the subject matter to be of a most fascinating nature, but certain aspects of the presentation began to strike a large resounding bell.

It is not a work of fiction nor is it a technical analysis of anything. It is simply a presentation of certain verifiable facts coupled with photographic evidence taken at various locations on Earth, but put into a context that challenges much of what we thought we knew, and almost defies the imagination.

The producer contends that sometime **beyond** 7,500 years ago, Earth was almost unimaginably different to how it is now. For all standing forests today are little more than dwarf shrubberies compared to those which stood upon Earth in the primordial world. Mind-blowing and as impossible as it may seem, the height of those ancient trees he claims, extended for thousands of feet (in some cases several miles) heavenward.

What we perceive to be a Mesa or table-top mountain such as the 264-meter (867-foot) rock formation known as Devil's Tower in Wyoming, USA, he explains, is actually the **petrified stump** of a former gigantic **tree**. For the huge hexagonal (six-sided) basalt columns which form its exterior, are nothing more than the gigantic vascular fibres of an ancient petrified tree. Furthermore, these hexagonal columns or cones are the backbone of every mountain on earth which in its local surroundings seems to be out of place.

Before switching off and closing your mind completely to such an outrageous notion, please pause to consider this. Traditional text-book-taught Geologists can only speculate how Devil's Tower was formed. They say that it probably formed underground, but only gradually became visible over millions of years as the natural elements (water and wind) eroded the surrounding landscape. Although quite how 'wind' erosion can possibly occur deep underground beggars belief.

The prevailing theory rests entirely upon ancient lava flows, and that being said, without any evidence whatsoever of volcanic activity in the region. Yet even though they are quite content to describe the structure as a 'Volcanic Sentinel', geologists know full well that 1) the structure was never part of a volcano. 2) It is not possible for a stream of molten lava to cool and solidify to form these amazing hexagonal structures. This one factor alone, has caused a major issue for geologists, because there is really no other way the structure and thousands of others like it, can be explained.

Such is also the case with the 'Giant's Causeway', an area of about 40,000 interlocking hexagonal basalt columns, located on the coast of Northern Ireland. Lost for a satisfactory and reasonable explanation, geologists can only claim this truly remarkable phenomena to be the result of an ancient volcanic fissure eruption. Once again being fully aware that it's not possible for molten lava to cool and solidify to form these incredible interlocking hexagonal structures. If you've ever seen photos of solidified molten lava, I'm sure you can understand why.

Some Botanists however, point to the fact that plants have the same kind of subsection, which are effectively pipes carrying food and water. These hexagonal stone columns they claim, are the **petrified** sections or sub-sections of an ancient colossal tree. In other words, wood turned to stone.

Although I've not been able to trace the original source, a few years ago the following article appeared on the Internet.

A huge and startling discovery has been made at the Devils Tower in Wyoming. Scientists from the Wyoming State Parks Department were conducting photographic seismic readings below the tower when they discovered an incredibly large petrified root system below the tower. The parks department released a statement saying, "We have discovered, what looks like a giant root system stemming from the base of The Devils Tower. The root system has been measured at 4 miles deep by 7 miles wide. We are currently conducting studies and tests to confirm that this is actually a root system and not a coincidence." This discovery is on the edge of rewriting history and science as we know it.

Whether or not the article is genuine I really cannot say, although at the time, the Wyoming State Parks Department issued a statement denying all knowledge of the article, and completely rejected the claim.

I think it reasonable and safe to assume however, that a discovery of such magnitude would amount to a full-blown and head-on challenge for both conventional historians and the foundational theories of geologists alike, hence will almost certainly be suppressed. In the main, Academia does not want to know the Truth, preferring instead to remain wilfully ignorant.

For the bizarre phenomena of petrification where life turns to stone must surely reveal the true history of Earth, which has been given to mankind by God. And Peter the apostle once warned how most folk will prefer to remain ignorant of such an inconvenient truth.

For when when an image of Devil's Tower (or other similar landmark) is viewed alongside an image of the stump of a recently felled oak tree for example, there is no apparent observable difference whatsoever between the two. Apart from the sheer scale of course.

If structures like Devil's Tower really are the petrified remains of ancient tree stumps, it does raise the question of who cut them down? When? And Why?

Figurative maybe, but are you aware that mountains have roots?

Job 28:9. He [God] putteth forth his hand upon the rock; he overturneth the mountains by the roots.

Daniel Chapter 4 tells of a strange dream or vision received by Nebuchadnezzar II the once proud king of Babylon. In his dream the king witnessed an enormous tree standing at the very centre of the earth. (Only possible if earth is a circular plane of course). This central tree was so large in fact, that its branches spread across the entire earth, and its top extended to heaven.

As he observes this remarkable tree, a holy watcher comes down from heaven, and decrees that the tree must be chopped down and destroyed. The stump of the tree however, complete with the roots, must be left firmly in the ground, as a sign that the heavens do rule.

Daniel 4:23. And whereas the king saw a watcher and an holy one coming down from heaven, and saying, Hew the tree down, and destroy it; yet leave the stump of the roots thereof in the earth.....

Daniel 4:26. And whereas they commanded to leave the stump of the tree roots; thy kingdom shall be sure unto thee, after that thou shalt have known that the heavens do rule.

The purpose of the vision was that Nebuchadnezzar should learn the lesson once and for all of God's sovereignty; "the King of Heaven whose works are Truth, and who is able to abase (bring down low) those who walk in pride." *(Daniel 4:37)*. For seven years the king has his mind overtaken by the mind of a beast and lives out in the wilds eating grass like an ox. As the seven years come to an end, the madness passes, Nebuchadnezzar regains his right mind and comes to his senses and immediately praises God.

Because one of his prophecies was recorded in the Book of Jude, Enoch deserves to be taken seriously. Interestingly, *Enoch 26:1* states;

And from there, I went to the middle of the earth, and saw a blessed, well watered place, which had branches which remained alive, and sprouted from a tree which had been cut down.

Again, and just like Nebuchadnezzar's dream, a tree located at the centre of the earth only makes sense on a circular and level terrain. Whilst no mention of roots being left in the ground, living branches growing from the stump of a felled tree, strongly indicates such was the case. Could it possibly be that the vision received by King Nebuchadnezzar was founded upon the truth of a far earlier event?

A reference to the ruler of the prehistoric world (aeon) maybe, who much like Nebuchadnezzar in this present world, was also brought down low by God due to his arrogance and pride? The high one of stature hewn down, the person charged by God as being the man responsible for the previous aeon/ world becoming a wilderness?

Isaiah 14:12. How art thou fallen from heaven, O Lucifer, son of the morning! how art thou *cut down to the ground*, which didst weaken the nations!

Two Gardens

Trees are mentioned in the Bible more than any living thing other than God and people. The Bible begins with a Tree and ends with a Tree and the Saviour of the world was put to death on a Tree. The term 'Tree of Life' appears ten times in the Bible, 10 signifying the completion of divine order. The Number 3 in the Bible represents divine wholeness, completeness and perfection. The Number 5 in the Bible is a symbol of God's grace; i.e. his undeserved kindness and favour to mankind. The fifth time the name Noah appears in the Bible, he found grace in the eyes of the LORD *(Genesis 6:8)*.

When added together we have *eight*, the biblical number of new beginnings, for 8 represents new life, regeneration, resurrection, and commencement, and 8 people survived the flood.

The term 'The garden *of* God' appears *three* times in the entire Bible, hence denoting divine completeness and perfection. The term 'The garden *of* Eden' appears on *five* occasions, hence denoting God's grace toward mankind.

For 'Eden', the garden *of* God and the garden *of* Eden are two entirely different Gardens in two entirely different worlds. Whilst for obvious reasons I cannot be certain, I would suggest that in the beginning the entire Earth itself was the original Eden, the Garden of God. For when this present world began, and for the benefit of Adam, God planted a garden eastward in *Eden. (Genesis 2:8).* An inference I suspect, to the eastern part of the earth.

Around 6,000 years ago, when this present aeon (world) began, God placed the newly created Adam into the newly prepared Garden *of* Eden. Apart from the tree of life and the tree of the knowledge of good and evil in the midst of the garden, every tree that grew from the ground was of a fruit-bearing variety, from which Adam could freely eat. Hence the Garden *of* Eden could actually be likened to an orchard.

Genesis 2:16. And the LORD God commanded the man, saying, Of *every* tree of the garden thou mayest freely *eat*:

On the other hand, all the trees in Eden, the Garden *of* God, are deciduous and named as the chestnut, the cedar, and fir. Yet one in particular was unique and unlike all the others.

Ezekiel 31:8. The *cedars* in the garden *of* God could not hide *him*: the *fir* trees were not like *his* boughs, and the *chesnut* trees were not like *his* branches; nor any *tree* in the garden *of* God was like unto *him* in his beauty.

Ezekiel 31:9. I have made *him* fair by the multitude of *his* branches: so that *all* the trees of *Eden*, that *were* in the garden *of* God, envied *him*.

Please note, these Trees are symbolic of mighty personal beings, the one in particular in reference to Lucifer, the anointed cherub, the only person named in the scriptures as once having been in Eden, the garden *of* God. *(Ezekiel 28:13).*

I think it also worth noting that after having fallen, Adam was cast out of the garden *of* Eden, whilst the fallen Lucifer who had been in Eden the garden *of* God, was cast out as profane from the mountain of God.

Ezekiel 28:16. By the multitude of thy merchandise they have filled the midst of thee with violence, and thou hast sinned: therefore I will cast thee as profane out of the mountain of God:

Genesis 3:24. So he drove out the man; and he placed at the east of the garden of Eden Cherubims, and a flaming sword which turned every way, to keep the way of the tree of life.

High Ones

When prophesying of the Assyrian (a name for the Anti-Christ), 'the day of visitation' and the desolation which shall come from afar, Isaiah makes an interesting observation, for he records that although haughty in character, the term 'high ones' refers not to their proud demeanour, but to the great height of their stature, and I really don't think he was talking about a group of men who just happen to be ten or twelve feet tall. The prophet of God was talking serious giants.

Between them, Ezekiel and Isaiah show the Assyrian, who is also of high stature, to be one and the same person as Lucifer.

Ezekiel 31:3. Behold, the Assyrian was a cedar in Lebanon with fair branches, and with a shadowing shroud, and of an high stature; and his top was among the thick boughs.

Ezekiel 31:8. The cedars in the garden *of* God could not hide him [the Assyrian]: the fir trees were not like his boughs, and the chestnut trees were not like his branches; nor any tree in the garden *of* God was like unto him in his beauty.

Ezekiel 28:13. Thou [Lucifer] hast been in *Eden* the garden *of* God; every precious stone was thy covering,......

While speaking a proverb against the human king of Babylon, just like Ezekiel his counterpart, the prophet Isaiah also simultaneously addressed the malevolent spirit person operating unseen in the background. He also likened a group of persons (angels), to cedars in Lebanon, and how one in particular, was considered to be untouchable.

Yet the prophet has named the now fallen 'untouchable one.'

Isaiah 14:8. Yea, the fir trees rejoice at thee, and the cedars of Lebanon, saying, Since thou art laid down, no feller [axe-man] is come up against us.

Isaiah 10:33. Behold, the Lord, the LORD of hosts, shall lop the bough with terror: and the high ones of stature shall be *hewn down*, and the haughty shall be humbled.

Isaiah 14:12. How art thou *fallen* from heaven, O Lucifer, son of the morning! how art thou *cut down* to the ground, which didst weaken the nations!

Now please don't get me wrong here. I'm not suggesting for one moment that table-top mountains or mountains in general, are the petrified remains of fallen angels. Yet in a strange and unexplained way the high ones who frequented *Eden*, the garden *of* God, seem to have had a personal connection with trees. Maybe those living trees were in effect a celestial portal, giving angels access between heaven and earth. I really have no idea.

But I do believe the scriptures indicate that enormous trees once stood upon earth, and for whatever reason, yet by the decree of God, those gargantuan primordial trees were hewn down and destroyed. Yet He demanded their stumps were to be left firmly rooted in the ground. Why? For man's benefit today I suspect, as a sign that the heavens indeed do rule.

So yes, it's quite possible, that presumed 'geological' features, such as Devil's Tower in Wyoming, are in fact, the petrified stumps and root-systems which were left in the ground, when the gargantuan trees were hewn down, back in the primordial world.

Either way, it would seem that everything we've taken for granted concerning the surface of the earth has been based upon mistaken identity. For what academia would have us believe to be sedimentary layering that has developed over millions or billions of years, is the permineralized tissues of some type of gigantic, biological entity, that has molecularly transitioned to stone, most likely in a mud-fossilization process.

Much of Geology is Biology, **not** molten rocks evolving over time from a theoretical big bang. Visual evidence for this can be found at the YouTube channels 'Mud Fossil University' and 'Tyson's Mud fossil Adventures'. Here you will see 100% evidence of a 600ft long exposed section of a bilipid membrane from a leviathan creature, the size of which is literally off the charts. Furthermore, Harvard and Max Planck Universities have certified that mud-fossils and what erodes from mud-fossils as mud, contains DNA as 100% valid, exactly as Mud Fossil University has claimed. Titled *Massive 600ft long bilipid membrane of a leviathan creature,* can be found on You-Tube, and is well worth checking out.

When researching this most bizarre phenomena, one's world-view largely depends upon what sort of lens, window, or looking glass we are seeing through, and there is no better lens to peer through than the word of God. A glimpse back into the deep past, the heavens and earth of old, of an age which ended abruptly, and a world which was plunged into darkness, the deep, the bottomless pit.

Let there be Light

Often referred to as 'The Genesis Gap', there's a teaching contained within the pages of the AKJV, the completeness of which, has been systematically removed from most all other versions of the Bible. For a major cataclysm occurred in the distant past, a deluge of such intensity, that the earth God had created for the purpose of being inhabited, was plunged into total darkness and became a watery wasteland, desolate and barren.

Genesis 1:1. In the beginning God created the heaven and the earth.

Isaiah 45:18. For thus saith the LORD that created the heavens; God himself that formed the earth and made it; he hath established it, he created it **not** in vain, he formed it **to be inhabited**: [.........]

2 Peter 3:5-6. for this they willingly are ignorant of, that by the word of god the heavens were **of old**, and the earth standing out of the water and in the water:whereby the **world that then was**, being overflowed with water, **perished**:

Jeremiah 4:23. I beheld the earth, and, lo, *it was* without form, and void; and the heavens, and they *had* **no light**.

Genesis 1:2. And the earth was without form, and void; and **darkness** *was* upon the face of the **deep**............

Job 38:30. The waters are hid as *with* a stone, and the face of the deep is *frozen*.

Genesis 1:3. And God said, Let there be *light*: and there was light.

Genesis 1:5. And God called the light Day, and the darkness he called Night. And the evening and the morning were the *first day*.

Genesis 1:9. And God said, Let the waters under the heaven be gathered together unto *one* place, and let the dry *land* *appear*: and it was so. And God called the dry land *Earth*.

Psalms 104:30. Thou sendest forth thy spirit, they [mankind] are created: and thou *renewest* the face of the earth.

Exodus 20:11. For *in* six days the LORD made heaven and earth, *the sea*, and all that in them *is*, and rested the seventh day: wherefore the LORD blessed the sabbath day, and hallowed it.

Note the precise grammar, and how 'the sea' is separated between two commas, for as we will find out later, this is not in reference to any sea on earth. In fact, there is no reference anywhere in the Scriptures, of God creating any individual sea on earth.

The harsh reality is, that from the moment God said; 'Let there be light', the heavens and the earth were destined for a fiery destruction. For it is written; "But the heavens and the earth, *which are now*, by the same word are kept in store, reserved unto *fire* against the day of judgment and perdition of ungodly men". *(2 Peter 3:7.)*

it is very likely that each of the 6 days represent a millennium, hence the world or age beginning with Adam, will last for a total period of 6,000 years.

Ruin-Restoration

The entire theme of the Bible, is about the battle over a kingdom, and the rightful ruler of that kingdom. This controversy goes back long before Abraham, and even long before Adam's day. For it began at some point *after* God had created the heavens and the earth, back in the *beginning*. Back in the distant past when God laid the foundations of the earth, and the entire host of celestial beings celebrated and burst into song. Why were they so joyful? Most likely because their Creator had established the *earth* for a specific purpose; that it should be *inhabited*.

Job 38:4. Where wast thou when I laid the foundations of the earth? declare, if thou hast understanding.

Job 38:7. When the morning stars sang together, and all the sons of God shouted for joy?

*Isaiah 45:18.*For thus saith the LORD that created the heavens; God himself that formed the *earth* and made it; he hath *established* it, he created it *not* in vain, he formed it to be *inhabited*: I *am* the LORD; and *there is* none else.

There is every indication in the Scriptures, that the original creation, or kingdom of heaven, was placed under the governance of Lucifer and his angels. When they rebelled and sinned against God, unrighteousness entered the realm, and by the word of God, waters of death were unleashed upon the aeon, or the world, that formerly existed in the heavens of old. In his second epistle, Peter refers to this primordial aeon or age as, "the world that then was" and tells us that it once existed in the heavens and the earth *of old*.

Lucifer's Flood

The Book of Job, (*Chapter. 22*) records a flood event that affected 'men', which is generally assumed to refer to the flood of Noah. This particular flood however, occurred '*out of time*', and hence *prior* to the six days of Genesis, and the beginning of time as we know it.

The author tells of the mighty men who once *had* the earth, a race of unjust and wicked men who walked in darkness, and thus were spiritually blind. He records how these men who once had the earth, met an untimely and drastic end, due to their foundation being destroyed by a flood.

Job 22:8. But as for the mighty man, he had the earth; and the honourable man dwelt in it.

Job 22:15. Hast thou marked the old way which wicked men have trodden? Which were **cut down out of time**, whose foundation was **overflown with a flood:**

Nevertheless, God is merciful and gracious, and Job 22 closes with a verse that offers the hope of deliverance to some. I've no idea what 'the island of the innocent' refers to, but it would suggest dry land surrounded by water.

Job 22:30. He shall deliver the island of the innocent: and it is delivered by the pureness of thine hands.

This cataclysmic flood mentioned briefly in Job, is not specifically recorded in the Bible. Neither is the catastrophic Judgement event which was witnessed in a vision by a young shepherd boy, a giant-slayer, who later became the most famous King of Israel.

In Psalms 18, David describes this earth-shaking catastrophe, which bears no resemblance whatsoever to the flood of Noah. Although he tells of the fearful 'floods of ungodly men' *(Psalms 18:4)* David makes no mention of water and rain, but rather records a time of terrible hailstones and coals of fire. (most likely meteorites).

Psalms 18:7. Then the earth shook and trembled; the foundations also of the hills moved and were shaken, because he was wroth.

Psalm 18:12. At the brightness that was before him his thick clouds passed, hail stones and coals of fire.

Noah's flood certainly affected the earth, but there is no record in Genesis of the earth being shaken. Nor did Noah's flood affect the heavens. Yet David records how the earth was shaken, and the heavens above were bowed (bent out of shape). He tells how at the rebuke of God, the foundations of the world (habitable age) were 'discovered' (meaning denuded in a most shameful way).

Psalm 18:15. Then the channels of waters were seen, and the foundations of the world were discovered at thy rebuke, O LORD, at the blast of the breath of thy nostrils.

Noah's flood rid the world of the ungodly *(2 Peter 2:5)* but it had no bearing on the foundation of the world. I cannot prove it of course, but David's vision almost certainly refers to the wicked men cut down out of time, those whose foundation was overflown with a flood. In turn, this can only refer to the flood recorded by Peter, whereby 'the **world that then was' perished**. *(2Peter 3:7).*

Who then, were these mighty men of old who once possessed the earth? It would be completely wrong to assume that they were men made in the image and likeness of God. Such a notion would contradict Scripture, for this world (habitable age) alone, was founded for the benefit of Modern-day man made in God's image.

This then begs the question of just whose image the inhabitants of the former world may have resembled? The rebel angels perhaps? Those whose once perfect leader had boasted, "I will exalt my throne above the stars of God? *(Isaiah 14:13).* Those traffickers of Lucifer, who became violent, corrupt, and dishonest in their trading? Much like the Luciferian kings of the earth today.

Ezekiel 28:18. Thou hast defiled thy sanctuaries by the multitude of thine iniquities, by the iniquity of thy traffick; therefore will I bring forth a fire from the midst of thee, it shall devour thee, and I will bring thee to ashes upon the earth in the sight of all them that behold thee.

There are striking similarities between the judgement of the gods in Psalms 82, and the judgement of the mighty men who once had the earth, as recorded in the Book of Job. The children of the most High, the gods, also walked in darkness, at a time when the very foundations of the earth were shaken.

Psalms 82:5-6. They know not, neither will they understand; they walk on in darkness: all the foundations of the earth are out of course. I have said, Ye are gods; and all of you are children of the most High.

In neither case was immediate redemption made available. The gods were sentenced to fall like the princes and to die like men, and the mighty men told God to leave them be, and rhetorically asked what He was able do for them?

Job 22:17. Which said unto God, Depart from us: and what can the Almighty do for them?

The prophet Isaiah charged the fallen cherub Lucifer as being the MAN responsible for the ancient world becoming a wilderness. Thus the term 'Lucifer's Flood' is often applied to the destruction of the former age back in the heavens of old.

It was this earlier water judgement upon 'the world that then was', and *not* Noah's flood, of which Peter warned that men during the last days would prefer to remain ignorant. For whilst the majority of folk today, may well believe it merely a fable, nobody is actually ignorant of the flood of Noah. The apostle Peter, refers to this aeon, or age, way back in the heavens of old, as "the world that then was", and relates how it was completely wiped out, or perished by deluge, and how the earth became at least partially submerged by this great flood, on the scale of an Extinction Level Event.

Many have been told, that Peter was referring to the flood of Noah, which should come as little or no surprise, for the apostle himself warned, that most would prefer to ignore this prehistoric flood, back in the heavens of old. Yet Peter makes a clear distinction between the heavens and the earth *of old*, and the heavens and the earth *which are now,* and which are destined for a fiery destruction. And we know for certain, that Noah's Flood occurred in this *present* heavens and earth.

2 Peter 3:5-6. For this they *willingly* are *ignorant* of, that by the word of God the heavens *were of old*, and the *earth* standing out of the *water* and in the *water*: Whereby *the world that then was*, being overflowed with water, *perished*:

2 Peter 3:7. But the heavens and the earth, *which are now*, by the same word are kept in store, reserved unto fire against the day of judgment and perdition of ungodly men.

At Genesis 2:4, we read; These *are* the **generation**s of the heavens and of the earth when they were *created*, in the day that the LORD God *made* the earth and the heavens.

We can be absolutely certain there has only been the *one* creation, for it is referred to as the *first* heaven and the *first* earth *(Revelation 21:1).* Yet each has existed for two generations, the initial and perfect creation at Genesis 1:1, which Peter referred to as the heavens and earth *of old*, followed by a restored or renewed creation over a period of six literal days,starting at Genesis 1:3. Which Peter referred to as the heavens and the earth, *which are now,*

So, the big question is this. Which generation of the heavens and the earth did Adam, Noah et al dwell in? The heavens and the earth WHICH ARE NOW? Or the heavens and earth which were OF OLD? The answer of course, should be a no-brainer. Yet it still surprises me just how many folk will insist, that Peter was talking about the flood of Noah.

Furthermore, if we take the word of God *literally*, the earth had already been flooded during an age *prior* to the flood of Noah. Solomon argued that there was nothing new under the sun. He then posed a rhetorical question; Is there anything of which it can be said, see, this is new?

Hardly, because it's already been (taken place) in a time of antiquity, which was before us. Simply put; history repeats itself.

Ecclesiastes 1:9-10. The thing that *hath been*, it *is that* which *shall be*; and that which *is* done *is* that which *shall be* done: and *there is* no new *thing* under the sun. Is there *any* thing whereof it may be said, See, this *is* new? it *hath been already* of old time, *which was before us.*

To the very best of my knowledge, the only portion of scripture an "old time before us" can possibly refer to, is "the world that then was" back in the heavens "of old", as recorded by Peter.

There is little wonder then, that in the wake of a mega-flood on the scale of an extinction level event, that the second verse of Genesis describes the earth as being "without form and void", in total darkness, and submerged beneath the "face of the deep" which according to the Book of Job was FROZEN. The earth itself remained underwater, until God commanded the dry land to appear.

Jeremiah 4:23. I beheld the earth, and, lo, *it was* without form, and void; and the heavens, and they *had* no light.

Genesis 1:2. And the earth was without form, and void; and darkness *was* upon the face of the deep. And the Spirit of God moved upon the face of the waters.

Job 38:30. The waters are hid as *with* a stone, and the face of the deep is *frozen.*

Genesis 1:9. And God said, Let the *waters* under the heaven be gathered together unto one place, and let the dry *land appear*: and it was so. And God called the dry land Earth......

Is this making sense yet? For vast amounts of water without heat and light =ICE. Exactly who, or what existed back in this primordial kingdom, we are not told. We can be assured however, that it was *not* modern-day man, made in the image and the likeness of God.

For how long the earth remained in this lifeless and barren state, we're not told. Only that the Spirit of God moved upon the face of the waters, and God said "Let there be Light", and there was light, at the start of the *first* Day (Genesis 1:3-5) of this present aeon or world.

In Exodus 20:11, we read how in six days the LORD *made* heaven and earth, the sea, and all that in them is. The word "made" however, has an entirely different meaning to the word "created", as found in Genesis 1:1. for when God creates a thing, it is from out of nothing, but by the power of his word. When God *makes* a thing, it is from out of the material which he *created* in the beginning. Hence we read that Adam's physical body was formed from the dust of the ground. *(Genesis 2:7.)*

For the six days are *not* an account of the original pristine creation of the Heavens and the Earth recorded at Genesis 1:1. Known as 'The Foundation of the World' (literally, the Conception of the Age) the six days are a record of God restoring/renewing his ruined creation and creating modern-day man in his own image and likeness.

Psalms 104:30. Thou sendest forth thy spirit, they are created: and thou renewest the face of the earth.

With the exception of Adam and Eve, the first modern-day man and woman, directly created in the image and likeness of God, every other form of life was brought forth *after*, or *according* to its *kind*. From the flora and fauna, the creepy-crawlies, the beast of the field etc. to the birds, the fowl and marine life. For a kind or type, had previously existed back in the primordial world.

Genesis 1:11. And God said, Let the earth bring forth grass, the herb yielding seed, *and* the fruit tree yielding fruit after his *kind*, whose seed *is* in itself, upon the earth: and it was so.

Genesis 1:25. And God made the beast of the earth *after* his *kind*, and cattle *after* their *kind*, and every thing that creepeth upon the earth *after* his *kind*: and God saw that it was good.

The six-day restoration of the earth, the foundation of this present world (habitable age) and new beginnings. No DNA cross-over of species from one side of the gap to the other, but a completely new order of life, and placed under the governance of man. All the plant, animal, and human-like fossils upon the earth today were caused by this prehistoric flood and do not bear any genetic relationship with the plants, animals and humans living today.

I'm no expert on the matter, far from it, but I suspect the demise of the primordial aeon, known as *the world that then was,* produced the ideal conditions for the strange, but well-documented, natural process of *petrification*, where former living things are turned to *stone*.

There is also some evidence which would indicate that these life forms which existed back in the prehistoric world, were silicon-based, as opposed to the carbon-based life-forms of this present world. Either way, the evidence for this catastrophic flood, on the scale of an extinction level event, is scattered right across the entire realm of the earth.

This catastrophic deluge of epic proportion is generally written-off as the Younger-Dryas impact hypothesis. Which is hardly surprising when Peter warned of man's willing ignorance to accept this event was by the word of God. *(2Peter 3:5.)* Whose judgements are a Great Deep. *(Psalms 36:6.)*

But Satan and his earthly cohorts, would have us believe, that the geological and fossil record, which first and foremost, is undeniable evidence for the destruction of life, and on a massive scale, is in fact, evidence for life evolving. A bold-faced lie, straight from the bottomless pit, where Satan was formerly bound for one thousand years. For not only is he murderer and a liar, but he is also the father of the lie. *(John 844.)*

Rahab

The Bible records the mysterious and unexplained 'cutting' or splitting of Rahab, whose destruction affected the Serpent/Dragon. Administered by the word of God, an event occurred way back in the generations of old, and one of such violence it shook the very pillars of heaven. This is most likely the catastrophe referred to by both Job and David the Psalmist.

Psalms 89:10. Thou hast broken *Rahab* in pieces, as one that is slain; thou hast scattered thine enemies with thy strong arm.

Isaiah 51:9. Awake, awake, put on strength, O arm of the LORD; awake, as in the ancient days, in the generations of old. Art thou not it that hath cut *Rahab*, and wounded the *dragon*?

Job 26:11. The pillars of *heaven* tremble and are astonished at his reproof.

My personal belief and one shared by others is, that Rahab was a celestial body which existed in the heavens of old. Many believe Rahab was located between the orbits of Mars and Jupiter, and when judgement struck, the planet split into a myriad pieces. The shattered fragments of this ancient land area, formed the present-day Asteroid Belt.

In 1949 the well-known Soviet astronomer, Orlov Sergey Vladimirovich, gave the 'hypothetical' planet the name '*Phaeton*'. In Greek mythology, Phaeton (Shining One) was the son of the sun god Helios, who attempted to drive his father's solar chariot for a day with disastrous results, and was ultimately destroyed by Zeus. In Roman mythology, Saturn's chariot is led by serpents or dragons.

Lucifer means 'light bringer' and the single verse in the King James Bible where Lucifer is mentioned by name, is in Isaiah 14:12 where it reads;

How art thou fallen from heaven, O Lucifer, son of the morning!

During the Renaissance the story of Phaeton's unsuccessful efforts were equated with Lucifer's attempts to get too close to God. Scenes of Phaeton falling from his chariot were thus very popular in Renaissance art. Whether of any significance, the tale of Phaeton appears in Plato's 'Timaeus', where Critias, a leading and violent member of the Thirty Tyrants, tells the story of '*Atlantis*' as recounted by an Egyptian priest.

However distorted they may have become, most if not all ancient mythology is based on original truth. The ancient mythologies taught by the Priesthood of Cain, which continued after Noah's flood with the Egyptians, Romans and Greeks, were it would seem, partially based upon the catastrophic events leading up to the earlier Flood of Lucifer.

Did this catastrophic event recorded in Scripture which wounded the dragon and shook the very heavens, cause an Extinction Level Event? Did this cause the ancient world to become a wilderness, and leave the barren earth standing both in the water and out of the frozen water? It certainly seems very likely. All the plant, animal, and human fossils upon the earth today were caused by this prehistoric flood and do not bear any genetic relationship with the plants, animals and humans living today.

A wilful ignorance, or refusal to believe this Doctrinal Truth, has opened the door for the Militia of Zeus and the Cult of Saturn to introduce their invented Doctrine of Evolution. The fossil record which first and foremost is a record of mass death and destruction, has been presented as evidence for life evolving.

The theological concept of God Almighty having destroyed an ancient civilization long before he created man in his own image, is one which many find hard to grapple with. Yet the Bible clearly speaks of a former world (habitable age) which perished due to a deluge of unimaginable proportion, and implies that it affected both the heavens and the earth.

2 Peter 3:5-7. For this they willingly are ignorant of, that by the word of God the heavens *were of old, and the earth* standing out of the water and in the water: Whereby the world that then was, being overflowed with water, perished:

The Deep

The first mystery we come across in the Book of Genesis, is why the heaven (singular) becomes the heavens (plural) in the space of one chapter.

Genesis 1:1. In the beginning God created the *heaven* and the earth.

Genesis 2:1. Thus the *heavens* and the earth were finished, and all the host of them.

From a ruin-restoration understanding of Scripture, the once perfect earth which God created 'in the beginning' was now without form and void. This raises the intriguing question as to what had become of the heaven? For in the second verse of Genesis the word 'heaven' is conspicuous by its absence. Heaven is not mentioned by name, but in the Hebrew tongue is recorded as the 'teh-home', a swirling, watery abyss which was covered with *darkness*, and rendered in the KJB as '*the deep*'. The same Hebrew word translates in *Psalm 36:6* as "the great deep", and used in direct reference to the judgements of God.

Darkness is synonymous with evil *(Isaiah 45:7; Jeremiah 23:12)*. The darkness upon the face of the *deep* was the result of sin and rebellion against God back in the heavens and the earth of *old*. A spiritual darkness far beyond just the absence of light, but a darkness which portrays a sense of sorrow, misery, death and foreboding.

Genesis 1:1. In the beginning God created the heaven and the earth.

Genesis 1:2. And the earth was without form, and void; and ***darkness*** was upon the face of the deep.

In the *Septuagint* (Greek Old Testament) the word translated as "***the deep***" is ἀβύσσου (abussos), which carries a far more sinister tone, for the Greek Dictionary defines *abusssos* as the bottomless pit, the abyss; the subterranean world of the dead. The word *abusssos* also appears in the Greek *Textus Receptus* (Received Text) which constituted the translation-base used for the English version of the King James New Testament.

'Abussos' appears nine times in total in the Greek New Testament text, and the number 9 signifies judgement, especially divine judgement. On the only two occasions where abusssos is translated as 'the deep', the surrounding context has nothing whatsoever to do with the oceans. Without exception, the Greek word used for the depths of the sea is *Bathos*, as in;

Luke 5:4. Now when he had left speaking, he said unto Simon, Launch out into the ***deep***, and let down your nets for a draught.

On both occasions where abussos translates as 'the deep', it refers ***not*** to the watery depths, ***but*** to the realm of the dead, and the void into which the devils fear to be cast before the appointed time.

Romans 10:7. Or, Who shall ***descend*** into the ***deep***? (that is, to bring up Christ again from the dead.)

Luke 8:31. And they [devils] besought [Jesus] that he would not command them to ***go out*** into the ***deep***.

To further our understanding, on each of the other 7 occasions where abussos appears in the Greek text, it translates as 'the bottomless pit'. With this primary meaning of the word abussos in mind, *Genesis 1:2* effectively states:

And the earth was (had become) a wilderness, an undistinguishable ruin, and darkness (both literal and spiritual) encroached upon the face of the Deep, the Abussos, the Bottomless Pit.

To be clear on the matter, *abussos* is never translated as hell. Hell always translates from either *haides*, or *gheh'-en-nah*, except for the one occasion where *tartarow* refers to the deepest part of hell. *(2 Peter 2:4).* Now although one might well be a portal of sorts to the other, the bottomless pit and hades or hell, are two separate entities. The latter is generally considered to be within the bowels of, or beneath the earth, whereas the bottomless pit lies somewhere beyond. Hence why souls of man *descend* into the deep, whilst the devils are *cast out* into the deep. *(Romans 10:7- Luke 8:31.)*

It would seem then, that the Abyss, Hell included, was not a part of the original, pristine creation. The bottomless pit came into existence at the destruction of 'the world that then was', back in the heavens and the earth of old, and as the result of rebellion toward God. This would explain the absence of the word "heaven" in the second verse of the Bible, for the heaven of old was reduced to the Deep aka the Bottomless Pit.

If this understanding is correct, the irony here is, that Lucifer, the light bringer, who was charged with making the world a wilderness, effectively sealed his own destiny. By introducing the bottomless pit, where now known as Satan, the deceiver and the accuser of the brethren, he would be cast for one thousand years, during which time he was unable to deceive the nations.

Noah's Flood

The second day of the Genesis week, is the only day out of the six, which God didn't immediately bless by declaring it good. Why? Because it was a day of division, which was necessary, but *not* of itself good. For God divided the lower waters from the upper waters, by placing the firmament between each level. On the third day, God gathered the waters under the heaven (firmament) into *one* place, and said, 'let the dry land appear'. At this stage, because the lower waters are gathered into one place, I think it safe to infer it was a singular body of water. It was from out of this vast body of water that the dry land appeared.

Genesis 1:7. And God made the firmament, and divided the waters [of the deep] which were *under* the firmament from the waters which were *above* the firmament: and it was so.

Genesis 1:9-10. And God said, Let the waters under the heaven be gathered together unto *one* place, and let the dry land *appear*: and it was so. And God called the dry land Earth; and the gathering together of the waters called he *Seas*: and God saw that it was good.

Notice how "Seas" is capitalized and plural, yet there is no reference to God creating individual oceans on earth. In fact the first sea to be named is the Salt Sea, *(Genesis 14:3)* and this is well after Noah's flood, and the later earthquake event which divided the earth in the days of Peleg. *(1 Chronicles 1:19.)* Things changed dramatically from this point, and today we have individual oceans, continents, thousands of islands and thousands of rivers.

In fact, the picture presented in Genesis, of the earth *prior* to Noah's flood, is of a vast circular landmass, with no individual oceans, just four major rivers and completely surrounded by water. Every equal-arm cross in existence today, is based on this massive and circular landmass with its 4 major rivers, which emerged from the waters of the deep.

Furthermore, the earth itself is established upon water. Adam and Eve were created innocent, hence it is quite possible that the dry land which emerged from the waters of the deep, was the 'island of the innocent', which God spared from total destruction.

Job 22:30. He shall deliver the island of the innocent: and it is delivered by the pureness of thine hands.

Psalms 24:2. For he hath founded it [the earth] upon the seas, and established it upon the floods.

Psalms 136:6. To him that stretched out the earth above the waters: for his mercy endureth for ever.

Throughout the Scriptures deep waters exist beneath the earth, which itself is located beneath the firmament (which God formed to contain the celestial bodies), and is firmly fixed and stationary. At no time does the Bible even suggest the earth to be an integral moving part of the Solar System. Because water always finds its own level, this then indicates that the earth, which is established upon the floods, exists upon a horizontal plane.

A close reading of the Genesis flood account shows that Noah and his family boarded the Ark *seven* days before the flood started in earnest, because it would seem the waters of the great deep surrounding the habitable circular earth were already encroaching upon the dry land. *(Genesis 7:7).* According to the Bible, the flood was instigated when the fountains of the great deep broke open *(Genesis 7:11)* followed by more than a month of torrential rain.

The covenant promise God made with Noah never to flood the entire earth again is unconditional, and made to all of Noah's descendants and all creatures of the earth and sealed with the sign of the rainbow. Hence after the floodwaters had receded from the face of the earth,

God set a boundary to prevent the waters from returning and flooding the earth ever again.

Genesis 8:14. And in the second month, on the seven and twentieth day of the month, was the earth dried.

Psalms 104:9. Thou hast set a ***bound*** that they [the waters] may not pass over; that they ***turn not again*** to cover the earth.

By way of reasoning, that bound or boundary was clearly ***not*** in place ***prior*** to the flood of Noah, but the waters certainly were. For the waters did indeed once turn to cover the earth. The word 'again' is the key which indicates the waters that once 'turned' to cover the earth's surface still exist, but are now restrained by some form of boundary established by God.

Though not actually stated, it would seem to indicate that as the flood-waters receded from the face of the flat circular earth, they froze around the entire circumference to form a massive barrier of ice. What better way to ensure the waters "turn not again to cover the earth" than to solidify them?

Again, whilst not explicitly stated, the Bible plainly informs us that the oceans of the earth stretch to a certain point, beyond which they cannot pass. This boundary which encircles all of earth's continents and oceans will serve its purpose until the very end of the age. It may even help to protect the earth from what lies beyond the recognized extremities.

Job 26:10. He hath compassed the waters with ***bounds***, until the day and night come to an end.

Job 38:11. And said, Hitherto shalt thou come, ***but no further***: and ***here*** shall thy proud waves ***be stayed***?

Yes, I'm well aware that this is all somewhat speculative, but nevertheless such speculation comes by reasoning from the scriptures along with that which the word of God firmly indicates. Likewise, although there is no actual evidence available to the likes of you and I, that the circular earth and its oceans are completely surrounded by a barrier of ice, neither is there any evidence that we live on a spinning globe. Multiple photographs of the Antarctic region can be found on the Internet, many of which show towering walls of ice rising perpendicular from the ocean. Some of these images are nothing short of stunning, the likes of which I've never seen before. Not even on David Attenborough's otherwise truly remarkable, 'Blue Planet' Series.

The generally accepted flat earth model is that Earth is in the form of an enormous disc with the Magnetic North Pole situated somewhere in the centre. Rather than being an isolated continent at the bottom of a globe, Antarctica is thought to be an impassable barrier of ice, an inhospitable frozen terrain which encircles the entire habitable earth, and serves to contain all of the continents and oceans. Apart from the handful of completely land-locked bodies of water such as the Dead Sea, all of the earth's seas and oceans are inter-connected which ensures that sea-level remains constant world-wide.

Sea of Glass

In *Genesis 1:10*, the word *Seas* refers to the two gatherings of water, those God placed **beneath** the firmament and those he placed **above** the firmament. Those who hold with the doctrine of ruin-restoration seem to agree that the waters above the firmament are frozen, and form a crystalline 'sea' that effectively acts as a barrier between the entire physical creation which is subject to death (the Law of Entropy) and the third heaven, or paradise, the abode of the Most Holy God, who is life everlasting.

Revelation 4:6. And before the throne there was a *sea of glass* like unto crystal.

Psalms 148:4. Praise him, ye heavens of heavens, and ye **waters** that *be* **above** the heavens.

Job 26:5. Dead things are formed from **under** the waters, and the inhabitants thereof.

Ezekiel witnessed 'the sea' or the upper firmament in a vision, and described it as 'the colour of the terrible crystal.' *(Ezekiel 1:22)*. The sea can also be seen 'in type' as the molten sea in King Solomon's temple.

2 Chronicles 4:2. Also he made a molten sea of ten cubits from brim to brim.....

Jesus referred to this 'contained' creation when he informed his disciples that he was not of this world (cosmos), but from above [the sea] whilst the inhabitants of this world are from beneath[the sea].

John 8:23. And he said unto them, Ye are from **beneath**; I am from **above**: ye **are** of this world; I am **not** of this world.

The heaven which contains the sun, the moon and the stars should not be confused with the *third* heaven or paradise, the abode of God the Father. *(2 Corinthians 12:2-4)*. Central to the Christian faith, is the belief that Jesus Christ, the Word made flesh, came down from heaven (paradise) as the Lamb of God to do the will of the Father and erase the sin of the *world*.

John 1:29. The next day John seeth Jesus coming unto him, and saith, Behold the Lamb of God, which taketh away the sin of the world.

John 6:38. For I came *down from heaven*, not to do mine own will, but the will of him that sent me.

Luke 23:43. And Jesus said unto him, Verily I say unto thee, To day shalt thou be with me in *paradise*.

The 'sea of glass ' didn't exist in the heavens and earth *of old*, but was constructed after God declared "Let there be Light", and on the Second Day, the day of division, and purely for the generation of the heavens and the earth *'which are now'*. Ultimately, all that is subject to the ravages of death (the Law of Entropy) must either be fully cleansed and restored, or utterly destroyed. My personal understanding is that the entire creation will in effect become the everlasting fire *prepared* for the devil and his angels. For the heavens and the earth, *which are now*, are destined for a fiery destruction.

2 Peter 3:7. But the heavens and the earth, *which are now*, by the same word are kept in store, reserved unto fire against the day of judgment and perdition of ungodly men.

2 Peter 3:10. But the day of the Lord will come as a thief in the night; in the which the heavens shall pass away with a great noise, and the elements shall melt with fervent heat, the earth also and the works that are therein shall be burned up.

2 Peter 3:12. Looking for and hasting unto the coming of the day of God, wherein the heavens being on fire shall be dissolved, and the elements shall melt with fervent heat?

Revelation 20:10. And the devil that deceived them was cast into the *lake of fire* and brimstone, where the beast and the false prophet *are*, and shall be tormented day and night for ever and ever.

Revelation 20:14. And death and hell were cast into the lake of fire. This is the second death.

Revelation 20:15. And whosoever was not found written in the book of life was cast into the lake of fire.

When this death-ridden *first* heavens and *first* earth finally pass away, the 'Sea' which acts as a barrier between the profane physical creation and the Glory of the Holy Creator, will have served its purpose, and in the future 'new heaven and new earth' will no longer be necessary. Note we have now returned to a new, but *singular* heaven.

Revelation 21:1. And I saw a new heaven and a new earth: for the *first* heaven and the *first* earth were passed away; and there *was no more sea.*

It is worth noting, that when speaking of the day of the Lord and the coming day of God, Peter was *not* referring to the day of Christ, the coming of Jesus in the clouds of heaven. For whilst Jesus returned with fiery vengeance, the heavens and earth were *not* burned out of existence, for if such were the case, there would have been no earth for the kings and priests to reign upon for a thousand years. Peter was referring to a cataclysm of fire at the end of the ages, when the heavens and the earth *which are now,* are burned out of existence.

2 Peter 3:7. But the heavens and the earth, which are now, by the same word are kept in store, reserved unto fire against the day of judgment and perdition of ungodly men.

2 Peter 3:13. Nevertheless we, according to his promise, look for *new* heavens and a *new* earth, wherein dwelleth righteousness.

Full or extreme Preterists, who tend to spiritualize nearly everything when it comes to prophecy, claim we are already in the new heavens and the new earth. But there is no empirical evidence for this whatsoever. On the other hand, the empirical evidence for humanity living during the little season, a time of great Satanic deception, can clearly be observed all around us, and on a daily basis.

Israel

It may not sound 'politically correct' but the high calling of the children of Israel was straight from the heart of God who chose them out of all the nations of the earth.

Deuteronomy 7:6. For thou art an holy people unto the LORD thy God: the LORD thy God hath chosen thee to be a special people unto himself, above all people that are upon the face of the earth.

That 'choosing' however did not automatically assure that all Israel would live the part, for they were required to live in obedience, and would receive either blessing or cursing accordingly. Of the 12 Hebrew tribes, Judah was the most faithful and the most active in making converts, especially after they teamed up with the Levites. Their converts became known as the proselytes (i.e. the ones who prayed to Jehovah, the God of Judah). The other 10 tribes, collectively known as Israel, did not fulfil their calling and separated from Judah and always did evil in God's eyes. Israel as a whole worshipped false gods and went into sin, and God had to cast her out of the land. Shortly before his death, Moses reminded the people of this, and issued dire warning that due to their profane life-style, great evil would come upon them, especially during the *latter* days.

Deuteronomy 31:29. For I know that after my death ye will utterly corrupt yourselves, and turn aside from the way which I have commanded you; and evil will befall you *in the latter days*; because ye will do evil in the sight of the LORD, to provoke him to anger through the work of your hands.

Judges 2:11. And the children of Israel did evil in the sight of the LORD, and served Baalim:

Time and again over the course of their turbulent history, the children of Israel rejected their God in favour of serving the pagan gods of the surrounding nations, and time and again they suffered as a result. You can read about their history in the Book of Kings 1&2.

Considered one of the minor prophets, the Book of Amos was likely written between 760 and 753 B.C. making the Book of Amos the first Biblical prophetic book written. More than almost any other book of Scripture, the book of Amos holds God's people accountable for their ill-treatment of others. Amos can see that beneath Israel's external prosperity and power, internally the nation is corrupt to the core. Of all the multitudes delivered out of Egypt, Amos brings the word of God specifically against the children of Israel, saying;

Amos 3:2. You only have I known of all the families of the earth: therefore I will punish you for all your iniquities.

In Chapter 5, Verse 2, Amos makes the astounding statement;

"The virgin of Israel is fallen; she shall no more rise: she is forsaken upon her land; there is none to raise her up."

The 'virgin of Israel' is never mentioned again in the Bible, for as God said, "there is none to raise her up." Why would God say this? Worship of the 6-pointed Star of Saturn!

Amos 5:26. But ye have borne the tabernacle of your Moloch and Chiun your images, *the star* of your god, which ye made to yourselves.

Acts 7:43. Yea, ye took up the tabernacle of Moloch, and the *star* of your god Remphan, figures which ye made to worship them: and I will carry you away beyond Babylon.

The Exile

Jesus has zero-tolerance for child sacrifice and strictly forbids it. One of, if not the primary reason for the 70 year captivity of the Jews in Babylon was the abominable practice of child sacrifice by fire to Molech. *(Jeremiah 32: 35-36)*.

The Book of Jeremiah, which was written between 630 and 580 B.C. records the final prophecies to Judah, warning of oncoming destruction if the nation does not repent of its idolatrous and immoral lifestyle. Jeremiah foretold how the nation would remain in Babylon for 70 years, before returning to their homeland. *(Jeremiah 29:10)*.

In 589 B.C. the armies of King Nebuchadnezzar laid siege to Jerusalem for over a year, killing many people, taking captive many thousand more, and destroying the First Temple built by Solomon, leaving Jerusalem in ruins.70 yeas later and just as Jeremiah foretold, Babylon was conquered by Cyrus II of Persia, who allowed the exiles to return to their homeland, and rebuild the City of Jerusalem and the Second Temple.

The Babylonian Exile opened 'Pandora's Box' so to speak, for though in the earlier years of captivity they still feared the LORD, (which is the beginning of wisdom *Proverbs 9:10)*, the children of Israel began to seek after and serve the strange pagan gods which were released.

2 Kings 17:33. They *feared* the LORD, *and* served their own gods, after the manner of the nations whom they carried away from thence.

After decades of intermarriage, and having been born in exile, it was a new generation who returned from Babylon, and Israel was largely replaced with Canaanites, Medeans, and Babylonians. So the new residents no longer feared the LORD, and appointed for themselves priests of all sorts to serve in the groves, and erect shrines on the high places.

2 Kings 17:25. And *so* it was at the beginning of their dwelling there, *that* they feared *not* the LORD: therefore the LORD sent lions among them, which slew *some* of them.

During the 70 year exile, the Jewish folk and their priests were exposed to Chaldean science, pagan ritual, magic and mysticism, and one has to wonder how much that influenced Jewish thought. Certainly it led to the development of the astrology and numerology for which the Chaldean Magi became famous. This developing mixture of Babylonian paganism and Old Testament teachings, was responsible for the spiritual blindness of the Jewish leaders in the days of Christ. The Virgin of Israel had fallen, and since their return from Babylon the foreigners now in Jerusalem feared *not* the Lord, hence lacked the wisdom to recognize the arrival of the promised Messiah.

2 Kings 17:34. Unto this day they do after the former manners: they *fear not* the LORD, neither do they after their statutes, or after their ordinances, or after the law and commandment which the LORD commanded the children of Jacob, whom he named Israel.

Due to no inspired written instruction from God, the four hundred years between the completion of Malachi the final book of the Old Testament, and the birth of Jesus Christ, are sometimes called 'the silent years'. During this period Kabbalists, Pharisees, Sadducees, Essenes, Samaritans, Zealots, Herodians (Edomites) and the Hasmoneans codified the Gnostic texts of the Apocrypha. These 'hidden texts' were then used by Essenes in Qumran who wrote the 'Dead Sea Scrolls', which were later used to write the 'Nag Hamadi Scrolls', The 'Talmud' and the 'Zohar'.

In an attempt to justify man's failure and weakness, during the silent years the Jewish religious leaders issued a whole variety of new laws and interpretations. While publicly retaining the appearance of Godliness, they became more elaborate and complex in an attempt to circumvent the written law as given by God to Moses.

These rules and regulations which have since been written down and compiled in 'The Babylonian Talmud' include, three chapters on how to behave in an outdoor toilet, much about bodily discharges especially faeces, and hand-washing from dawn to dusk to ward off unclean spirits or devils, against which Christ declaimed. Just the rules of the Sabbath alone would leave one scratching one's head in bewilderment.

For example, can you imagine being homeless in today's society, and a holy 'man of the cloth' comes down on you like a 'ton of bricks' for having the audacity to pick up your sleeping-bag, on a Sunday of all days, and cart your belongings to another shop doorway in the adjacent street. That's how crazy things had become in Jesus' day, for the religious authorities had determined that such an act constituted 'carrying a load' on the Sabbath. Therefore it was in breach of the commandments of God.

This is why the rulers of the Synagogue were so outraged with Jesus when he healed a man on the Sabbath. Not because he'd broken the law of God, but because he had broken the law of the Pharisee. Jesus didn't mince his words, but told the Pharisees outright that their spiritual father was the devil.(*John 8:44*). He also told them their religion was based on the traditions of man, that it was not of God nor did they derive it from the Old Testament. Hence His words recorded in Matthew 15:6;"Ye have made the commandment of God of none effect by your tradition."

Although some of the more dubious doctrines were concealed from the general public, they were rigorously upheld by the religious leaders. The Pharisees took great pride in their piety and as was their daily custom, prayed on the streets so as to be seen by the public. They were the ones responsible for stirring up dissent among the Jews by claiming Jesus to be a blasphemer and an imposter, which led to his mock trial and crucifixion.

These were the men Jesus accused of being hypocrites, and likened their religion to white-washed sepulchres, indeed beautiful from the outside, but inside full of dead men's bones and of all uncleanness. *(Matthew 23:27)*. Jesus also warned the scribes and the Pharisees, that the shed blood of all the prophets slain since the foundation of the world, would be required of their generation.

Luke 11:50. That the blood of all the prophets, which was shed from the foundation of the world, may be required of *this generation*;

In fact, Jesus had much to say, and many dire warnings for this particular generation in the latter days, which Moses too, had previously warned of. For these were the days also foretold of by the prophet Daniel, who, in a night vision saw one like the Son of man coming in the clouds. A vision which would come to pass "*at the time of the end.*" *(Daniel 8:17.)*

Deuteronomy 31:29. For I know that after my death ye will utterly corrupt yourselves, and turn aside from the way which I have commanded you; and evil will befall you *in the latter days*; because ye will do evil in the sight of the LORD, to provoke him to anger through the work of your hands.

The birth of a King

Daniel 7:13. I saw in the night visions, and, behold, *one* like the Son of man came with the clouds of heaven, and came to the Ancient of days, and they brought him near before him.

Daniel 10:14. Now I am come to make thee understand what shall befall thy people in the *latter days*: for yet the vision *is* for *many* days.

Daniel 9:24. Seventy weeks are determined upon thy people and upon thy holy city, to finish the transgression, and to make an end of sins, and to make reconciliation for iniquity, and to bring in everlasting righteousness, and to seal up the vision and prophecy, and to anoint the most Holy.

Sixty nine weeks out of Daniel's prophetic seventy weeks of years, namely, 69x7=483 years, were perfectly fulfilled, when Jesus started his public ministry. This is why there was an air of expectation and excitement in Israel at the time, for the religious Jews rightly understood that Daniel's prophetic seventy weeks of years, were almost at the point of conclusion. And why John the baptist, who was in prison at the time, sent his disciples to ask of Jesus, if he truly were the coming one, or should they look for another? *(Matthew 11:3.)* And why the people cried out; "Hosanna; Blessed is he that cometh in the name of the Lord:" *(Mark 11:9.)*

Whether aware of Daniel's prophecy, or not, even the magi, the wise men from the east, recognized the imminent birth of the new king of the Jews. They had followed the star they had seen in the east, all the way to Jerusalem.

Saying, Where is he that is born King of the Jews? for we have seen his star in the east, and are come to worship him. *(Matthew 2:2.)*

For these wise men, the magi, were learned in the art of astrology, and had recognized that the world was entering the Age of Pisces, which began in AD 1, the year King Jesus was born. Which is why the fish symbol has long been associated with Christianity. It has nothing to do with his followers being fishers of men, but represents the dawn of the age Jesus was born into.

Spiritual warfare at the highest level was underway at the birth of Christ, for I suspect that the guiding star was Satan himself who can appear as an angel of light. For Satan knew that the only way he could ever be defeated by the seed of the woman (as prophesied in Genesis 3:15), was if God himself were to come in the flesh.

Hence the picture presented by Matthew, is one of Satan, working through the hearts of wicked men, to destroy Jesus as a young child, whilst God the Father was always one step ahead, by protecting his only-begotten Son. Yet the scriptures are crystal clear, prophecy was being *fulfilled*, every step of the way.

Ultimately, by following the star, the wise men encountered king Herod, a wickedly jealous and unscrupulous man, who told them to report back to him once they had found the new born king. For according to the lying Herod, he too wanted to worship the king, but in truth, he wanted to destroy him. Herod then called for the chief priests and scribes, demanding to know where the Christ would be born.

And they said unto him, In Bethlehem of Judaea: *for thus it is written* by the *prophet*. *(Matthew 2:5.)*

From here, the star appeared once again, leading the wise men to Bethlehem, and to the very house where the young child Jesus, was with Mary, his mother.

Matthew 2:11. And when they were come into the house, they saw the young child with Mary his mother, and fell down, and worshipped him: and when they had opened their treasures, they presented unto him gifts; gold, and frankincense, and myrrh.

Having worshipped Jesus and presented their regal gifts, God warned the wise men in a dream, not to return to Herod, but to take a different route back to their homeland. Which much to Herod's disgust, they duly obeyed.

Matthew 2:13-15. And when they were departed, behold, the angel of the Lord appeareth to Joseph in a dream, saying, Arise, and take the young child and his mother, and flee into Egypt, and be thou there until I bring thee word: for Herod will seek the young child to destroy him. When he arose, he took the young child and his mother by night, and departed into Egypt: And was there until the death of Herod: *that it might be fulfilled* which was spoken of the Lord by the *prophet*, saying, Out of Egypt have I called my son.

In the meanwhile, Herod was livid that the wise men had not reported back to him, and in a fit of murderous rage issued orders for what would become known as the 'Massacre of the Innocents'. The execution of all male children who were two years old and under in the vicinity of Bethlehem. This was Satan's attempt to kill Jesus, by working through the evil, murderous heart of a willing human king, but it also fulfilled prophecy.

Matthew 2:17-18. Then *was fulfilled* that which was spoken by Jeremy the prophet, saying, In Rama was there a voice heard, lamentation, and weeping, and great mourning, Rachel weeping *for* her children, and would not be comforted, because they are not.

Matthew 2:19-20. But when Herod was dead, behold, an angel of the Lord appeareth in a dream to Joseph in Egypt, Saying, Arise, and take the young child and his mother, and go into the land of Israel: for they are dead which sought the young child's life.

Having duly returned to Israel, Joseph became fearful for his family, because Herod's son, Archelaus, was now reigning in Judaea. Having been warned of God in a dream, Joseph now headed towards Galilee.

Matthew 2:23. And he came and dwelt in a city called Nazareth: *that it might be fulfilled* which was spoken by the *prophets*, He shall be called a Nazarene.

Luke 21:32. Verily I say unto you, This generation shall not pass away, till *all be fulfilled*.

On the day of Pentecost, Acts 2:16 reads; " But this is that which was spoken by the prophet Joel;"
According to Jesus, all would be fulfilled during the lifetime of the first generation of believers.. This would have included all of Joel's prophecies. Such as;

Joel 2:1. Blow ye the trumpet in Zion, and sound an alarm in my holy mountain: let all the inhabitants of the land tremble: for the day of the LORD cometh, for it is nigh at hand;

Joel 2:10. The earth shall quake before them; the heavens shall tremble: the sun and the moon shall be dark, and the stars shall withdraw their shining:

Time and again throughout the gospels, Jesus warned His audience that *all* of the Old Testaments prophecies would be *fulfilled* during their generation. Furthermore, many of them would still be alive to witness the Son of man coming in the clouds of heaven, just as *prophesied* by Daniel

Daniel 7:13. I saw in the night visions, and, behold, *one* like the Son of man came with the clouds of heaven, and came to the Ancient of days, and they brought him near before him.

Matthew 16:28. Verily I say unto you, There be some standing here, which shall not taste of death, till they see the Son of man coming in his kingdom.

Mark 13:26. And then shall they see the Son of man coming in the clouds with great power and glory.

It is quite clear, that Jesus spent his ministry years, preaching the gospel of the kingdom of heaven and the kingdom of God, to a generation of people living in the last days and at the time of the end for *Israel*. Some of whom would still be alive to witness his coming in the clouds.

The Kingdom of Heaven and the Kingdom of God

Did you know that neither of these terms are to be found in the Old Testament? I didn't, or not until I done a word search a number of years ago now. Of course, they are alluded to throughout the Old Testament, but never mentioned by name. Both terms are used to a degree interchangeably in the New Testament, but nevertheless each term conveys a different meaning. The kingdom of God is primarily a spiritual kingdom, whereas the kingdom of heaven is primarily a literal and physical kingdom.

It was the kingdom of God, the spiritual kingdom, that the Jews failed to grasp hold of. It came in fully at the Cross, and is a message that is accepted within the heart of a man, by faith, which produces the fruits of the Spirit.

It is the kingdom which Jesus said we should first seek, and is experienced from the moment faith comes and a man becomes born again. Not of water via the womb this time, as Nicodemus once supposed, but born directly of the Spirit of God. The very moment he is delivered from the kingdom of darkness, and is the work of the Father, Son and Holy Spirit. This is the kingdom that can never be forcibly taken away from the believer in Christ.

When asked by the Pharisees (whose idea of the kingdom was a literal, physical one that would bring freedom to the nation from their Roman oppressors) when the kingdom of God would come, Jesus replied;

The kingdom of God cometh not with observation: neither shall they say, Lo here! or, lo there! for, behold, the kingdom of God is *within* you. *(Luke 17:20-21.)*

Yet when Jesus was questioned by Pilate in similar vein, his reply was completely different;

My kingdom is not of this world: if my kingdom were of this world, then would my servants fight, that I should not be delivered to the Jews: but *now* is my kingdom not from hence. *(John 18:36.)*

Note the emphasis of the word *now*, because several Bible versions omit the word 'now' altogether. Now indicates that although not yet, the time would come when Jesus would indeed have a literal kingdom on earth. Jesus was referring to the kingdom of heaven, rather than the kingdom of God, although eventually they will be inseparable. The term 'kingdom of heaven' is primarily a literal and physical kingdom, and the battle for dominion of this kingdom has brought about untold amounts of bloodshed and war.

Matthew 11:12. And from the days of John the Baptist until now the kingdom of heaven suffereth violence, and the violent take it by force.

The kingdom of God *within* you can never be taken by force by violent men. It is the literal kingdom of heaven, *not* the kingdom of God, that the battle has been waged over, even to this day.

Jesus came to his own and preached a dualistic message. To the Jews, the heirs of the promised political kingdom, the Lord preached the gospel of the kingdom of heaven—a literal, physical kingdom *soon* to come: 'From that time Jesus began to preach and say, Repent:for the kingdom of *heaven* is at hand.' *(Matthew 4:17.)*

To the entire world, he preached the coming kingdom of *God*—righteousness and holiness: 'Now after that John was put in prison, Jesus came into Galilee, preaching the gospel of the kingdom of God, and saying, the time is fulfilled, and the kingdom of God is at hand, *repent* ye, and believe the gospel.' *(Mark 1:4.)*

Acts 17:30. And the times of this ignorance God winked at; but now commandeth all men every where to *repent*:

When rightly dividing the word, we can see that Jesus was preaching two components of the kingdom. And the Jews who accepted him, would see him return in the clouds, just as he had foretold. Hence the millennial reign primarily fulfilled the literal and political kingdom of heaven upon earth. The *first* resurrection of the blessed and holy, *(Revelation 20:6)* who reigned upon the earth for one thousand years, as the kings and priests of God.

Revelation 5:10. And hast made us unto our God kings and priests: and we shall reign *on* the earth.

The spiritual kingdom of God, that Jesus said cannot be observed by others, because it is "within you", will collectively remain within the body of Christ, for as long as born-again believers still walk upon the face of the earth.

Interestingly, the term 'kingdom of God' appears seventy times in the King James Bible, and 70 signifies forgiveness, wholeness, healing and salvation. Jesus sent out seventy disciples, expressly to preach the good news of the kingdom of God.

*Luke 10:1-9.*After these things the Lord appointed other *seventy* also, and sent them two and two before his face into every city and place, whither he himself would come..[.......] and say unto them, the kingdom of God is come nigh unto you.

The term 'kingdom of heaven' appears thirty three times in the King James Bible and the number 33 relates to king David, Jerusalem and Jesus. David was thirty three generations from Adam, had 33 mighty men, and reigned from Jerusalem for 33 years. Jesus, the true king of that great city, lived for thirty three years before the cross.

When Jesus made urgent statements of immanency, such as 'the time is nigh', he meant exactly as he said. Jesus was referring to the generation he spoke to directly, not a future generation of believers 2,000 plus years down the line. The Scriptures make clear that the expectation of the first generation of those who believed that Jesus was the Christ, included the great tribulation, the coming of the Son of man in the clouds of heaven, and the first resurrection/rapture. Furthermore many expected to still be alive to witness this truly astounding event. Although Jesus didn't explicitly say so, his disciples rightly understood what he meant. John was not going to die, but would remain here on earth, until the coming of Jesus in the clouds of heaven.

John 21:23. Then went this saying abroad among the brethren, that that disciple should not die: yet Jesus said not unto him, He shall not die; but, If I will that he tarry till I come, what is that to thee?
Whilst he may not have fully understood it at the time, by faith, John himself believed Jesus would keep his promise, and to the extent he encouraged his fellow-believers to share the same confidence.

1 John 2:28. And now, little children, abide in him; that, when he shall appear, we may have confidence, and not be ashamed before him at his coming.

Matthew 24:33. So likewise ye, when ye shall see all these things, know that it is near, *even* at the doors.

Luke 21:28. And when these things begin to come to pass, then **look up**, and lift up your heads; for your redemption draweth nigh.

Luke 21:32. Verily I say unto you, This generation shall not pass away, till all be fulfilled.

Luke 9:27. But I tell you of a truth, there be some standing here, which shall not taste of death, till they see the kingdom of God.

Matthew 24:21. For then shall be great tribulation, such as was not since the beginning of the world to this time, no, nor ever shall be.

1Thessalonians 4:17. Then we which are alive and remain shall be caught up together with them in the clouds, to meet the Lord in the air: and so shall we ever be with the Lord.

1 Corinthians 15:51-52. Behold, I shew you a mystery; We shall not all sleep, but we shall all be changed, In a moment, in the twinkling of an eye, at the last trump: for the trumpet shall sound, and the dead shall be raised incorruptible, and we shall be changed.

It wasn't just the early Christians who knew the time of the end was fast approaching, for John even wrote that Satan was exceedingly angry, because he knew that his time was fast running out. *(Revelation 12:12.)* Because that old Serpent knows the Scriptures far better than you and I, the reason for his great wrath, I suspect, was because he knew it was written, that he would be bound within the bottomless pit for the entire one thousand years.

For the last thirty years or so, I have always accepted the futurist interpretation of end times prophecy, so know from personal experience how it can be quite a struggle to believe otherwise. But, through re-reading the Scriptures, from a fresh perspective, how is it possible to refute the historicist view, and the literal past-fulfilment of these end time prophecies?

The battle for dominion over the kingdom of heaven, was resolved at the Cross, and death was finally defeated, but the out-workings of Christ's victory, continue to this very day. And will do so until the final judgement at the great white throne, and "death", the last enemy of Christ, is destroyed in the lake of fire forever. In the meanwhile, and although the millennial reign, the kingdom of heaven upon earth, has been and gone, the kingdom of God remains within the hearts of all those born again, until all is 'delivered up' to God the Father.

1 Corinthians 15:24-26. Then *cometh* the end, when he shall have delivered up the kingdom to God, even the Father; when he shall have put down all rule and all authority and power. For he must reign, till he hath put all enemies under his feet. The *last* enemy *that* shall be destroyed *is* death.

Full or Extreme Preterism would have us believe that even this prophecy has been perfectly fulfilled, hence we are now living in the new heavens and the new earth. For the earth that we dwell upon, and the heavens above us, are not the heavens and the earth that God created in the beginning, for the first heaven and the first earth have previously been burned out of existence in a maelstrom of fire. They will claim that all we need to do, is worship God. For beyond death, collectively, each member of the "church" or the "body of Christ", will constitute the city of God which is New Jerusalem. *(Revelation 3:12.)*

All I can say is, if this really is the new earth, then I dread to think what life on the *first* earth was like. For where is God's promise of abundant righteousness which Peter told us about? Why is Satan deceiving the nations like never before, when according to Full Preterists, he has already been cast into the lake of fire?

Surely the only answer can be, is that we, and the few generations immediately before us, have all been born into the Little Season? An open-ended period of time, during which Satan has been released from the bottomless pit, for the sole purpose of deceiving every nation on earth.

This Generation

When reading the Bible, I've long come to the conclusion, that unless the surrounding context dictates otherwise, the simplest understanding of the plain written text, is generally the right one. Take the term 'this generation' for example. For although I was originally taught that Jesus was referring to a generation in the far distant future, our generation for example, a simple reading of the plain written text, declares otherwise. Jesus was referring directly to the generation of folk in his presence. Which is exactly what his disciples believed. For good old-fashioned common sense alone, should be enough to convince us that the early disciples did *not* believe that Jesus wasn't being entirely honest with them, when he used the term, "this generation". Likewise, logic and reason should tell us they did *not* believe that what Jesus really meant, was folk who wouldn't be born for at least another two millennia, would be the generation who would see him coming in the clouds.

Mark 13:26. And then shall they see the Son of man coming in the clouds with great power and glory.

Mark 13:30. Verily I say unto you, that this generation shall not pass, till all these things be done.

In an attempt to get around this dilemma, the naysayers will turn to the Greek text. I have even been told that Jesus didn't tell folk back in the day, that they would see him *coming* in the clouds at his return. Because what Jesus really meant was, that folk would see him *going* up in the clouds at his ascension. Evidently, or so I was told, it's a translation issue, for in the Greek language, the word "coming" really means "going". Hence those darned King James Bible translators, didn't know whether they were coming or going half of the time, and have much to answer for, wouldn't you say?

Matthew 23:36. Verily I say unto you, All these things shall come upon *this generation*.

Luke 11:50. That the blood of all the prophets, which was shed from the foundation of the world, may be required of *this generation*;

Luke 21:32. Verily I say unto you, This generation shall not pass away, *till all be fulfilled.*

Jesus was referring to the fulfilment of **all** the Old Testament prophecy concerning himself, which would include the seventy weeks *determined* by Daniel, to make an end of sins.[....] and seal up the vision and prophecy.*(Daniel 9:24.)*

Luke 22:22. And truly the Son of man goeth, as it *was determined*: but woe unto that man by whom he is betrayed!

Who determined this prophecy? That's right, it was Daniel. Hence the seventy weeks have already been fulfilled.

Jesus also told those at the time how the law and the prophets ended with John, after which the gospel of the kingdom of God would be preached. *(Luke 16:16.)* Yet he also warned his disciples that they wouldn't have enough time to preach this gospel throughout all the cities of Israel, before the Son of man would be seen coming in the clouds.

Matthew 10:23. But when they persecute you in this city, flee ye into another: for verily I say unto you, Ye shall not have gone over the cities of Israel, till the Son of man be come.

In light of this warning, as well as the fact that on numerous occasions Jesus told those in his presence that many would still be alive to witness his coming, Jesus returned in the clouds within a few decades of his ascension to heaven. Most likely a period of 40 years, which is generally accepted as being God's number of testing and cleansing. In the days of Noah for example, torrential rain fell from the heavens above over a prolonged period of 40 days and 40 nights. The Israelites were wandering in the desert for 40 years, Jesus Christ was tempted in the wilderness for 40 days and 40 nights, and for the people Jesus addressed, to know and remain faithful in Christ for the final 40 years before his return.

This then, would have been coincident with the fall of Babylon aka Jerusalem, in 70 AD. We are often told that Rome is the city which sits upon the seven hills (mountains), that the 'whore' is the Vatican, or even Mecca, and that the killing of prophets and saints is a reference to what Rome or some anti-Christian world power will do. When one looks at the subject carefully however, there is only one city on earth that fits the bill, and that is the City of Jerusalem, which is also built on seven hills or mounts.

At the time of the apostles, Jerusalem did have a lot of power over many kings of the earth, because Jerusalem was the centre of worship of God, as well as being a centre of commerce. Jerusalem (spiritual Sodom and Egypt) the great city where the Lord Jesus was crucified, is none other than Babylon! How do we know? When writing to the church at Jerusalem, Peter referred to 'that great city' as Babylon.

Revelation 11:8. And their dead bodies shall lie in the street of the great city, which spiritually is called Sodom and Egypt, where also our Lord was crucified.

1 Peter 5:13. The *church that is* at **Babylon**, elected together with *you*, saluteth you; and *so doth* Marcus my son.

Biblically it is neither Rome nor Mecca, but Jerusalem alone, who is charged by Jesus, with the unholy offence of killing the saints and the prophets. Furthermore Jesus told those in his presence that they were the generation which would be required to answer for the slaying of each and every Old Testament prophet. For the Law and the Prophets ended with John the Baptist. *(Luke 16:16.)*

Matthew 23:37. O Jerusalem, Jerusalem, thou that killest the prophets, and stonest them which are sent unto thee, how often would I have gathered thy children together, even as a hen gathereth her chickens under her wings, and ye would not!

Luke 11:50-51. That the blood of all the prophets, which was shed from the foundation of the world, may be required of **this generation**. From the blood of Abel unto the blood of Zacharias, which perished between the altar and the temple: verily I say unto you, It shall be required of **this generation**.

In 70 AD, when judgement came upon Babylon, aka Jerusalem, and 'that great city' fell, we are told, that in her was found the blood of the prophets, which Jesus said would be required of the generation he had directly spoken to.

Revelation 18:24. And in her was found the blood of prophets, and of saints, and of all that were slain upon the earth.

This was the same generation whom Jesus assured, that some would still be alive to witness him coming in the clouds, and likely concurrent with the rapture of believers and the first resurrection. Little wonder then, that Peter addressed these early Christians, as a "chosen generation". *(1 Peter 2:9.)*

If Jesus required pay-back from those he was speaking to at the time, it makes perfect sense that he would return in their generation.

Logically speaking, this is what the disciples must have expected. There is nowhere in Scripture, to indicate that the blood of all the old testament prophets slain from the foundation of the world, would be required from a future generation more than 2,000 years later. Especially in light of the fact, that the prophets were until John the Baptist. In fact, this 2,000 plus year gap, which cannot be found anywhere in the Bible, is perhaps the greatest hoax to have been played upon millions of Christians world-wide to date. And I too, once fell for it, hook, line and sinker. Even though I inwardly knew that "this generation" referred to the generation of people that Jesus was directly speaking to.

At the end of the day, both the historicist and the futurist view of the fulfilment of end-time prophecy, depends entirely upon who the term, "this generation", refers to. Traditionally, our generation today, and the many generations before us, have all been taught it referred to them/us. Yet the generation living during the time of His ministry, were told directly by Jesus, that some of those in his presence, would still be alive, to witness His coming in the clouds.

Logic and reason therefore dictate, that the early disciples believed, wholeheartedly, that the term "this generation", referred directly to themselves. In fact, from the New Testament alone, there is no valid reason whatsoever to suggest otherwise. The first generation of Christians, expected Jesus Christ to return within their own lifetime. Peter in fact, was so convinced that he would write to his fellow believers to inform them they were a *chosen* generation. *(1 Peter 2;9.)* And even Jesus himself declared; "Surely I come quickly". *(Revelation 22:20.)* What right do we then have, to even assume, that Jesus, who warned this generation that he would be seen coming in the clouds, was *not* true to his word? Even though I assumed this myself for many years.

Indeed, when writing a letter of encouragement to his fellow believers in Christ, John reminded them, how they could be certain that they were living in the *final* days. Because many a Christ-denier had appeared on the scene, of which Jesus had warned would be one of the many signs to watch out for, leading up to his return.

1 John 2:18. Little children, it is the *last* time: and as ye have heard that antichrist shall come, even *now* are there many antichrists; whereby we *know* that it is the *last time*.

Time and again throughout the gospels, Jesus assured his audience that some of them would still be alive to witness his coming in the clouds of heaven.

Matthew 16:28. Verily I say unto you, There be some standing here, which shall not taste of death, till they see the Son of man coming in his kingdom.

Matthew 24:30. And then shall appear the sign of the Son of man in heaven: and then shall all the tribes of the earth mourn, and they shall see the Son of man coming in the *clouds* of heaven with power and great glory.

Luke 21:32. Verily I say unto you, *This generation* shall not pass away, till *all* be fulfilled.

Mark 13:30. Verily I say unto you, that this generation shall not pass, till all these things be done.

Mark 13:26. And then shall they see the Son of man *coming in the clouds* with great power and glory.

This would be in reference to the prophet Daniel's night vision, who saw one like the Son of man come in the clouds of heaven.

Daniel 7:13. I saw in the night visions, and, behold, *one* like the Son of man *came with the clouds of heaven*, and came to the Ancient of days, and they brought him near before him.

John records in the Book of Revelations, how even those who *pierced* him, would see Jesus as he comes in the clouds. This too, would be the fulfilment of Old Testament prophecy, and Jesus told the generation he was speaking to, that *all* would be fulfilled, and how some of those listening to him, would still be alive to witness his return.

Zechariah 12:10. And I will pour upon the house of David, and upon the inhabitants of Jerusalem, the spirit of grace and of supplications: and they shall look upon *me* whom they have *pierced*, and they shall *mourn* for him, as one mourneth for *his* only *son*, and shall be in bitterness for him, as one that is in bitterness for *his* firstborn.

Revelation 1:7. Behold, he cometh with **clouds**; and every eye shall see him, and they *also* which *pierced him*: and all kindreds of the earth shall *wail* because of him. Even so, Amen.

Those who *pierced* him of course, were the Roman soldiers, while Jesus hung on the cross according to *John 19:34*. Hence they were still alive when Jesus returned. As too was Caiaphas the high priest. For having confirmed who he truly was, Jesus had previously told

Caiaphas directly that he would see the Son of man coming in the clouds.

Mark 14:62. And Jesus said, I am: and ye shall see the Son of man sitting on the right hand of power, and coming in the clouds of heaven.

There is so much internal evidence within the Scriptures themselves, which would bear witness to the fact that the entire New Testament, including the Book of Revelations, was written and **completed** several years earlier than we've always been led to believe. Which immediately throws the proverbial spanner into the works, and overturns man's traditional, theological apple-cart. For according to what the majority of us have always been taught, there should be no internal evidence to support such a claim. Yet that evidence has always been there, hidden away in plain sight. But we failed to see that evidence, **not** because it was **not** there, **but** because it was **not** supposed to be there. For that would mean the end-time prophecies, which by far the majority of Christians, are looking forward to today, were actually fulfilled more than two thousand years ago. And that would be unthinkable.

Hence why many would argue, that Jesus didn't actually mean what he said. His followers would **not** literally witness the Son of man arrive in the clouds, for that was merely a figure of speech. What Jesus really meant, was that the people would see the result of his coming judgement against Jerusalem. "Coming in the clouds" was simply synonymous with the destruction and wrath of God. Therefore they would witness the destruction, but not the Son of man in the clouds himself. Even though Jesus had declared otherwise.

But that is merely a cop-out, and much like saying that the disciples did not literally see Jesus when he was taken up to heaven in a cloud. *(Acts 1:9.)* For the term 'taken up in a cloud', is simply synonymous with Jesus disappearing in a puff of smoke.

In *Acts 1:11* the angels tell the disciples that Jesus will return in the same way they saw him ascend up into heaven. In other words, they would see Jesus return from heaven, in the same manner as they saw him rise up to heaven; in the clouds.

Many would argue that when the Bible says that God was to come on the clouds of heaven that this expression did not mean that he was actually coming on literal clouds. This is not true, for the clouds that mask the brightness of God's presence are indeed literal clouds. For in the Book of Exodus when God appeared to the Israelites he did so amidst literal clouds. If this were not so, how then, could the Israelites follow these clouds to the Promised Land?

When reading the scriptures there's no doubt that the early disciples and followers of Jesus, expected to see him return in the not too distant future. The apostle John, was even told directly, that he was to remain alive on earth until the day when Jesus would return. Peter, on the other hand, was told by Jesus, that he would suffer and be put to death, but in a manner that would bring glory to God.

*John 21:19.*This spake he, signifying by what death he [Peter] should glorify God. And when he had spoken this, he saith unto him, Follow me.

John 21:22. Jesus saith unto him [Peter], If I will that he [John] tarry till I come, what *is that* to thee? follow thou me.

Between them, these two disciples represent "the dead in Christ" who would be the "first" to rise (i.e. the first resurrection), and the living which remain, and be instantaneously changed and caught up (the rapture) into the air, to join the first resurrection at His return.

1 Corinthians 15:52. In a moment, in the twinkling of an eye, at the last trump: for the trumpet shall sound, and the dead shall be raised incorruptible, and we shall be changed.

1 Thessalonians 4:16-17. For the Lord himself shall descend from heaven with a shout, with the voice of the archangel, and with the trump of God: and the dead in Christ shall rise first: Then we which are alive *and* remain shall be caught up together with them in the clouds, to meet the Lord in the air: and so shall we ever be with the Lord.

The Jew First

Let's cut to the chase here, and call a spade a spade. For first and foremost, Jesus was **not** sent to bring the gospel of salvation to the Gentiles, but rather, to the lost sheep of the House of Israel. *(Matthew 15:24.)* Furthermore he commanded his disciples to do the same, and not to preach the gospel to the Gentiles, nor even to enter their cities.

Matthew 10:5-6. These twelve Jesus sent forth, and **commanded** them, saying, Go **not** into the way of the Gentiles, and into any city of the Samaritans enter ye **not**: But go **rather** to the lost sheep of the house of Israel.

Yes, I know that by and large, Jesus was rejected by his own, and for this very reason, the message originally intended for the lost sheep of Israel, was eventually preached throughout the Gentile world. But nevertheless, the principle remains the same; it is the Jew **first**, and **also** to the Gentile.

And if you're thinking; "Hey, that's a little unfair", then rest assured, for the same principle also applies to times of great tribulation and sorrow. **First** the Jew and **also** the Gentile. It was the children of Israel who first received the promise of a future Messiah. It was they who first received the promise of a future time of peace and great prosperity, referred to in the Book of Revelations as the one thousand years. But it was also these very same people, who due to their disobedience to God, were warned of a coming tribulation, referred to as the time of Jacob's Trouble.

Jeremiah 30:7. Alas! for that day *is* great, so that none *is* like it: it *is* even the time of Jacob's trouble; but he shall be saved out of it.

Romans 1:16. For I am not ashamed of the gospel of Christ: for it is the power of God unto salvation to every one that believeth; to the Jew **first**, and **also** to the Greek.

Romans 2:9. Tribulation and anguish, upon every soul of man that doeth evil, of the Jew **first**, and **also** of the Gentile;

Romans 2:10. But glory, honour, and peace, to every man that worketh good, to the Jew **first**, and **also** to the Gentile:

Maybe I'm overthinking here, but what if the years of great

tribulation leading up to the destruction of Jerusalem aka Babylon, were primarily God's judgement upon the Jews? Which we know was the case, because Jesus told the generation he spoke to so. He even addressed the Pharisees and the Sadducees with;

"O generation of vipers, who hath warned you to flee from the **wrath** to come?" *(Matthew 3:7.)*

On the other hand, Jesus encouraged his followers thus;

And when these things begin to come to pass, then look up, and lift up your heads; for your redemption draweth nigh. *(Luke 21:28.)*

Matthew 24:33. So likewise ye, when ye shall see all these things, know that *it is near*, even at the doors.

Paul also encouraged believers to heed Jesus' words, and wait for His coming in the clouds of heaven, as he had promised, for they would be delivered from the **wrath** to come. *(1 Thessalonians 1:10.)*

The prophets of old warned of great tribulation to come upon Jerusalem and the people of Israel, referred to as the time of Jacob's trouble. Yet there's also a principle in Scripture, that history tends to repeat itself, because there is nothing new under the sun.

Ecclesiastes 1:9. The thing that hath been, it *is that* which shall be; and that which is done *is* that which shall be done: and *there is* no new *thing* under the sun.

As noted earlier, the events taking place throughout the gospels were fulfilling that which was written in the law and the prophets. On the day of Pentecost, Acts 2:16 reads;" But this is that which was spoken by the prophet Joel;"

According to Jesus, all would be fulfilled during the lifetime of the first generation of believers.. This would have included all of Joel's prophecies. Such as;

Joel 2:1. Blow ye the trumpet in Zion, and sound an alarm in my holy mountain: let all the inhabitants of the land tremble: for the day of the LORD cometh, for it is nigh at hand;

Joel 2:10. The earth shall quake before them; the heavens shall tremble: the sun and the moon shall be dark, and the stars shall withdraw their shining:

Matthew 16:28. Verily I say unto you, There be some standing here, which shall not taste of death, till they see the Son of man coming in his kingdom.

But first, it needs to be said, that whoever was responsible for dating the completion of the Book of Revelations as being *after* 90 AD, made a cracking good job of concealing the truth. For once this date became accepted, then it could no longer be possible for John to have *foretold* the fall of Jerusalem aka Babylon in 70 AD. For Jerusalem was destroyed more than 20 years *before* he'd completed his book of prophecy.

Let's assume for a moment however, that the Book of Revelations was completed more than twenty years *after* the destruction of Jerusalem. Do you not think it strange, that John didn't get round to mentioning the fall of that "great city"? Especially in light of the fact that Jesus had previously warned of its destruction, along with the second temple. And how do we account for the fact John conveyed a sense of immanency to his first-century readers, when saying on three occasions that "the time is at hand"?

Or the fact that John recorded the words of promise declared by Jesus; of how he would come *quickly?* Not just the once, but six times. Can we really believe that Jesus didn't keep the promise he made to the first generation of Christians? Man's personal belief system apart, do we find within the Scriptures any legitimate reason to think that when saying "Behold, I come quickly", Jesus was addressing a future generation of believers, two millennia down the line?

When writing to the brethren at Corinth, the Apostle Paul, also conveyed the same sense of immanency, when encouraging the brethren not to be troubled for "the time is short". *(1 Corinthians 7:29),* and how the day of Christ is at hand. *(2 Thessalonians 2:2.)* Likewise, Peter encouraged believers to remain sober and prayerful, because the end of *all things* is at hand. *(1 Peter 4:7.)*

When writing to the brethren concerning the coming of the Lord, and how one thousand years in his sight is merely but one day, Peter was *not* suggesting that Jesus was going to postpone his return for another 2,000 plus years. Not at all; for he was encouraging his fellow believers not to give up hope. For whilst a few decades might seem like a long, drawn-out wait to them, such is not the case with God.

Unlike the prophet Daniel, who was told to "shut up the words, and *seal* the book, even to the time of the end:' John was told *not* to seal the prophecy, because there was very little time to wait. In other words, Daniel's prophecy was sealed because the better part of 500 years would pass before it was fulfilled. Whilst John's prophecy was to remain unsealed, because its fulfilment would shortly come to pass.

Daniel 12:4. But thou, O Daniel, shut up the words, and *seal* the book, *even* to the time of the end: [.......]

Revelation 1:1. The Revelation of Jesus Christ, which God gave unto him, to shew unto his servants things *which must shortly come to pass.*

Revelation 22:10. And he saith unto me, Seal *not* the sayings of the prophecy of this book: *for the time is at hand.*

Even so, the disciples still didn't have enough time to preach this message of the kingdom throughout all the cities of Israel, before Jesus, the Son of man, returned in the clouds of heaven. Which once again suggests the time period between Jesus saying these things, and his return to fulfil his own prophecy, was only a few decades at most.

Matthew 10:23. But when they persecute you in this city, flee ye into another: for verily I say unto you, Ye shall not have gone over the cities of Israel, till the Son of man be come.

If the first generation of believers didn't have enough time to preach the gospel throughout the land of Israel, it immediately raises the question, what about the nations of the Gentiles? For Jesus first came to minister to the Jews, that through Israel, he would then preach the gospel of the kingdom of God to the Gentiles. Indeed, Jesus himself said "the gospel of the kingdom shall be preached in all the world for a witness *unto all nations*; and then shall the end come". *(Matthew 24:14.)*

After his resurrection, Jesus commanded the apostles to remain in Jerusalem and begin their ministry there. In the Book of Acts, we read how the gospel went first to the Samaritans, and then to the Gentiles, and how, through the ministry of Paul, the good news of salvation went throughout the Roman Empire.

But how about all the other nations of the world, the rest of Europe, Asia, Africa and the Americas etc.? How could the gospel possibly be preached to all the nations on earth, if Jesus returned during the lifetime of at least some of the first generation of believers, as he had promised? Realistically, and humanly speaking, it would be an impossibility for the gospel to be preached to all the nations on earth, if the first generation of believers didn't have enough time to share the gospel throughout Israel, before the coming of the Son of man in the clouds of heaven.

Tradition would have us believe that when writing the Book of Revelations, John was referring to a generation of folk in the far distant future. Yet it is Written, that John recorded "things which MUST shortly come to pass", and "for "the time is at hand." *(Revelation 1:1.)*

Things which must shortly come to pass, included an angel preaching the everlasting gospel throughout all the nations of the earth, and this BEFORE Jesus returned in the clouds of heaven and the destruction of Babylon aka Jerusalem in 70 AD.

Revelation 14:6. And I saw another angel fly in the midst of heaven, having the everlasting gospel to preach unto them that dwell on the earth, and to every nation, and kindred, and tongue, and people,

This supernatural, worldwide preaching of the gospel to all the nations was also PRIOR to the millennial reign of Jesus Christ.

All things considered, and unless one's head is buried in the sand, it's extremely hard to deny that Jesus, as the Son of man, returned in the clouds of heaven, to be witnessed by the generation he made this promise to. The scriptures confirm without doubt, that the expectation of the first generation of Believers in the Lord Jesus Christ included the fulfilment of Old Testament prophecy, the great tribulation, the second coming of Christ, and the rapture at the first resurrection. So, what if God's judgement, primarily for the Gentile world, finally arrives *after* the Little Season, and *after* the war of Gog and Magog?

there are other reasons which seem to suggest there's a dual fulfilment of prophecy within the Scriptures, concerning the end-times. Not in the least, because a first resurrection demands a second, at least. We are told that "the rest of the dead lived not again until the thousand years were finished". *(Revelation 20:5.)* But are not told how long after the millennium this resurrection takes place.

Everything we know about "the rest of the dead" is contained within this one sentence, but we do know they were *not* part of the "first resurrection",i.e. those who are Christ's at his coming. *(1 Corinthians 15:23 .)*

The very term a *first* resurrection demands at least a second however, and there are those who believe that an entire generation of the dead were resurrected immediately after the millennial reign came to a close, but such a concept would amount to reincarnation. A highly popular belief, but one not supported by the word of God. We do not get a second chance at life.

However, because a person's death is by appointment, followed by the judgement *(Hebrews 9:27)*, we can only assume this second, and final resurrection occurs at the very end of the world, and the final judgement at the great white throne. *(Revelation 20:11.)* But whether or not there is another rapture beforehand for believers in Christ, we are not told. Personally, I suspect there will be, but that is just my own opinion.

Full or Extreme Preterists tend to spiritualize the past-fulfilment of all end times prophecy, and claim that for one thousand years, the redeemed kings and priests reigned from **heaven** with Jesus, and **not** on the earth itself. Their office of government may well indeed have been in heaven, but the King James Bible clearly states how they would reign as kings and priests **on** the earth. Not over it. This would have been in their new glorified, resurrected spiritual bodies of flesh and bone, incorruptible and immortal. For we are told that beyond death and the grave, a new body awaits us, one formed like the glorious resurrection body of Jesus Christ. *(Philippians 3:21.)*

A body that can exist in the physical world, and is able to talk, perform tasks, eat and drink etc. but an illuminated body, as in a being of light, which is not restricted by the physical laws.

It could even be said, that the kings and priests of Jesus Christ, reigned on the earth for a thousand years, as extra-terrestrial beings, meaning persons not of this earth. But certainly not as semi-transparent, wraith-like beings, or extra-terrestrial entities arriving in warp-speed space-craft, as presented by the likes of Hollywood.

Mounting evidence suggests a lot of published research and history is false, and relatively few ever think beyond what they want to hear. There is a war taking place for the souls of mankind which the majority fail to see; having been blinkered by a fantasy world of falsehood, materialism and toxic manufactured realities. Evidence for a highly advanced and unified civilization that once inhabited the earth can be found everywhere. As too can evidence be found for a major earth-changing event and a series of cataclysms, most likely beginning at around 1,000 AD.

What if certain agencies have been re-writing history? Could it be that so-called 'Universal Classic World History' prior to the sixteenth century, is a carefully crafted construct of lies and deception, fabricated in the 16th-18th centuries upon the 'firm' foundation laid down by an assortment of Italian scholars, Roman clergy and humanists from the 14th -15th centuries? If the conspiracy is true, how far was it pursued? What if the history of Western Civilization is both drastically shorter and dramatically different from the version taught in our schools?

"History is the version of past events that people have decided to agree upon".—Napoleon Bonaparte

"The very ink with which history is written is merely fluid prejudice."—Mark Twain.

"History is a pack of lies about events that never happened, told by people who weren't there".—George Santayana, American philosopher (1863-1952)

"The most effective way to destroy people is to deny and obliterate their own understanding of their history".—George Orwell.

Tribulation Years

There were endless trials and tribulations, and thousands upon thousands of deaths for the Israelites prior to Jesus returning in the clouds. Which he had foretold of course, most likely around forty years earlier. There's no doubt whatsoever, that the people living in Israel at the time, endured and suffered the time of great tribulation, as warned of by Jesus in *Matthew 24:21*.

Yet it needs to be understood, that Scripture does *not* describe a 7 year Tribulation; it describes a period of 7 Seals where 4 Horsemen ride and a period of 7 Trumpets (begins at Revelation 8) called the Great Tribulation, lasting 1260 days or 42 months. The last day is the 7 vials/bowls of God's wrath which was the Second Coming of Jesus, and most likely shortly before, the dawn of the Millennium.

Futurists would disagree here, as I once did, by saying, "of course there will be 7 years of Tribulation". It says so in the Bible. But they can't tell you where it says so. For it is an understanding that comes from interpreting the 70 weeks recorded by Daniel as being 70 weeks of years. Simply put, 69 weeks of years ended with the death of Jesus, followed by an open-ended age of Grace, with the final 70th week being the 7 year tribulation, which they claim has not yet happened, but will do shortly.

But if the 70th week is still in the future, as claimed, then why did Jesus say "the *time* is *fulfilled*" in *Mark 1:15*? If there is a 2000+ year gap between the 69th and 70th week of Daniel, why doesn't Daniel, or any other scripture mention it? Because the presumed massive space of time between the 69th and the 70th week comes from Bible study notes, which are the word of man, and *not* the word of God.

Study Bible Notes began in earnest with con-man Cyrus A Scofield, the Zionist Congress and the Bible Revision Committee in the 1880s. They all have the same theme, Dispensationalism; i.e. The 7 year Tribulation, the Rapture and a new Covenant with Israel. All are untrue, because the rapture and the first resurrection occurred more than 2,000 years ago, and the new Covenant, which is available to all, is for those whose faith is in the Lord Jesus Christ.

This is why, more than 2,000 years later, the majority of Christians still await the Second Coming. To justify this 2,000 year wait, they will say; "well, it's only been like a couple of days in God's sight. Disregarding the fact, that the context of this passage, was for the people at the time, who Peter encouraged by reminding them that God is not slack in fulfilling his promises. *(2 Peter 3:9.)*

For sixty nine weeks out of Daniel's seventy weeks of years, namely, 69x7=483 years, was perfectly fulfilled, when Jesus started his public ministry. If the seventieth week is still in the future, then why, during the time of the Apostles, did the religious Jews believe the seventieth week was on their own door-step, so to speak? Or put another way; if the seventieth week is still in the future, why does scripture say Jesus confirmed the covenant in *Galatians 3:17,* which refers to *Daniel 9:27?*

One of the admins of a group I belong to says; "I think Daniel's seventieth week is 66-73 AD, as mid week the city is destroyed". Which I believe is likely correct, for this would be a period of approximately 40 years, or a ***generation*** since the crucifixion of Christ. Daniel's seventieth week was fulfilled with the desolation of Jerusalem and the second Temple. There is nowhere in the Scriptures to indicate the seventieth week was postponed for yet another 2,000 plus years. It may well be comfortable to think so, but the teaching is just not there.

The law and the prophets were until John. *(Luke 16:16.)* Jesus told the generation he spoke to, that the blood of the prophets slain since the foundation of the world. would be required of THEM. Not some random generation in the far distant future. Just as foretold by Jesus in the Gospels, and John in Revelations, Jerusalem aka spiritually Sodom and Egypt aka Babylon would fall, and in her was found the blood of the saints and the prophets. *(Revelation 17:6.)*We are told this took place in 70 AD.

The great tribulation for Israel was the desolation of Jerusalem, and things were so horrific during the time of Jacob's trouble, many parents even ate their own children, as foretold by the prophets. Bear in mind that Jesus warned how all the Old Testament prophecies would be fulfilled during the lifetime of "this generation."

Deuteronomy 28:53.And thou shalt eat the fruit of thine own body, the flesh of thy sons and of thy daughters, which the LORD thy God hath given thee, in the siege, and in the straitness, wherewith thine enemies shall distress thee:

According to Josephus, hundreds hundreds of thousands of dead bodies were stacked in Jerusalem or thrown over the city wall into the valleys around it. J ews that tried to find food outside of the city were tortured and crucified outside the city, so that all of the trees around Jerusalem were filled with decaying corpses.

Josephus describes some of the horrors of the Roman-Jewish war in *Of The War Book VI;*

> Thus did the miseries of Jerusalem grow worse and worse every day; and the seditious were still more irritated by the calamities they were under, even while the famine preyed upon themselves; after it had preyed upon the people. And indeed the multitude of carcasses that lay in heaps one upon another was an horrible sight; and produced a pestilential stench; which was an hindrance to those that would make sallies out of the city, and fight the enemy.

Many pilgrims from the Jewish diaspora who, undeterred by the war, had trekked all the way to Jerusalem to be present at the Temple during Passover, became trapped in Jerusalem during the siege and perished. All three walls of Jerusalem were eventually destroyed as well as the Temple and the citadels. The city was then put to the torch, with most survivors taken into slavery; some of those overturned stones and their place of impact can still be seen, at the site where the Temple once stood.

The Man of Sin

Jesus came unto his own, and his own received him not. *(John 1:11.)* Jesus warned them that because he'd come in his Father's name and had been rejected, another would come in his own name, who they would receive. *(John 5:43.)*Apparently, any name would be received, as long as it was ***not*** the name of Jesus.

John 19:15. But they cried out, Away with him, away with him, crucify him. Pilate saith unto them, Shall I crucify your King? The chief priests answered, We have no king but Caesar.

Jesus foretold how many false Christ's and false prophets would arise, with the ability to perform signs and wonders, on a scale, which if it were possible, would deceive the very elect. (*Matthew 24:24.*) The most influential false Christ that Jesus had previously warned of, was undoubtedly Simon bar Kochba, whose followers revolted against Roman authority, which directly led to the death of 580,000 Jews. The resulting disease and famine in desolated Judea killed far more, and thousands were sold into slavery.

As a false Christ, Simon bar Kochba, was a "type" of beast, but not the man of sin who Jesus warned, would come in his own name, and be received. Although many Preterists believe that the Roman general Titus, fulfilled the role, there is plenty of evidence to indicate that Nero was in fact, the man of sin, the Beast of Revelations. As Caesar, Nero desired to be worshipped as a god, and the title 'Nero Caesar' fits the gematria code number "666." John used gematria in which numbers are used to represent certain letters, to reveal Nero without actually writing down his name.

Because most contemporary sources describe him as harbouring such a tyrannical and deep-rooted hatred toward Christians, there's no reason to doubt that the early believers in Christ, would have considered Nero to fit the Biblical character known as the beast down to a T.

Nero's evil was legendary and there was no end to his vices. According to the Roman historian *Suetonius*, Nero murdered his parents, wife, brother, aunt, and many others close to him and of high station in Rome. He was a torturer, a homosexual rapist, and a sodomite. He even married two young boys and paraded them around as his wives.

The *Sibylline Oracles* label Nero a "great beast." and the early Christian author, *Lactantius*, calls him a "noxious wild beast." It's a historical fact that Nero began to persecute the Christians throughout the Roman Empire in mid-November 64 AD. This intense persecution only ended when Nero committed suicide in June 68 AD. Thus he made war on the saints for a period of exactly 42 months.

Revelation 13:5. And there was given unto him a mouth speaking great things and blasphemies; and power was given unto him to continue ***forty and*** **two months**.

Mostly all the apostles and their followers were brutally killed by the Antichrist forces of the Beast, like in one of those first false flag operations of Nero. Nero was responsible for the great fire of Rome, but he blamed it on the Christians, whom he ended up torturing and slaughtering. One historian writes that the Great Fire ended up damaging Nero's "moral reputation and financial viability," largely because Nero used that excuse to burn alive "a despised minority"; namely the Christians. Tertullian [145-220 AD] credited "Nero's cruel sword" as providing the martyr's blood as seed for the church. At one point he urged his readers to "consult your histories; you will find there that Nero was the first who assailed with the imperial sword the Christian sect."

In June 68 AD Nero ended his life by thrusting his sword through his own throat, with the help of his personal secretary, Epaphroditus, in part because he realized that his popularity had waned and also because of an attempted coup. Nero lived by the sword, and died by the sword. The saints were called to endure and remain faithful in light of the fact that the beast who so often wielded the sword would himself be killed by the sword. *(Revelation. 13:10, 14).*

The Two Witnesses

Revelation 11:3-4. And I will give *power* unto my **two wit**nesses, and they shall prophesy a thousand two hundred *and* threescore days, clothed in sackcloth. These are the two olive trees, and the two candlesticks standing before the God of the earth.

Although I disagree with full, or extreme Preterism, one website, *Revelation/Revolution,* provides some interesting Biblical and historical evidence suggesting that the two witnesses recorded by John, are in fact one person, namely, the post-resurrected Jesus Christ.

What? I hear you say? No way could this be true, surely?

Yet Jesus is commonly believed to have made several appearances throughout the Old Testament. *(Genesis 16:7; 21:17; 22:11; 31:11; Exodus 3:2-15; 17:1-7; Judges 6:11; 13:21; Daniel 3:24-27; Micah 5:2).* In theological terms, these various comings or appearances of Christ are called "theophanies."

In view of this, the post-resurrected Christ may well have returned in the flesh to prophesy for three and a half years from the start of the Jewish War until the start of the siege of Jerusalem. The fact that the two witnesses are called "the two olive trees and the two candlesticks standing before the God of the earth", suggests that the two witnesses are indeed one man. In *Zechariah 4:11-14,* the two olive trees symbolize the king and the high priest. According to

Hebrews 5:10, Jesus "was called of God an high priest after the order of Melchisedec." *Hebrews 7:1* states; "For this Melchisedec, **king** of Salem, **priest** of the most high God." By saying that Jesus is a high priest in the order of Melchisedec means that Jesus is both king and high priest.

Given the fact that *Revelation 11:4* suggests the two witnesses are both king and high priest, does this mean that the two witnesses must be one man, Jesus Christ? The fact that Jesus Christ is called the two witnesses is also a suitable title in light of the fact that he seems to have divided his earthly ministry in 2 times three and a half year intervals. The 3.5 years of his public ministry leading up to the crucifixion, plus the post-death 1,260 days, clothed in sackcloth.

The two witnesses "have power to shut heaven, that it rain not in the days of their prophecy". *(Revelation 11:6.)* Is it a mere coincidence that Josephus tells of a prolonged drought that nearly dried up the pool of Siloam as well as all the other springs around Jerusalem before the arrival of the Roman army? Then when Titus arrived with the Roman army in 70 AD, Josephus says that the "water overflowed." In other words, there appears to have been a severe drought, followed by a great rainstorm upon the arrival of the Roman army to besiege Jerusalem in 70 AD.

Matthew 24:27. For as the lightning cometh out of the east, and shineth even unto the west; so shall also the coming of the Son of man be.

Lightning very often accompanies heavy rain storms. Perhaps the rainstorm that marked the arrival of the Romans at Jerusalem in 70 AD, was accompanied by lightning, as a sign that Christ, the Son of man, was coming on the clouds in judgment at that time? In fact, Josephus records in *The Wars of the Jews (4.4.5)* that in 68 AD;

> There broke out a prodigious storm in the night, with the utmost violence, and very strong winds, with the largest showers of rain, with continued **lightnings**, terrible thunderings, and amazing concussions and bellowings of the earth, that was in an earthquake. These things were a manifest indication that some destruction was coming upon men, when the system of the world was put into this disorder; and any one would guess that these wonders foreshowed some grand calamities that were coming.

Could it possibly be, that Jesus Christ himself, fulfilled his own prophecy of the two witnesses? Or is the very notion too outrageous? And how about Jesus ben [son of] Ananias? For according to

Josephus, his determination, his consistent warning cries against Jerusalem, and his characteristics, mirrored those of Jesus Christ in the most extraordinary and remarkable way.

Writes Josephus in The Wars of the Jews (6.5.3);

> But, what is still more terrible, there was one Jesus, the son of Ananus, a plebeian and a husbandman, who, four years before the war began, and at a time when the city was in very great peace and prosperity, came to that feast whereon it is our custom for every one to make tabernacles to God in the temple, began on a sudden to cry aloud, "A voice from the east, a voice from the west, a voice from the four winds, a voice against Jerusalem and the holy house, a voice against the bridegrooms and the brides, and a voice against this whole people!"

> This was his cry, as he went about by day and by night, in all the lanes of the city. However, certain of the most eminent among the populace had great indignation at this dire cry of his, and took up the man, and gave him a great number of severe stripes; yet did not he either say any thing for himself, or any thing peculiar to those that chastised him, but still went on with the same words which he cried before. Hereupon our rulers, supposing, as the case proved to be, that this was a sort of divine fury in the man, brought him to the Roman procurator, where he was whipped till his bones were laid bare; yet he did not make any supplication for himself, nor shed any tears, but turning his voice to the most lamentable tone possible, at every stroke of the whip his answer was, "Woe, woe to Jerusalem!"

> And when Albinus (for he was then our procurator) asked him, Who he was? and whence he came? and why he uttered such words? he made no manner of reply to what he said, but still did not leave off his melancholy ditty, till Albinus took him to be a madman, and dismissed him. Now, during all the time that passed before the war began, this man did not go near any of the citizens, nor was seen by them while he said so; but he every day uttered these lamentable words, as if it were his premeditated vow, "Woe, woe to Jerusalem!" Nor did he give ill words to any of those that beat him every day, nor good words to those that gave him food; but this was his reply to all men, and indeed no other than a melancholy presage of what was to come.

> This cry of his was the loudest at the festivals; and he continued this ditty for seven years and five months, without growing hoarse, or being tired therewith, until the very time that he saw his presage in earnest fulfilled in our siege, when it ceased; for as he was going round upon the wall, he cried out with his utmost force, "Woe, woe to the city again, and to the people, and to the holy house!" And just as he added at the last, "Woe, woe to myself also!" there came a stone out of one of the engines, and smote him, and killed him immediately; and as he was uttering the very same presages he gave up the ghost.

Make of this historical account whatever you will, but it has been suggested by some, that this extraordinary individual was actually one and the same as the two witnesses, both the king and the high priest, the embodiment of the post-resurrected Jesus Christ.

Impossible; I hear you say? I would tend to agree, except for one simple fact. All things are possible with God. *(Luke 18:27.)* Which is not to suggest that any one of us should formulate a doctrine based upon the secular historical record. From Scripture alone, all we know for certain is, that Christ appeared the **one time**, to put away sin by the sacrifice of himself. *(Hebrews 9:26.)* Yet we also know that after his resurrection, and over a period of 40 days, Jesus made at least ten bodily appearances, and was seen alive by more than 500 people in total. Although at times he wasn't immediately recognized visually, which suggests he could change his appearance at will.

Nevertheless, and regardless of who Jesus, son of Ananus, actually was, I think it safe to say that the selfless and consistent seven and a half year long message of warning he conveyed to the inhabitants of Jerusalem, came from the very heart of God. For He is "not willing that any should perish, but that all should come to repentance". *(2 Peter 3:9.)*

And yes, I realize that this is all rather speculative, and partly based on extra-biblical sources. Nevertheless, whilst secular historians like Josephus and Tacticus were not actual eye-witnesses of the events of Jesus' life, both men are considered unbiased and trustworthy, and both made reference to Jesus in their writings.

The Abomination of Desolation

For more than 25 years I was half awaiting a third temple to be built on the Temple Mount in Jerusalem. Even though a third temple is not mentioned by Jesus or the Apostles. One of the reasons being, or so I was told, that certain prophecies, such as the abomination of desolation standing where it should not, could not be fulfilled until a third temple is built.

Yet some historians believe that when they ransacked the Jerusalem temple in 68-70 AD, the Romans sacrificed a pig to Mars, the god of war, and most likely in the inner court on the altar of holocausts that stood before the sanctuary building.

According to Wikipedia; the suovetaurilia or suovitaurilia was one of the most sacred and traditional rites of Roman religion: the sacrifice of a pig (sus), a sheep (ovis) and a bull (taurus) to the deity Mars to bless and purify land. Josephus says the Roman *ensigns* were an *abomination* to the Jews *(Antiquities. 18.3.1; 18.5.3).*

Writes Lynn Louise Schuldt in her 2001 book, *Prophecy Paradox: The Care for a First Century End Time*, (revised edition. p. 73).

> Josephus says the Roman army worshipped the *ensigns* on the eastern gate of the Temple. Was this blasphemous worship done at the gate facing inside the Temple or outside? Josephus does not say. It seems probable that this sacrifice was done on the inside of the Temple as the Roman army consisted of a large contingent of up to 20,000 local Jewish troops. These Jewish troops could not be relied upon and so they would have been assigned to various mundane tasks at and around the Roman camp to free-up the better trained, more reliable
>
> Roman troops who would have been the ones to enter the city especially the Temple and do the dirty work. It is likely this abominable worship was done on the inside of the Temple out of view of the Jewish local troops. If this sacrifice was done on the outside of the Temple in view of the Jewish soldiers it might have caused a riot. After all a big part of what caused the Jews to revolt against Rome was the fact that a provocateur sacrificed birds outside of a synagogue in Caesarea. Josephus says, "This thing provoked the Jews to an incurable degree, because their laws were affronted, and the place was polluted." *(Wars 2.14.5.)*
>
> The fact that the synagogue was polluted even though this blasphemy occurred outside the door of the synagogue implies the same concerning the blasphemous sacrifices at the Temple's eastern gate: Whether or not this **blasphemous** worship and *pig sacrifice* occurred inside or just outside the Temple is irrelevant as the Temple would be seen to have been defiled either way. Thus it is likely that this blasphemy occurred inside the Temple out of view of the Jewish local troops. [*emphasis*; mine]

It would therefore seem extremely likely, that Daniel's prophecy was *fulfilled* more than 2,000 years ago, causing many in Judaea to heed Jesus' warning and flee to the mountains.

The Second Coming, which by far the majority of Christians have been taught is still future, is recorded in Roman history. Please don't get me wrong here, for I'm sure we were taught the futurist view of end-times prophecy in good faith. In much the same way that our parents and school teachers taught us in good faith, that we live on a rapidly spinning ball. But somebody somewhere has been hell-bent on deceiving us. Now I wonder who that might have been? The

Great Deceiver of all the nations on Earth, maybe?

The Second Coming

If Jesus did *not* return in the clouds of heaven as he promised to, then he was guilty of deceiving the early disciples and the first generation of believers in Christ.

Luke 9:27. But I tell you of a *truth*, there be some *standing here*, which shall not taste of death, till they see the kingdom of God.

Luke 10:1. After these things the Lord appointed other seventy also, and sent them two and two before his face into every city and place, whither he himself would come.

Matthew 10:23. But when they persecute you in this city, flee ye into another: for verily I say unto you, Ye shall *not* have gone over the cities of Israel, *till* the Son of man be come.

Mark 13:26. And then shall they see the Son of man coming in the clouds with great power and glory.

As noted in my previous book, and which is easily verifiable, there were three reliable historians, namely, Josephus, Tacticus, and Pseudo-Hegesippus, who each recorded that a figure of "tremendous size" , followed by an army of fiery angels, appeared over Jerusalem during Passover, three and a half years before its destruction in 70 AD.

Although Jesus is not mentioned by name, as pagans who were unfamiliar with the teachings of Christian eschatology, Tacitus and Josephus would never have been expected to make such an identification. Yet, whilst one gets the distinct impression these three unbiased historians didn't know quite what to make of it all, the parallels between these historic accounts with Revelation 19 are quite striking.

Writes Josephus in *The Wars of the Jews (6.5.3);*

> On the twenty-first day of the month of Artemisius [Jyar], a certain prodigious and incredible phenomenon appeared; I suppose the account of it would seem to be a fable, were it not related by those that saw it, and were not the events that followed it of so considerable a nature as to deserve such signals; for, before sunsetting, chariots and troops of soldiers in their armor were seen running about among the clouds, and surrounding of

cities. Moreover, at that feast which we call Pentecost, as the priests were going by night into the inner [court of the temple,] as their custom was, to perform their sacred ministrations, they said that, in the first place, they felt a quaking, and heard a great noise, and after that they heard a sound as of a great multitude, saying, "Let us remove hence."

Tacticus records in *The Histories (5.13)*

"In the sky appeared a vision of armies in conflict, of glittering armour."

Pseudo-Hegesippus also describes the coming of Christ on the clouds with His mighty angels, when in *Pseudo-Hegesippus 44.* he writes;

A certain figure appeared of tremendous size, which many saw, just as the books of the Jews have disclosed, and before the setting of the sun there were suddenly seen in the clouds chariots and armed battle arrays by which the cities of all Iudaea and its territories were invaded.

The medieval Jewish historian Sepher Yosippon, expounds upon this angelic army in the sky of 66 AD by saying;

Moreover, in those days were seen chariots of fire and horsemen, a great force flying across the sky near to the ground coming against Jerusalem and all the land of Judah, all of them horses of fire and riders of fire.

Yosippon's description of the angelic army of fire in the sky in 66 AD fulfils the prophecies of the coming of the Lord in *Isaiah 66:15, Psalm 68:17* and *Habakkuk 3:1-8* in a surprisingly literal way. Yosippon adds the fact that this angelic army in the sky of AD 66 was composed of cavalry that blazed with fire, hence fulfilling *2 Thessalonians 1:7-8.*

And to you who are troubled rest with us, when the Lord Jesus shall be revealed from heaven with his mighty angels. In flaming fire taking vengeance on them that know not God, and that obey not the gospel of our Lord Jesus Christ:

Notice that this army is described exactly as the angelic army seen by Elisha and his companion in 2 Kings 6:17—chariots, horses and horsemen of fire. Also in Wars of the Jews 6:5:3 are the words, "Thus there was a star resembling a sword, which stood over the city, and a comet, that continued a whole year".

Jesus himself said "I will shew wonders in heaven above, and signs in the earth beneath; blood, and fire, and vapour of smoke." *(Acts 2:19.)* Could this sword-like star have been the "sign of the Son of Man" mentioned in Matthew 24:30? The "sign" could, of course, have been the Son of Man himself, but a sword seen in the heavens above the city, could certainly have been a sign to the Jews that judgment was coming upon them.

A few days, or possibly a week or so later, at the start of the Jewish revolt, when writing about the construction of the Corinth Canal in 66 AD, the Roman historian, *Lucius Cassius Dio*, records another strange supernatural event; of blood and vapour of smoke.

In *Roman History 63.16*, Cassius Dio writes;

> [W]hen the first workers touched the earth, blood spouted from it, groans and bellowings were heard, and many phantoms appeared. Nero himself thereupon grasped a mattock and by throwing up some of the soil fairly compelled the rest to imitate him.

When recording the same event in *Lives of the Twelve Caesars 6.19*, the historian, *Suetonius*, indicates that the rising of these phantom-like figures, was coincident with the sound of a trumpet.

It would seem likely in fact, that each of the seven trumpet judgements of the Apocalypse, were fulfilled during Israel's first century war with Rome. At various stages throughout the war each stage was marked, or heralded by a Roman trumpeter, whilst the Book of Revelation tells us an angel in heaven blew the trumpet. There is probably far more truth in the term "As above so below" than we care to realise.

Daniel 4:35. And all the inhabitants of the earth *are* reputed as nothing: and he doeth according to his will in the army of **heaven**, and *among* the inhabitants of the **earth**: and none can stay his hand, or say unto him, What doest thou?

Just as the grains of sand on the sea shore are innumerable, so too are the multitude of stars in the heavens.*(Hebrews 11:12)*. But there also exists another 'host of heaven' which is also described as 'innumerable,'and these are the angels. *(Hebrews 12:22)*. There is an unexplained correlation between the angels and the stars throughout Scripture, and it would seem that under the sovereign will of God, this mutual relationship in the heavens above can play a determining role on the physical battlefield of earth.

*Judges 5:20. **They** fought **from heaven**; the **stars** in their **courses fought** against Sisera.*

The meaning of Sisera is 'Servant of Ra' (the sun god) and in an extraordinary, but unexplained way, God had lured the entire enemy army to one particular place, and caused great vexation for Sisera their leader. It was almost certainly due to the influence of "the stars in their courses", the angels who played a role in the battle on earth, but from the vantage point of being "the army of heaven".*(Daniel 4:35.)* How this can even be possible, we're not told, but the surrounding context indicates that all of Sisera's horses were suddenly spooked and bolted, and in the confusion which followed, both horse and rider plunged headlong into the fast-flowing river Kishron and were swept away.

There's both a human element and a divine element to war at times, or so it would seem, for there's no doubt the Canaanite army was defeated and slain by the weapons of man. *(Judges 4:16)*. Sisera himself was killed when the heroine Jael drove a metal tent-peg straight through his temple, and pinned Sisera to the ground. *(Judges 4:21)*.Yet apparently, this defeat of the entire enemy army would not have been possible without the interaction of the stars in their courses, fighting from heaven. So yes, it's quite possible that each time an angel in heaven sounded a trumpet during the great tribulation, it was coincident with a Roman soldier sounding a trumpet on earth, during their war with the Jews. Like I said, there's probably far more truth to the paraphrase "as above so below" than we care to realise.

The fact that something of a supernatural origin occurred, is evidenced by the numerous stone buildings, rocks and mountains with a molten facade, which can be found at various locations across the earth, especially around the area of Petra, in southern Jordan.

Dating of Revelations

Without question, Revelation with all its symbolism, is a very difficult book to get one's head around, and because I'm not a theologian, my understanding of John's writings is very limited. I have come to realise however, that the approximate date it was written is of great significance, especially during the times of distraction, deception and outright lies that embrace us today.

Both the historicist and the futurist view of the fulfilment of end-times prophecy, depend largely upon when John wrote the Book of Revelations. Traditionally, it's generally claimed that the Book of Revelations was written while John was at Patmos, around AD 91-96, and well after AD 70. There's no doubt John was on the isle of Patmos, for it is written! *(Revelation 1:9.)*

Yet the internal evidence within the Scriptures, indicates that not only were the Gospels, the Book of Acts, all of the Epistles, and the Book of Revelations, completed prior to 70 AD, many, if not the majority, of the prophecies therein, have already been fulfilled. Including the one thousand year reign of Christ.

And if you're wondering how it's possible for the Bible itself to indicate it was completed several years before 70 AD, may I suggest by reasoning from the Scriptures. But first, if John had written the Book of Revelations *after* 90 AD, do you not think that he would have mentioned the destruction of Jerusalem, which had taken place twenty years *earlier*? Especially as Jesus had foretold its destruction during his ministry years.

On the contrary, John had actually prophesied the fall of Jerusalem aka Babylon, likely between 5 and 10 years *before* it happened. Jesus foretold the destruction of Jerusalem, and when writing to the church at Jerusalem, of which he was an elder, Peter referred to the city as Babylon.

1 Peter 5:13. The church that is at Babylon, elected together with you, saluteth you; and so doth Marcus my son.

John doesn't mention Jerusalem by name in the entire Book of

Revelations,but instead, refers to her as; "The great city, which spiritually is called Sodom and Egypt, where also our Lord was crucified". *(Revelation 11:8.)* He then goes on to foretell the *fall* of that great city, Babylon aka Jerusalem. Which fell in 70 AD. Hence the prophecies of both John and Jesus, were recorded a few years *prior* to 70 AD. Which doesn't sit well with tradition. Hence, many find it hard to get their head around.

Furthermore, if Revelation was written by the Apostle John (which I believe it was), Jesus had previously declared that John was to remain alive, until He returned. It is therefore most likely that whilst at Patmos, John's body was changed in an instant, in the twinkling of the eye, and he was taken up, along with all the resurrected bodies of the dead in Christ, including Peter, and together, they met the Lord in the air. For this was the promise, as recorded by the apostle Paul.

Secular Historians recorded the appearance of a huge Christ-like figure, along with fiery chariots, horses of fire and warriors in the skies above Jerusalem in 66 AD. If this supernatural event truly were the second coming of Jesus, this would mean the Book of Revelations had already been completed, and most likely during the two or three years leading up to 66 AD. It is my opinion, that the later dating of its completion to well after 70 AD, was a deliberate attempt, to hide the fact that Jesus had already returned.

The great tribulation that Scripture refers to, were the last days of the age for Israel-Judah-Jerusalem-Judea, and **not** the last days leading up to the end of the world. Don't fall for the **big lie** about the modern day, Anti-Christ State of Israel being a fulfilment of prophecy. Today's Israel is a British/Rothschild creation, and still comes under the banner of the 6-pointed star of Saturn.

Three World Wars

In the early 1700's the mystical rabbi, Israel ben Eliezer who became known as Baal Shem Tov, created 'Hassidic' Judaism, to trick Jew and Gentile alike into creating a pre-millennial kingdom on earth led by a human messiah from the genealogical line of King David.

In the late 1800's, England was awash with the erroneous semi-political Christian doctrine of Anglo-Israelitism, wherein the British Christians were taught that they were one of the lost tribes of Israel; therefore they should support the Zionist Jews venture to create a Jewish state: Israel. In 1871, the Confederate war general, and head of Scottish Rite Freemasons in America, Satanist Albert Pike, received a channelled vision. In a letter dated August 15 (the feast day of Lucifer) 1871, Pike described his vision to fellow Luciferian Mason, and founder of the Italian Mafia, Giuseppe Mazzini. Both men were Jesuit handled by Catholic priest, Jean Pierre DeSmet.

Pike's letter, which was available for many years at the London Museum, and is still catalogued there, detailed the need for 3 World Wars which would be necessary to produce Antichrist. WW1 would be necessary to end Czarist Russia, and build up Nazism. WW2 would be necessary to end Nazism and replace it with Communism. WW3 would then be necessary to allow a man of peace to end world wide hostilities between the entire Muslim world and the Christian World. Such would bring an end to Christianity and Atheism.

Writes Albert Pike:

> The war must be conducted in such a way that Islam and political Zionism mutually destroy each other. Meanwhile the other nations, once more divided on this issue will be constrained to fight to the point of complete physical, moral, spiritual and economical exhaustion. We shall unleash the Nihilists and the atheists, and we shall provoke a formidable social cataclysm which in all its horror will show clearly to the nations the effect of absolute atheism, origin of savagery and of the most bloody turmoil.

The reality is, that the first world war was deemed necessary to introduce the warped ideology of Zionism, and the second world war was necessary to produce the modern-day State of Israel. Churchill,

Hitler, Stalin and Roosevelt waged a merciless war on humanity murdering approximately 60 million people, and the whole bloody shambles including the 'holocaust', was essential for Zionists to establish modern-day Israel. The 1918 Treaty of Versailles economically devastated Germany, and the Ottoman Turks were forced to give up control of Jerusalem in exchange for the guarantee of a Palestinian State. They did so without a fight, to comply with the 1917 'Balfour Declaration'.

Nicknamed 'Bloody Balfour,' the British Foreign Secretary and Freemason Arthur Balfour, was an inner-circle member of the London-based Round Table Group which had been financed by the Rothschild's in 1909. His letter of November 1917, was addressed to Freemason Baron (Lionel Walter) Rothschild, expressing the British government's support for a Jewish homeland in Palestine.

This served two functions: it would ensure safe passage through the Suez Canal and trade with India; and it would placate both Zionist Jews and British Christians who had been fooled into thinking they should support Zionist Jews in obedience to God and the Bible.

There is nothing prophetic about the 1948 occupation of Palestine, it was a pay-off to Lord Rothschild for the earlier sinking of the Lusitania and blaming it on the Germans, thus dragging the US into WW1 as an ally of England. Without their European and American assets, Jewish supremacism of ruling the world from Jerusalem is not feasible, and the rise of anti-Semitism in Europe served to create the racist/apartheid State of Israel.

Zionism

In 1896 Theodor Herzl, a Rothschild agent, founded the Zionist Movement, and on August 29, 1897, the first Zionist Congress was held in Basel, Switzerland. At this initial Zionist gathering, and obviously with something rather unpleasant in mind for his fellow countrymen to further the Zionist cause, Theodor Herzl stated;

> It is essential that the sufferings of Jews—become worse—this will assist in realization of our plans," and ended his discourse by saying; "I have an excellent idea".

He then predicted with uncanny accuracy, that within fifty years there would be a Jewish state. Three years later on June 11, 1900, Zionist Rabbi Stephen S. Wise, hinted what Herzl's "excellent idea" might involve, by stating;

"There are 6,000,000 living, bleeding, suffering arguments in favour of Zionism."

In 1906 the periodical, 'British Israel Truth' stated :

"We must prepare our-selves for big changes in a Great War which faces the peoples of Europe."

In 1909, the Oxford University Press, published the Scofield Reference Bible. Financed by the House of Rothschild, this Bible was purposefully designed to alter the Christian view of Zionism by creating and promoting a pro-Zionist subculture within Christianity.

Having been awarded a phony PhD, ex-convict Cyrus Scofield's role, was to re-write the King James Version of the Bible by inserting hundreds of Zionist-friendly notes in the margins, between verses and chapters, and at the bottom of the pages. Below are just 3 of the many examples taken from the revised 1967 Edition:

"A curse laid upon those who persecute the Jews."

"For a nation to commit the sin of anti-semitism brings inevitable judgment."

"God made an unconditional promise of blessings through Abram's seed to the nation of Israel to inherit a specific territory forever."

In September 1947, and exactly fifty years since Theodor Herzl had made his famous prediction, the British government announced that the Mandate for Palestine would end at midnight on 14 May 1948. In November 1947, the UN General Assembly adopted UN Resolution 181. The resolution recommended the creation of independent Arab and Jewish States in Palestine, and a Special International Regime for the city of Jerusalem.

Since the Second World War, three groups have converged and come to dominate American policy for the benefit of Israel: the neoconservatives, the Republican evangelicals (Christian Zionists), and Jewish Zionists.

Zionists simply must have control of Jerusalem, and the land promised to Abraham known as Eretz Israel, in order to falsify end-times prophecy, by building the Third Temple and to present their false Messiah to the world.

With an over-emphasis on; 'And I will bless them that bless thee, and curse him that curseth thee' *(Genesis 12:3)* Christian Zionism has led millions of so-called Christians to justify their support for war rather than peace, which includes the merciless killings of millions of people in Iraq, Afghanistan, Syria and Palestine.

In the New Covenant, there is no authorization whatsoever for violence. Jesus said to love your enemies, *not* slaughter those who reject him. How then, can people who claim to follow Christ be so misled? Because they have been bewitched into believing the Bible teaches something it does not teach. Christian support of Israel is, in fact Antichrist, because Israel denies that Jesus is the Christ, hence rejects both the Father and the Son. *(1 John 2:22)*.

An awkward situation arises however, because it's not unusual for an anti-Zionist to stand accused of being anti-Semitic. In the majority of cases, nothing could be further from the truth. Anti-Zionism and anti-Semitism are two entirely different things. Many Jews, including certain rabbis have been anti-Zionism, but it would be quite ridiculous to suggest they're anti-Semite. Let's be very clear, for there has been a deliberate ploy that folk should confuse Zionism with Judaism. Not all Zionists are Jewish by any means, and not all Jews are Zionists. In fact, whilst millions of Christians are Zionist, a great many Jews are strongly opposed to it, which I repeat, would hardly amount to anti-Semitism now, would it? Generally speaking, when either Zionism or Israel are mentioned, most folk automatically think of the Jewish people, which due to the propaganda-induced mind-set is understandable, but it's also very misleading. Zionist Christians and Zionist Jews dominate both political parties in the US Congress, as well as the overall direction and policies coming from the White House. It's pretty much the same here in the UK, where Zionist Jews have an almost total grip on the British Media, and it's reckoned that Zionists have effectively been running the show for at least 100 years. The nation of Israel (Isis Ra El) is not Jewish, nor the Lion of Judah, nor God's gathering of Jacob to the promised land. It is a British-Rothschild created mixture of Ashkenazis (Germanic Pagans), Canaanites, Medeans and Edomites as listed in 2 Kings 17:30, and flying the Star of Molech. This is not the star of David as they would have us believe; it's the Six Pointed Star of Saturn, the Primeval Sun and Black Star of the Chaldeans.

Although they call themselves Jews, and whilst they may well represent the interests of the Rothschild's, we need to remove the blinkers and stop thinking 'Jew', but think 'Gnostic' instead. These people who claim to be Jews, were and still are, Gnostics posing as Jews. Every Jewish Encyclopedia will certify this, and more importantly so does the Word of God.

Revelation 2:9. I know thy works, and tribulation, and poverty, (but thou art rich) and I know the blasphemy of them which say they are Jews, and are not, but are the synagogue of Satan.

They and the people they influence, are descendants of the Canaanites. In public, they fight each other, but in private they pledge oaths to Lucifer. They establish drug enforcement agencies, yet have a drug czar and make billions of dollars growing heroin. They make weapons, run the military and sign peace accords. They start world wars, and then claim to want world peace. They give themselves Nobel peace prizes, honorary PhDs, Cabinet positions, UN leadership roles, University chairs, Supreme and World Court positions, and an assortment of humanitarian awards. They make the laws, interpret the laws, and let each other violate the laws at will. They swear to God and seek the light of Lucifer.

It's time to stop blaming Jews for the Crucifixion and Catholics for the Crusades and Inquisitions. All of it was orchestrated by the 'Synagogue of Satan', the guardians of 'Satan's Seat', the sorcerers from behind the scenes who are currently running the worldwide stage show. The Great Tribulation happened, the millennial reign of Christ has happened. The events that are unfolding right now, I believe, are a simulation of what happened during the tribulation, the time of Jacob's trouble, where without the mark of the beast, no one can buy or sell etc.

Dominion

Under the authority of God, Adam, who was made a little lower than the angels, would have been the ruler of the kingdom of heaven upon earth, so to speak. But after having disobeyed God, and succumbed to the adversary, he lost this opportunity, sin and death entered the aeon or world, and by default, Satan became the god of this world, who now held the power of death. *(Hebrews 2:14.)*

Psalms 8:5-6. For thou hast made him [Adam] a little lower than the angels, and hast crowned him with glory and honour. Thou madest him to have **dominion** over the works of thy hands; thou hast put all *things* under his feet:

Formerly known as Lucifer, Satan was the one who was initially crowned with glory, and had dominion over the creation, and now, here was a man and a woman, made a little lower than himself, receiving from God, the crown he had lost. Pride had been his downfall, and what a jolt to his pride this must have been. If for no other reason, surely this stirred up his hatred of mankind, created in the image and the likeness of God. And what a kick in the teeth it must have been, knowing the earth he once had dominion over, had now been given to these lesser beings.
Few today believe the Earth and its fullness belong to the Lord. *(Psalm 24:1).* Nor believe he has given the Earth to the children of men. For this makes the Earth unique.

*Psalms 115:16 .*The heaven, even the heavens, are the LORD'S: but the *earth* hath he given to the children of men.

Sadly, the subtlety of the Serpent god, led to Adam's sin, and he too lost his crown. But even *before* the foundation of the world, God had made provision for Adam and his fallen sons, in his only begotten Son, Jesus Christ, who was also made a little lower than the angels. Satan, who had once deceived a *sinless* man, made a little lower than the angels, and who now held the power of death, was finally defeated at the cross, by a *sinless* man, also made a little lower than the angels.

Hebrews 2:9. But we see Jesus, who was made a little lower than the angels for the suffering of death, crowned with glory and honour; that he by the grace of God should taste death for every man.

Hebrews 2:14. Forasmuch then as the children are partakers of flesh and blood, he also himself likewise took part of the same; that through death he might destroy him that had the power of death, that is, the devil;

2 Corinthians 5:21. For he hath made him *to be* sin for us, **who knew no sin**; that we might be made the righteousness of God in him.

1 Peter 1:20. Who verily was foreordained **before** the foundation of the world, **but** was manifest in these last times **for you.**

Ephesians 1:4. According as he hath chosen us in him before the foundation of the world, that we should be holy and without blame before him in love:

The old Serpent

Since the dawn of time, Snake or Serpent worship is present in many ancient cultures, which should come as little or no surprise, for it is a form of Satan worship. The old Serpent or Dragon is another name for Satan, the Devil *(Revelation 20:2)* and Jesus says that Satan is the god of this world. *(2 Corinthians 4:4).* Hence the Bible indirectly informs us that the god of this world is an ancient serpent god.

During the millennial reign of Christ, Satan was unable to deceive the nations, because he was bound within the bottomless pit for the entire thousand years. At the end of the thousand years Satan was released, and able to get up to his old tricks again, by deceiving the nations of the world. *(Revelation 20:3.)* Make no mistake. Satan, **not** Jesus Christ, is the god of this world (age).

Although God the creator is sovereign to rule and over-rule in all world affairs, according to Jesus, the god of this world is a deceiving, murderous liar, and always has been. *(John 8:44).* Supernatural beings known as the principalities and powers, are the invisible rulers of this world. *(Ephesians 6:12).* Along with a legion of lesser entities known as evil spirits, devils or demons, they operate under the leadership of Satan, who in exchange for acknowledgement and worship, has the authority to offer men kingdoms, riches, and glory. *(Luke 4:5-6).*

Whilst far from easy to understand, under the sovereign rule and will of God, and by decree of the 'Watchers', the kings of the earth tend not to be righteous men, but are the **basest** (most morally reprehensible) of men. *(Daniel 4:17).* It's a question of putting things into perspective, for the rulers of nations have not attained that position of authority by their own wisdom, nor due to their own efforts. Though he is the god of this world, neither does Satan ordain kings and queens. It is the Lord God alone who removes and sets kings in their kingdoms. *(Daniel 4:17).*

Jesus was not, and is not a 'Jew' nor a 'Christian'; he was Judean. Jews killed Jesus as well as many of their own prophets, they persecute the followers of Jesus, do not please God, and are contrary to everyone. *(1 Thessalonians 2:15.)* Judaism is Pharisaism, and Rabbinical Judaism is the driving force behind world events, for they are in control of most every psychotic world leader. Driven by the principalities and the powers, which rule the darkness of this world, they are the Synagogue of Satan *(Revelation 2:9)*, the descendants of Amalek, who are in a generational war with God.

Ephesians 6:12. For we wrestle *not* against flesh and blood, *but* against principalities, against powers, against the rulers of the darkness of this world, against spiritual wickedness in high *places*.

Exodus 17:16. For he said, Because the LORD hath sworn *that* the LORD *will have* war with Amalek from generation to generation.

God told Saul to destroy the Amalekites. He failed to do what God asked of him *(1 Samuel 15:2-3)* and so the war continues to this very day. Amalekites control world leaders toward War as they have since t he first war in Genesis 14:1. Amalek is the real 13th Tribe, in the form of the spiritual, physical and religious House of Esau. God hates them and they know it. *(Romans 9:13).* Yet it's foretold they will gain worldwide Dominion. *(Genesis 27:39-41).*

Whilst new Bible versions have muddied the waters, in *Genesis 27:40* the *Authorized King James Version* makes perfectly clear, it is Esau who achieves 'Dominion' (sovereign authority to rule the earth) and his intent is to slay the house of Jacob.

Genesis 27:39-40. And Isaac his [Esau's] father answered and said unto him, Behold, thy dwelling shall be the fatness of the earth and of the dew of heaven from above. And by thy sword shalt thou live, and shalt serve thy brother; and it shall come to pass when thou shalt have the *dominion*, that thou shalt break his *yoke* from off thy neck.

This dominion falls into three main categories, for the "fatness of the earth" speaks of Wealth, "the dew of heaven from above" speaks of Spirituality and Religion, and living "by the sword" speaks of Military. Sovereignty means 'No higher authority'. And Switzerland is the only sovereign nation, and home of the Knights Templar and Knights of St John (aka Hospitallers), along with the world's

International Bankers and the worldwide Intelligence Services (CIA) and CERN.

The Gnomes of Zurich are the Saturnian priest-kings, the secret chiefs, aka the shadow government, who control the world on behalf of the god of the world, Satan. The Sorcerers, who from behind the scenes control the Vatican (spiritual arm) and the City of London Corporation (financial arm), enforced by Washington DC (the military arm). Each of the three districts is classified as a Sovereign Territory, free from their respective national laws.

Jesus warned that creditors make slaves of debtors *(Luke 7:41),* and the Edomites are the robber-barons, the creditors making slaves of debtors. This is the reason why Esau was prophesied in *Genesis 27:39-41* (KJV) to obtain Dominion, the sovereign authority to rule the Earth. Ultimately the robber-baron's world-wide financial system is a rigged game designed to enslave everyone on Earth. Hence why Mortgage means 'Death Note'.

In 1994, 160 Nations agreed to a timeline for reducing world population from 6Billion to 800Million by 2030; today called 'UN Agenda 2030'. The 30 year old plan calls for the fluoridation of drinking water, the release of toxic chemtrails in the atmosphere to sicken and sterilize the population, and releasing man-made mutated Influenza. Everything that is going on in the world today, is all by design of the World Economic Forum New World Order to create a one world socialist Nazi government. Our very own government is effectively at war with the people, whilst Mainstream media is being used to promote their propaganda to brainwash the public and to keep humanity in a constant state of fear, confusion and distraction, while they pull off one of, if not the greatest deception in history.

A recent article from *The Expose* reads;

> The central players in this very real conspiracy (and there is definitely no 'theory' involved here!) are the elitist, unelected and unaccountable private individuals at *the World Economic Forum* and the extremely powerful but virtually unknown *Bank for International Settlements*. Between them, they are covertly conspiring to collapse the entire global economy to their ultimate political and fiscal advantage. This is being done to create the right conditions needed to implement their so-called Great Reset. This drive to destabilise the governance of sovereign nations involves using the 'climate change' pseudo-science peddled by a

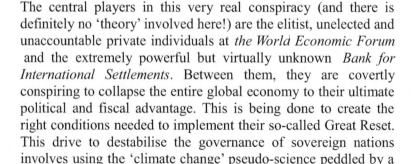

corrupt, bought-and-paid-for academia which is integral to the fake *Green New Deal*. The world is being deceived by a cocktail of outright lies and carefully planned subterfuge, all reinforced by shutting down any form of real debate by the mainstream media, that is enabling a criminal mind-set to unlawfully seize control.

Genuine scientists, who practise real science by always following the evidence, know that so-called 'climate change' is occurring naturally as it has done throughout the ages, and that Carbon Dioxide, which only accounts for 0.04% of the Earth's atmosphere, is in fact a benign gas whose concentration actually lags temperature trends. Indeed, it is considered by real ecologists to be the "gas of life" for all living creatures and that we actually need more of it, not less!

But the most frightening aspect of 'climate change' is how the UK's mainstream media, especially the BBC, ITV and Channel 4, along with universities and schools, have completely and deliberately shut down any further balanced debate on this subject, as they all promote a carbon-free future that endorses the globalist's agenda for the *Great Reset* and the *Green New Deal*.

Simple common sense, not to mention fairness, tells you that this is not right, and that this UN-led official narrative is completely unable to meet public challenges from highly qualified climatologists. You cannot ever close down scientific debate unless, of course, there is something to hide!

And please don't get me started on the worldwide vaccine agenda. Which, of course, are not vaccines in the traditional sense, but rather, are a form of artificially-intelligent, bio-synthetic, self-replicating, nano-technology. Moderna chief scientist calls it 'Information Therapy', an operating system that essentially "hacks the software of life."

Having gas-lit the population into believing the shot-in-the-arm was fully authorized, safe and efficient, the Office for National Statistics has revealed that England and Wales suffered another record-breaking week of deaths in the week ending 21ˢᵗ October 2022, with an extra 1,714 people dying compared to the five-year average. Excluding the weeks affected by the Jubilee Bank Holiday in early June, and the late Queen's funeral in September, this means England and Wales have now recorded significant numbers of excess deaths every week for the past 27 weeks, bringing the grand total to 34,237 since the week ending 24th April.

With further ONS figures proving 94% of all Covid-19 deaths since April have been among the triple/quadruple vaccinated, and also proving that mortality rates per 100,000 are highest among the vaccinated population in all age groups, this strongly suggests that the Covid-19 vaccines are to blame for why so many extra people are dying.

This is all being done as part of the United Nations General Assembly's 2030 Agenda, in which the UN Biodiversity Treaty and the UNESCO re-wilding program calls for world population reduction, and the elimination of 5 billion people from Earth, a return to an agrarian economy, no motorized transportation and vast areas of wilderness separating small controllable cities of less than 20,000 people. They call it 'Sustainability'. What they really mean is, the elimination of mankind created in His image and His likeness, and a world without God.

All of their plans can be viewed by looking up 'Project for a New American Century' (PNAC) written by Dick Cheney, Paul Wolfowitz, Jeb Bush, Richard Perle, and Bill Bennett, just as the Illuminati plans can be viewed by looking up 'Protocols of the Learned Elders of Zion', or Free masonry's goals by looking up 'Morals and Dogma of the Ancient and Accepted Rite of Freemasonry'.

The highly controversial text, 'The Protocols of the Learned Elders of Zion' are not a fake as many would have us believe; neither are they anti-Semitic for they are not Jewish. They are the Luciferian, Edomite blueprint of world wide domination. Make of it what you will, but Protocol 10 in part states;

"It is indispensable to utterly exhaust humanity with dissension, hatred, struggle, envy, torture, starvation *and inoculation of disease* so the Goyim see no other issue than our complete sovereignty in money and all else."

On February 25, 2009 at the World Health Organization Council on Eugenics, the endearing Satanist, Dr. Henry Kissinger is quoted with saying;

> Once the herd accepts mandatory forcible vaccination, it's game over! They will accept anything -forcible blood or organ donation-for the 'greater good'. We can genetically modify children and sterilize them-for the 'greater good'.

Control sheep minds and you control the herd, Vaccine makers stand to make billions, and many of you in this room today are investors. It's a big win-win! We thin out the herd and the herd pays us for providing extermination services. Now, what's for lunch, huh?

During an interview on Jan 10th 2016, founder of the World Economic Forum Klaus Schwab, explains that Human beings will soon receive a chip in their body in order to merge with the *digital world*. In March, 2019, University dropout Bill Gates, who has no medical qualifications applied for Patent #060606 for an injectable microchip interface for Digital Currency, and the European Union proposed a Covid/Passport Vaccination Card. The inclusion of 666 raised many an eyebrow at the time.

This nefarious program originated one hundred years earlier in 1917, when Theosophist and claimed clairvoyant Rudolph Steiner, gave a series of lectures about how one day a belief in God would be deemed a mental illness, and predicted a "Vaccine to end knowledge of the spirit and soul". Steiner further illustrated the goal;

> It is pathological for people to think in terms of Spirit and Soul. Sound people will soon speak of nothing but the body--- sickness is people who think of Soul and Spirit---a medicine will be found for this, the soul will be made non-existent---physicians will administer a vaccine to influence organisms as soon as it is born.

Whether this is possible remains to be seen, but in 2004 the war for souls gained Government Approval. FunVax is a US Government 'vaccine' program tested in Iran, designed to deactivate VMAT2 (the so-called God Gene) and suppress neuro-transmitters in the brain, in order to combat 'Religious Fundamentalism'.

Do I believe the current jab is the mark of the beast? No not exactly, for the mark of the beast was fulfilled back in the end times for Israel. But nevertheless in the end-times for the entire world, there is a war for the human soul, and who knows what the forthcoming 6 monthly boosters might contain, or ultimately be capable of? Personally, I think that along with seasonal Flu shots we can expect many more of them, finally ending up with Micro-Needle Quantum Dot delivery. Unprecedented times of hyper-inflation, energy failures and food shortages, homelessness, lawlessness and severe hardship lay ahead for us all, but especially I suspect, for those who've refused to accept the Needle.

Falsification of Prophecy

Anybody with the ability to reason and think things through logically, must surely realise by now that our corrupt national leaders, criminal governments and complicit mainstream media have deceived us in the most dark and malevolent way. The world we know is rapidly collapsing into a totalitarian medical police state, where governments claim the power to constantly monitor your location and your compliance with their demanded medical interventions. The ultimate goal is constant government surveillance of your location, your vaccine compliance, your medication compliance, your speech compliance and your total obedience to the medical police state regime that's killing you.

There is an international Edomite spiritual war going on for the souls of men which relatively few are aware of. Government at every level has been known to lie with impunity, and commit atrocities of epic proportions and then create lies for the public to swallow, in order to support and justify those atrocities. Why?

Because none are righteous, the love of money is the root of all evil, and every government on earth involved in the Satanic world-system has an otherworldly agency running in the background. This supernatural agency is more organized than the greatest army man has ever assembled, and their goal is to change or falsify the Word of God. Especially concerning end times prophecy. For the controllers of this world, are falsifying end times prophecy in an attempt to convince us that these prophecies have not yet been fulfilled, and it would seem they are actually following the blueprint of Scripture to do so. This is why millions of Christians world-wide, who look at what is going on around them, believe that the time draws near,when Jesus returns to rapture them out of this world. But the truth is, that the first resurrection occurred when Jesus returned, just as he promised the generation he spoke to, somewhere around 68-70 AD.

Matthew 16:28. Verily I say unto you, There be some standing here, which shall not taste of death, till they see the Son of man coming in his kingdom.

Matthew 24:21. For then shall be great tribulation, such as was not since the beginning of the world to this time, no, nor ever shall be.

America

The U.S. $ sign symbolizes the Serpent, and the Eagle carries the Serpent on the Dollar for a reason. America is the namesake of

Amurru, the Edomite serpent and shepherd god of the Amorites, and the Eagle symbolizes Edomite 'Dominion.' *(Genesis 27:40).*

Writes Manly P. Hall in The Secret Teachings of All Ages. (p. xc.)

> Not only were many of the founders of the United States Government Masons, but they received aid from *a secret and august body* existing in Europe, which helped them to establish this country for *a peculiar and particular purpose* known only to the initiated few. The Great Seal is the signature of this exalted body—*unseen* and for the most part *unknown*—and the unfinished pyramid upon its reverse side is a trestle-board setting forth symbolically the task to the accomplishment of which the United States Government was *dedicated* from the day of its inception. [emphasis mine]

Sourced from the back cover of 'The New World Order' (1990) by Ralph A. Epperson;

> Historian/author Ralph Epperson has spent many years researching the history of the Great Seal, and has discovered that those who designed the two circles committed America to what has been called 'A Secret Destiny.' This future 'destiny' is so unpleasant that those who wanted the changes it entails had to conceal that truth in symbols.

Writes Rhoda Wilson for the Expose;

> The FBI was born under the Teddy Roosevelt administration when Congress would not give his Attorney General the secret permanent police force he was demanding.
>
> J. Edgar Hoover – the Scottish Rite Masons' most honoured member, second only to Albert Pike who proudly proclaimed their god, Lucifer is the god of good and light that fights against the evil God of the Christians who is against humanity – worked diligently to commit atrocities against the American people from the start. Hoover, a cross-dresser and puppet of the Masons, even established a Masonic chapter of the FBI called the Fidelity Chapter which Hoover insisted his agents refer to as the "Seat of Government."
>
> To this day the FBI has been a force of dictatorship domestically that made way for the Babylonian Deep State CIA to work alongside other nation's Deep State Intelligence Agencies abroad and at home.

Former CIA Director William Casey, once said;

"We'll know our disinformation program is complete when everything the American public believes is false."

Benjamin Franklin was not a President, but he was America's first Grand Master (Philadelphia Lodge) Free Mason. Franklin was also an avid astrologer who said; "Astrology is one of the most ancient sciences, and no important affair was ever undertaken without consulting Astrology". Franklin chose America's birthday on July 4, 1776, because of a rare solar occultation of 5 planets. Both Franklin and Thomas Jefferson were initiates of the Masonic 'Nine Sisters Lodge' in Paris. Franklin was also a member of Sir Francis Dashwood's 'Hell Fire Society' (Stanley Kubrick's 1999 movie 'Eyes Wide Shut' may ring a Baal), holding nocturnal orgies and sacrifice rituals in London and Paris, as a revolutionary war diplomat with Britain's King George III.

America was created to be destroyed, and the Cult of Saturn plan to present New York City in ruins to the world as 'Babylon the Great is fallen is fallen', as per *Revelation 18:2*. Don't fall for the deception; Babylon, aka that great city Jerusalem, fell in 70 AD. America is coming down, but not because she is spiritual Babylon. America was purposefully created to be destroyed, and to become the Scapegoat for Babylon is fallen, is fallen. From her ashes will arise the New World Order aka New Atlantis.

This plan to make America the phoenix of the new age was put in writing in 1627 by Francis Bacon, who many now believe was the true esoteric founder of America. Inspired by Jesuit priest Tobie Matthew, his book 'New *Atlantis*: *A Work Unfinished*', and as gold was being robbed from the Americas, Free-Masonic Rosicrucian, Sir Francis Bacon, tells the story of an elite society of God Men called Salomon's House in New Atlantis. Salomon refers to Salomon Rothschild, George Washington's American Revolution financier. The author detailed the demise and rising of the Americas as a Phoenix to become the 'New Atlantis', and portrayed a utopian vision of the future of human discovery and knowledge. Bacon himself was a Rosicrucian and master of Jewish Kabbalah. New Atlantis being in reference to the great Atlantean pre-flood civilization described earlier by Plato. America would be used by both Jesuit and Rosicrucian occultists to return the world to pre-flood glory.

To do so, these Christ-hating parasites are not only carrying out their dark and wicked, world-wide depopulation agenda via an injectable gene-altering serum, but under the umbrella of climate change, they are also ***destroying*** the earth; whilst declaring their dual mantra of 'Build Back Better', and 'Order out of Chaos'. Hard to take in maybe, but America was created to be destroyed, which many speculate will be caused by the eruption of the volcanic caldera of Yellowstone National Park. Could this be the reason why NASA on occasion issue a D-Day warning? And why former Clinton CIA Director and Obama adviser, James Woolsey once said;

"Two thirds of America will die from ancient diseases, mass riots and worldwide economic chaos."

'The Great Reset', in my opinion, is symbolic of Esau achieving dominion, by finally breaking free from his brother, Jacob's yoke. *(Genesis 27:40.)* Jesus said he hated Esau, and to this day, the Edomites seem to take great pride in the fact. *(Romans 9:13.)*

Earth-Destroyers

Those Old Testament prophecies fulfilled in Israel in 68-70 AD, were coincident with the coming of the Son of man in the clouds of heaven. Supernatural events in the heavens above, and surrounding Jerusalem, which seem to have been recorded by secular historians such as Josephus. Yet whilst those same first century historians had much to say about the destruction of cities, such as Rome and Jerusalem, they have nothing whatsoever to say about men destroying the earth. But the Scriptures clearly say that at his coming, Jesus will destroy those which *destroy* the earth.

Revelation 11:18. And the nations were angry, and thy wrath is come, and *the time of the dead*, that they should be judged, and that thou shouldest give reward unto thy servants the prophets, and to the saints, and them that fear thy name, small and great; and shouldest destroy them which **destroy the earth**.

I'm not sure about you, the reader, but I cannot believe that mankind had the means to destroy the earth, back in 70 AD. So what does this verse actually mean? Was John referring to the coming of the Son of man, a little over 2,000 years ago? Or was he referring to the time beyond the 'little season', the final years leading up to the war of Gog and Magog followed by the final judgement? The time of the dead?

Revelation 20:12. And I saw the dead, small and great, stand before God; and the books were opened: and another book was opened, which is the book of life: and the dead were judged out of those things which were written in the books, according to their works.

For it's only been in more recent times, that man has had the weaponry to destroy the earth. In fact, man now has the capability to create hurricanes, tornados, earthquakes and tsunamis etc. In other words, man has the technology to cause folk to think, "Only God could do something like this". Hard to believe? Then consider this;

In **1871**, 33 degree Luciferian Freemason Albert Pike commented in *Morals And Dogma*:

> There is in nature one most potent force, by means whereof a single man, who could possess himself of it, and should know how to direct it, could revolutionize and change the face of the world.

In **1891**, the electrical genius, Nikola Tesla said;

> Throughout space there is energy. Is this energy static or kinetic? If static our hopes are in vain; if kinetic – and we know it is, for certain – then it is a mere question of time when men will succeed in attaching their machinery to the very wheelwork of Nature.

In **1899**, on the night of July 3-4, Nikola Tesla experimentally discovered the standing scalar wave potential in his Colorado Springs laboratory. He discovered it was being radiated from within a travelling thunderstorm, and recognized the phenomena as being an "electromagnetic sound wave". Strangely enough, Tesla himself would not take direct credit for his inventions, but claimed that his insights were a result of having tapped into some universal, or divine source of knowledge that was available which he, through some state of mind, simply became a conduit for, and then did his best to manifest that knowledge for the benefit of the world.

In **1900** Nikola Tesla published the plans for extracting limitless energy from the Sun and sequestering unlimited nitrogen from the atmosphere for the world-wide farming industry. He was eventually murdered for that in 1943.

In **1901**, Tesla began construction of the 57metre high Wardenclyffe tower in New York. Ostensibly for telegraphy, he used the tower to further his experiments into the transmission of electricity.

In **1908** Nikola Tesla claimed he could direct unbelievable amounts of wire-less energy to any 3 dimensional location on, in or above the earth at the speed of light and without any transmission loss.

That same year on June 17th, Tesla directed Electro-Magnetic energy from his Wardenclyffe Tower on Long Island, and over the North Pole along a Magnetic Field line ('Ley Line') in the Earth, into a remote location deep in the Tunguska forest of Siberia. The release of energy was estimated at between 5 and 30 megatons of TNT between 3-6 miles above the earth's surface.

Eye witnesses reported the sky was literally torn apart, but because of the remote location, coupled with the Russian Revolution and Civil War, an expedition did not reach Tunguska until 1927. The team of scientists found a 2,600 Sq Km swathe of forest lay scorched, with felled trees radiating out from the centre, but without any evidence of a meteor impact crater found. Even as far away as Scotland, it was reported that the skies were so illuminated, it was possible to read a book at midnight.

In **1912** (February) during a rare interview, Nikola Tesla said that it would be possible to split the earth by combining vibrations with the correct resonance of the earth itself.

In **1930** Tesla said his weapon could be used as a defence shield, for wireless communication and for wireless power transmission to locations anywhere on the earth without the use of any fuel source other than the Earth's magnetic field.

In **1934**, German physicist Dr. W.O. Schumann gave an address at the Faculty of Science University in Munich, in which he incorporated a spiritual element with Nazi technology, stating;

> Everything destructive is of Satanic origin, everything creative is divine. Every technology based upon explosion or combustion has thus to be called Satanic. The coming new age will be an age of new, positive, divine technology.

In **1947,** on January 7, aged 86, Nikola Tesla was murdered (suffocated) by Nazi SS initiates, Otto 'Scarface' Skorzeny and Reinhard Gehlen, in his rented room at the New Yorker Hotel. Although Tesla was an American citizen, after his death the FBI seized his entire estate, and secured it under the seal of the U.S. Office of Alien Property. The National Defence Research Institute called in MIT Scientist John G Trump, to review Tesla's inventions and papers. Donald's 'Uncle John' was then asked to develop Tesla's inventions as Weapons of War.

Copies of Tesla's papers on particle-beam weaponry were sent to the U.S. Air Force Institute of Technology at Wright-Patterson Air Base, Dayton, Ohio. Under the command of General L.C. Craigie, experiments were carried out to test the feasibility of Tesla's concept. No details were ever published and the project was discontinued. All copies of Tesla's papers mysteriously 'disappeared' with no record of what happened to them.

In the meanwhile, Dr. W. O. Schumann, who had previously spoken publicly in Munich, Germany on the subject of divine, or esoteric technology, was brought to America under the Jesuit-orchestrated Operation Paperclip, where he too worked at the Wright-Patterson Air Force Base. In 1948 Schumann returned to Munich.

Once Uncle John Trump had officially reported Tesla's work to be "primarily of a speculative nature, with little or no practical value", this new technology was given to Brotherhood of Death member and Freemason, Joseph Stalin and his communist regime. Churchill (a Freemason and initiated Druid) along with Roosevelt and Stalin, planned the Cold War Hoax to provide the necessary privacy across 12 time zones for thousands of scientists to develop this technology as electro-magnetic weather modifying weapons.

At this time the Rothschild-Zionist-Banking Cabal had financial control of both governments. The US-Soviet nuclear stand-off provided the defence contractors a lot of money, and kept the world in fear of a nuclear holocaust so the scientists could work on the device that will one day fool people into thinking only God could do something like that. After the war when people started reporting seeing odd unexplained lights in the skies, the newly formed Illuminati-controlled CIA, began spreading alien-propaganda to hide the theft of Tesla technology and their true agenda. Shadow governments and the military operate a form of black technology which is far more advanced than most can even begin to imagine.

In **1947**, Atomic Scientists introduced the world to the Doomsday Clock, a symbol which represents the likelihood of a man-made world-wide catastrophe.

In **1958**, on January 7, Senate Majority Leader and later President Lyndon Johnson stated;

> Control of space means control of the world. From space, the masters of infinity would have the power to control the earth's weather, to cause drought and flood, to change the tides and raise the levels of the sea, to divert the gulf stream and change temperate climates to frigid. There is something more important than the ultimate weapon. And that's the ultimate position. The position of total control over the Earth that lies somewhere in outer space.

In **1961**, Soviet Premier Nikita Khrushchev who married Stalin's daughter, said to the world's newspapers:

"We have a new weapon, just obtained which is so powerful if used unrestrained could wipe out all life on earth. It's a fantastic weapon."

In **1968**, 'Jason Society' member and UC Berkeley professor, Gordon MacDonald, wrote in 'Unless Peace Comes';"modification of storms and controlling hurricanes can be used for terrorizing population centres."

In **1970**, Obama advisor Zbignew Brzezinski, wrote in 'Between Two Ages'; "weather control is a key element of strategy."

In **1975**, Leonid Brezhnev said to the UN: "The frightening scalar electromagnetic (EM) weapons can be used, but only very, very gingerly indeed. If a slight mistake is made, everybody loses everything."

The same year that the 'Geneva International Disarmament Accord' issued a proclamation 'prohibiting the awakening of volcanoes, creating avalanches and landslides, creating tidal waves, harnessing lightning, artificially creating hail, fog and rain, altering the course of rivers, melting Polar Ice, or destroying the ozone layer'. Have you ever heard of it?

In **1995**, on May 26 'The Glasgow Herald' broke a story stating that Soviets had used hypnosis and high frequency radio waves to program human weapons to become fearless, conscienceless, fighting machines. These warriors were activated using numbered codes and passwords.

In **1997** (April) US Defence Secretary, William Cohen said;

Others [terrorists] are engaging even in an eco-type of terrorism whereby they can alter the climate, set off earthquakes, volcanoes remotely through the use of electromagnetic waves.

In **2006**: US Congress debates weather modification bills S 517 and HR 299.

In **2001**, five years earlier, and as proven beyond doubt with forensic science by Dr. Judy Wood in her most remarkable book, 'Where Did The Towers Go'? a directed free-energy weapon (DEW) was used to attack New York City.

Four weeks earlier, on 9/10/2001, the Federal Emergency Management Agency (FEMA) held a Terrorist Drill in New York City. Spokesman Tom Kennedy said on the evening news that FEMA was planning for a Terrorist Act in NYC followed by a Hurricane in New Orleans, followed by a 7.0 Earthquake in Los Angeles. Coincidence?

In **2010**, another intentionally created disaster caused the 'Deepwater Horizon' drilling rig to explode in the Gulf of Mexico on April 20, putting a stop to oil production. When an oil drilling rig catches fire from a well blowout, the well head shear ram is closed and the rig is severed from its mooring. This did not happen. Shear Rams, plus 7 separate Door Rams, and 2 annular valves all mysteriously failed during this orchestrated disaster.

You may recall photos from November 2009 of Prince Hall Freemason Barack Obama, bowing to Japan's Emperor Akahito (a member of the City of London Round Table, and 830th Knight of the Order of the Garter). Obama was delivering MOX (mixed oxide) uranium-plutonium fuel rods for Fukushima Reactor 3. Perhaps the most toxic sea and airborne man-made material known.

In **2011**, the Fukushima disaster began on Lent with an electro-magnetic scalar-wave induced earthquake and tsunami. The 48 hour EM signal ends precisely as the earthquake hits Fukushima. The location of Fukushima at the origin of the Pacific Jet Stream, and the use of seawater in the reactors caused the world's greatest disaster by order of magnitude. Far worse than Chernobyl which released radiation high into the atmosphere during the explosion; Fukushima is releasing radiation constantly into the ocean where its course east takes it to the North and South American continents, where it follows the Jet Stream east full circle.

To add insult to injury, the engineered Super Typhoon Hagibis, hit Japan on the Feast of Atonement 2019. 'Hagibis' was a record-setting storm in terms of speed of intensification, wind velocity and ground speed, tracking directly over Fukushima, sending millions of tons of radioactive debris bags into the Pacific Ocean. The Luciferian kings of the earth are intent on destroying one third of all oceanic life, as foretold in *Revelation* 8:9.

Simply put, the Earth and Ionosphere function as a Battery of nearly infinite energy. Discharging this energy as a capacitor can direct energy anywhere on, above or within the Earth. Man is capable of transmitting power and information without wires or satellites everywhere on Earth. Facilities like SuperDarn, SOUSY, EISCAT, HAARP, the Russian Woodpecker Grid and Duga Radar System in Chernobyl, transmit energy accurately all across the Earth. If you think the US, Russia and China are adversaries, guess again. Occultists/Satanists work together in every nation on Earth and Russia and the US are no exception. We have seen them working in unity in more recent times, for it's the same group of players who have been running the covid pandemic show, instigating the lockdowns and destroying the world economy.

Scalar technology has demonstrated the capability to alter jet stream winds, enhance or diminish ocean temperatures like El Nino and La Nina, and create strange fires, floods and drought. Earthquakes will happen in diverse places, as stated in the Bible, because evil men who serve Lucifer are creating them with Scalar technology. Fukushima was a HAARP induced ecological disaster, as was the Haiti earthquake, the India/Pakistan floods, the Sichuan earthquake in China, Hurricane Katrina, and the Indonesia earthquake/tsunami used to murder 250,000 human cattle on Yule 2004.

It would appear that we've entered a new chapter in the ongoing operations that utilize destruction in order to further particular agendas. Direct energy is now being used by drones, to create strange fire such as the multiple wildfires burning across California in 2015 and 2017, and the more recent wildfires burning in Greece. In one sense nothing has changed of course, as forest fires have always broken out randomly and naturally.

When you examine the video footage of these fires however, you see peculiar anomalies that just don't add up. Anyone with critical thinking ability, can look at the aftermath and know something's not right. Vehicles cannot be reduced to ashes within minutes, and houses do not burn from the inside, outwards. It's almost as if these fires are selective in what to consume, ignoring Fire Breaks, and skipping over one potential fuel source to devour another. Entire rows of houses turned to dust with very little debris, whilst nearby bushes and pine trees fail to ignite and remain standing untouched.

During the Valley Fire of 2015, in the Middletown, California area, 20 miles from Santa Rosa, strange 'fires' occurred with one observer stating;

"It wasn't even a fire. It was like fluorescent evil."

Beginning July 1, 2021, a series of supposed Lightning strikes over a geo-engineered heat dome ignited 180 wildfires, killing hundreds of people and destroying much property and the natural habitat in British Columbia. It would seem however, that genuine forest fires were used in some areas as cover for the use of Scalar Weapons, so that the public would be unaware of what actually occurred.

It's reckoned that Tesla technology is able to provide virtually cost-free energy to every residential and commercial property on earth.

Something no occult-led government in the world would allow. The controllers of this world have trillions of dollars invested in fossil-fuel technology, and will release the new technology only as and when it suits them. Which is most likely never.

Former American journalist, HL Mencken (deceased) once said;

> The aim of practical politics is to constantly menace the population with an endless array of hobgoblins, all of which are imaginary.

There is no doubt that the hobgoblin termed 'global warming' is in one sense very real, because the Amazon River and Asia's great rivers are retreating rapidly. Polar ice packs are melting faster than ever with both Antarctic and the Arctic regions situated under the largest holes in the ozone layer on record. One of the under-reported areas that affect literally billions of people is the Himalayas which supply water to all the great rivers of Asia, many of which are slowly drying up. Yet at the same time, all the rivers in Eastern Australia are FLOODING, causing all food crops, and livestock herds, to be washed away. Yet none of these disasters are the result of what we've all been led to believe, is the cause. For they have all been engineered and orchestrated by the controllers, whose end goal has always been a world population of no more than one billion, of which 500 million are slave labour.

Just like the bank-roller of chaos, George Soros, the environmentalist and 33 Degree Luciferian Freemason, Al Gore, knows full well that electromagnetic scalar and microwave energy (HAARP) is being used to tear holes in the ozone layer allowing more radiation to contact the northern and southern latitudes. Because back in April, 1997, during his term as Vice President, his Secretary of Defence, William Cohen, admitted to the world that this was happening.

Al knows full well, that directed radio frequency (RF) energy aimed at the ionosphere is reflected back to earth to intentionally melt polar ice caps. Al Gore knows scalar energy can be used to re-forest desert areas if desired, by moving jet streams anywhere they choose. He also knows that scalar weapons can be used to redirect weather fronts to increase or lower regional temperatures accordingly, if they so choose. His role in the grand Luciferian scheme is to publicize alternative causes of global warming and blame humans so they can be exterminated for the good of the 'planet' that he affectionately refers to as 'Mother Gaia'.

By promoting the CO2-related Global Warming Scam the world has been conned into taking a guilt-trip; a distraction from the real end-times agenda, which has caused most of the world to adopt the belief that humanity in general is accountable for any extreme change in the weather patterns.

I think it can be firmly established, that over the last seven decades, not only has man developed the technology capable of destroying the earth, he is actively trying to do so. For wicked men have an agenda. Which brings us back to the Book of Revelations. Why would John record that at His coming as the Word of God, Jesus will destroy those which are destroying the earth, when the technology to do so, just didn't exist at the time? The prophet Isaiah said the earth will be utterly broken and staggering to and fro like a drunkard *(Isaiah 24:20)*, and Jesus said he would return to destroy those who would destroy the earth. *(Revelation 11:18)*.

Which again begs the question; was John referring to the second coming of Christ, when he appeared in the clouds as the Son of man? Or was he referring to the end of the little season and after the war of Gog and Magog, when wicked men are annihilated by God's fire raining down from heaven? This time there will be no survivors, for it will result in the end of the ages, and the unsaved dead from across the ages being raised for judgement at the great white throne.

Revelation 20:9. And they went up on the breadth of the earth, and compassed the camp of the saints about, and the beloved city: and fire came down from God out of heaven, and devoured them.

Revelation 20:11. And I saw a great white throne, and him that sat on it, from whose face the earth and the heaven fled away; and there was found no place for them.

One other point I would like to make; Jesus told his disciples that "in the regeneration when the Son of man shall sit in the throne of his glory, ye also shall sit upon twelve thrones, judging the twelve tribes of Israel." *(Matthew 19:28.)* Yet when writing to the believers in Christ at Corinth, Paul also says; "Know ye not that we shall judge angels?" *(1 Corinthians 6:3.)* I think it safe to say that the judgement of the twelve tribes of Israel took place *after* the coming of the Son of man in the clouds, but *prior* to the millennial reign of Christ. For how else could the prophecies of Isaiah, Ezekiel and Zechariah be fulfilled? When examining them, it becomes clear that God would supernaturally gather a remnant of the 12 tribes of Israel and bring them back to the Promised Land at the end of the age, and prior to the beginning of the 1,000 year kingdom.

As for the judgement of the angels, the Scriptures indicate this takes place way *beyond* the thousand years, at the very end of the world, and *prior* to the eternal kingdom in the new heavens and the new earth. So yes, because the Scriptures foretell two judgements, separated by an undisclosed period of time, it is quite likely that the earth-destroyers are annihilated by Jesus at His coming *after* "the little season" and at the very end of the world. Whilst I cannot be too dogmatic about this, one thing is certain; both the prophet Joel and Jesus himself, said the horrors of "the great tribulation" during the last days for Israel were a one-off event. Never to be repeated.

Joel 2:2. A day of darkness and of gloominess, a day of clouds and of thick darkness, as the morning spread upon the mountains: a great people and a strong; there hath not been ever the like, *neither shall be any more after it,* even to the years of many generations.

Armageddon? or Gog and Magog?

Christians world-wide have been a persecuted minority since the time of the Apostles. But today it would seem, that our own governments, especially those in the Western world, are at war with the very people they are supposed to protect, regardless of race or religion. Whilst true Christians still remain a minority, it is not just Christianity, but humanity in general which is now under attack, and in a way never before experienced.

Like a Witch's Spell, and driven by the cleverly engineered government narrative of mixed messages, propaganda and lies, coupled with bribery, coercion and the Draconian lockdown measures, plus the complicit mainstream media's daily hype, a wave of Mass Psychosis has severely crippled the nations, especially those with a Christian heritage. Why? What is so different about the times that we live in?

I think it goes without saying, that all Christians would claim it's because we are living in the end-times. But which end-times? Those approaching the war of Armageddon? Or could it possibly be that we are approaching the end times of the Little Season? That unique period of time recorded in Scripture, where Satan is released, for the sole purpose of deceiving all the nations of the world.

Revelation 20:7-8. And when the thousand years are expired, Satan shall be loosed out of his prison, And shall go out to deceive the nations which are in the four quarters of the earth, Gog and Magog, to gather them together to battle: the number of whom *is* as the sand of the sea.

Here in the UK, the government is now controlling the NHS, and it is the government that is actually dictating what the NHS should do during Covid emergency measures. During a call made to Brian Gerrish of UK Column News on 18 April 2021, a deeply concerned senior NHS Board member, turned whistle-blower, warns that the result of the government's enforced Covid and vaccination policies can only be described as genocide.

She goes on to explain how government messaging to her senior NHS colleagues is removing their capacity for rational thought, and they are effectively being mind controlled to implement policies which, in more rational moments, they would challenge as wrong.

Fear prevails, and she and her board colleagues are being expected to toe an unwritten policy line, set predominantly in conference calls with no written record. She warns that if her privately troubled colleagues do not speak out, "your children will be next".

"And I think the long-term safety effects of these injections is still not known, yet we can see that the short-term impact is huge. And we're now moving into a territory where we are going into healthy, younger, fertile individuals, and — God forbid — children. And that, quite frankly, terrifies me".

And there lies the problem, for we can only speculate on the ultimate goal, the true reason for injecting billions of people world-wide with this experimental, fluidic technology. The big question is whether the nation is being run by a bunch of arrogant, lying buffoons, who, over the last few years have made one enormous error of judgement after another? Or are highly organized powers of darkness at work? Supernatural powers with malicious intent pulling the strings of our prestigious world leaders?

Hard for many to acknowledge, but it's obvious now that everything seems to be a deception. Education, medical, where we are in time, gender confusion, even down to the shape of the earth. Mankind is constantly bombarded by Luciferian imagery, symbology and numerology, in an attempt to deceive him into rejecting the truth in exchange for a lie. The All-seeing 'Eye of Horus' is everywhere, and humanity is caught in the midst of what some might call a generational shift in the way the world works and thinks. And it's all done by design.

For whatever one's view concerning where we are at in the Biblical time-line, one thing is unarguable. At some point in His-Story, there is an entire generation who are born into this world *after* Satan has been released from the bottomless pit. Hence it is unarguable that an entire generation is born into the time-period known as the Little Season. Furthermore, not only would this first generation have no idea of having been born into the little season, they would also be deceived into thinking the millennial kingdom is still to come.

Who can deny that we live in an unprecedented time of layer upon layer upon layer of lies and deception? How can anyone know for certain, that their generation and the few generations before them, are not descendants of that initial deceived generation?

In my previous book, *Tartarian Rule? Or Millennial Kingdom?* I presented a collection of my own personal thoughts, many of which are written from a Biblical perspective, and based around the diligent research carried out by various members of what is collectively termed "The Alternative History Community." It explores the possibility that a highly advanced civilization ruled the earth for a period of one thousand years, a period which by and large, has been erased from the official historical narrative. This civilization were the true builders of most of the grand architectural wonders we see in our cities worldwide. They also had the ability to extract and store free electro-magnetic energy direct from the Aether, and distribute it world-wide.

I covered the strong possibility that after this highly advanced civilization had seemingly disappeared, a series of mud-floods or other major catastrophes affected most all countries across the earth. Often hidden and explained away, but there is evidence everywhere of a major worldwide event and various unrecorded catastrophes in the official historical timeline.

We covered some of the many anomalies in world history, the almost sudden appearance, and the relocation of the millions of orphans, especially across Western Europe and America. The explosion of folk suffering from severe mental health issues, and the huge number of Lunatic Asylums which sprung up and opened their doors to contain them. In each case, the official given explanation or cause, doesn't quite ring true somehow.

If our entire generation and the two or three generations before us have indeed been born into the Little Season, how would we know it? What can we expect? My guess is, Satan's final attempt to falsify Bible prophecy as if it has not yet been fulfilled, and by following the blueprint of Scripture to do so. This would likely include the destruction of NYC, for America was purposefully created to be destroyed, and become the Scapegoat for Babylon the Great is fallen, is fallen. A prophecy which was fulfilled more than 2,000 years ago, with the destruction of Jerusalem. Which was foretold by John in the Book of Revelations, and by Jesus himself in the four gospels.

This plan to make America the phoenix of the new age was put in writing in 1627 by Francis Bacon, who many believe was the true esoteric founder of America. Inspired by Jesuit priest Tobie Matthew, his book 'New *Atlantis*: *A Work Unfinished*', was written as a vision of the Rosicrucian's 'Perfected Lodge'. It tells the story of the Jesuit/Rosicrucian plan to make America the phoenix of the new age. From out of her ashes, will arise Klaus Schwab's unholy vision of the Luciferian new world order. A world without God, where you will own nothing and be happy; a world which none can enter without first swearing allegiance to Lucifer.

To quote David Spangler, one of the founding figures of the modern New Age movement;

"No one will enter the New World Order unless he or she will make a pledge to worship Lucifer. No one will enter the New Age unless he will take a Luciferian Initiation."

To this very day, Satan, the god of this world keeps the unbeliever spiritually blind to the gospel of Christ. *(2 Corinthians 4:4.)* From my own personal experience, I would suggest that the god of this world, also has the ability to blind the minds of believers in Christ, to certain Biblical truths. Especially where he or she is reluctant to let go of traditional teaching and inherited theology, based upon what they've previously been taught.

Luke 9:27. But I tell you of a truth, there be some **standing here**, which shall not taste of death, till they see the kingdom of God.

In view of the fact that time and again, Jesus declared that many of those in his presence, would still be alive to witness his coming in the clouds of heaven, the rapture and the second coming of Christ has already been fulfilled. Which then begs the question as to why, more than 2,000 years later, by far the majority of Christians world-wide, have remained blissfully unaware of the Biblical fulfilment of this historic event?

To complicate things further, if as the Scriptures suggest, the return of Christ, and the first resurrection were fulfilled well over 2,000 years ago, then the millennial reign of Christ has already taken place, for it has been and gone. This in turn has resulted in one of the greatest cover-ups in history.

There is no doubt whatsoever, that we live in unprecedented times, a fact which I don't think anyone would argue with. But where exactly are we with respect to Biblical end-times prophecy? The futurist, including myself until fairly recently, would tell us that the four horse-men of the Apocalypse are all saddled-up and raring to go, as we fast approach the War of Armageddon. *(Revelation 16:16.)* Yet the Scriptures both directly and indirectly inform us that all these prophecies, culminating with the fall of Jerusalem aka Babylon, 'that great city', were fulfilled long ago. It's strikingly obvious that we're not living during the time of the one thousand year reign, nor do we inhabit the new heavens and the new earth, "wherein dwelleth righteousness". *(2 Peter 3:13.)*

Hence, the only point in the Biblical time-line we can possibly be living in, is the 'Little Season'. It is also very likely that many of the events which took place over 2,000 years ago, as these prophecies were being fulfilled, were 'types' or 'shadows', of events which will take place during the times leading up to the final battle on earth against the Lord Jesus Christ and his people.

Yet at the same time, methinks we can expect the second coming of Christ to be falsified, in order to convince folk that these prophecies, including the War of Armageddon and the fall of Babylon, have not yet been fulfilled. A third world war is certain to come, but don't fall for the deception. For it will NOT be the Biblical war at Armageddon *(Revelation 16:16)*, which has already occurred and disguised in our history books as being the fall of Jerusalem and the fall of Rome. The coming world war will be that of Gog and Magog. *(Revelation 20:8.)*

Gog and Magog, it's often said, refers to such nations as Russia and China. According to the Word of God however, Gog and Magog refers to all the nations from the four quarters of the earth.

Revelation 20:7-8. And when the thousand years are expired, Satan shall be loosed out of his prison, And shall go out to ***deceive the nations which are in the four quarters of the earth***, Gog and Magog, to gather them together to battle: the number of whom *is* as the sand of the sea.

It goes without saying, that this historicist or past-fulfilment of Bible prophecy, immediately raises the question of the millennial reign of Christ. When did it happen? And if it has already taken place, why don't we know about this? Where is the evidence? Why is it not recorded in our history books? All perfectly reasonable questions for which there are no definitive answers. Yet at the same time, there are numerous anomalies in the mainstream historical record, and many indicators to suggest an extensive period of time, possibly as much as a thousand years, remains pretty much unaccounted for in the generally accepted time-line. I found this in the Roman history archives at the hidden history website.

> piſe as it is before declared. After Iulius Ceſars death, Octa-
> uius ſucceaded in a ſole regimente, who raigned at the byrth
> of our Sauiour Chriſte. Then there was an vniuerſall peace
> ouer all the worlde. Octauius caughte the imperiall ſeate in

Here is what it says, with modernized spelling of the words:

"After Julius Cesars [sic] death, Octavius succeeded in a sole regiment, who reigned at the birth of our Saviour Christ. Then there was an universal peace over all the world."

Octavius was also known as Caesar Augustus, who shortly before the birth of Jesus, issued a decree that all the world should be taxed. *(Luke 2:1.)* I know nothing more about this image, nor which historian recorded it. or even if it's genuine. But could this time of worldwide peace be a veiled reference to the millennial kingdom?

The law and the prophets were until John (the baptist) whereas grace came by Jesus Christ. Nothing has changed in that respect. But if Jesus was true to his word, then he returned in the clouds of heaven, whilst some of those he spoke to directly, were still alive.

Matthew 16:28. Verily I say unto you, There be some standing here, which shall not taste of death, till they see the Son of man coming in his kingdom.

To those who believed they were still under the law, Jesus said;

Luke 3:7. Then said he to the multitude that came forth to be baptized of him, O generation of vipers, who hath warned you to *flee* from the *wrath* to come?

Whereas those who believed they were saved by grace (Jew and Gentile alike) through faith in Jesus Christ, he said;

1 Thessalonians 1:10. And to wait for his Son from heaven, whom he raised from the dead, even Jesus, which *delivered* us from the *wrath* to come.

Paul is believed to have died around 6 years prior to the destruction of Babylon, as foretold by John in Revelations. Hence he would have been resurrected when Jesus returned in the clouds, just as he promised the generation he spoke to. With Babylon aka Jerusalem in ruins, this was the time when the kings of the earth were punished, whilst Satan, the old Serpent, and the high ones on high, would be imprisoned for many days (1,000 years) within the abyss, the bottomless pit.

Isaiah 24:21-22. And it shall come to pass in that day, *that* the LORD shall punish the host of the high ones *that are* on high, and the kings of the earth upon the earth. And they shall be gathered together, *as* prisoners are gathered in the pit, and shall be shut up in the prison, and after **many days** shall they be visited.

Now was the time of the prophesied restoration by Christ of all things. *(Acts 3:21).* For having informed us that the lives of some men will be spared, Isaiah (like most of the prophets of old), foretells of a time period of great wonder and blessing, generally referred to as the 'millennial reign of Christ.' The purpose of the 1,000-year reign was to fulfil promises God made, that couldn't be fulfilled while Satan and the high ones on high are free, and the kings of the earth have political authority. Some of these promises, called covenants, were given specifically to Israel. Others were given to Jesus, the nations of the world, and the entire creation. Those promises include longevity, peace and harmony, with no fear of man in the heart of the beast.

Yet incredibly, even after many generations lived to enjoy such a time of great blessing, a generation arose who began to resent the Lord's authority over them. This would lead to the release of Satan from the abyss to deceive the nations again, and today the entire world is being deceived, as never before in human history. We are racing at break-neck speed towards the final rebellion against God, resulting in the Battle of Gog and Magog.

Revelation 20:3. And cast him into the bottomless pit, and shut him up, and set a seal upon him, that he should deceive the nations no more, till the thousand years should be fulfilled: and after that he must be loosed a little season.

Revelation 20:8. And shall go out to deceive the nations which are in the four quarters of the earth, Gog and Magog, to gather them together to battle: the number of whom *is* as the sand of the sea.

Those who partake in this ultimate rebellion against the Lord and his City, are innumerable, and will be directly destroyed by fire from heaven. This time there will be no survivors, for it will result in the end of the ages, and the ***unsaved*** dead from across the ages being raised for judgement at the great white throne. *(Revelation 20:9-11).*

Could it be possible, that by and large, our history books have been fabricated? And could it be possible that our perception of the timeline that we live in, has been manipulated? Some historians have believed this to be the case for decades, and a fast growing number of folk are, if you like, waking up to such a possibility. Even though it might seem highly improbable.

Did you know for example, that history has always been written by the victors, and the Roman Catholic Church has ruled over all since the Dark Ages, where no information, except Church doctrine, was allowed to get out?

Fabricated Chronology

The history we study in school is largely made up, and much is based around guesswork. In fact, what we call "mainstream science", "mainstream history", and mainstream news" etc. cannot really be trusted. If indeed we are currently living in the Little Season, it would be quite naïve to think that certain historical figures, dates and times have not been in some way distorted. If for no other reason, than to hide the fact that the second coming, and the millennial reign of Christ have already occurred. Hence the big question remains, as to what extent our perception of history, and even the time-line itself, has been manipulated and artificially shortened, or even extended?

We know for example, that we live in the year 2022 because our calendar dictates this. But do we really live a little over two thousand years since the time of Jesus Christ? Yes, I realize such a question sounds quite ridiculous. Yet believe it or not, there's a fair amount of evidence which would suggest that the "Church" and "Christianity" has been made out to be 1,000 years older than it actually is, and Jesus lived not much more than around 1,000 years ago.

Russian researcher and mathematician, Anatoly Fomenko (born 1945) dates the Book of Revelations to 1486, a little under 1500 years later than is currently accepted.

Whilst a great deal of controversy has always surrounded the 'Shroud of Turin' for example, it has been carbon-dated to between 1260 and 1390 AD, suggesting that Jesus lived roughly 1,000 years later than claimed. This world famous length of cloth, which was said to have come from the actual tomb of Christ, was taken from Judea to Constantinople, where it was stored and kept safe for several centuries, until it was discovered in France in 1353.

There is a spear mark on his side and nail marks through the wrists and feet, and a crown of thorns. There are no pigments on the linen, and the image depicts depths, i.e., it's not two-dimensional like a painting would be, suggesting the source casting the imagery was made at different distances from the cloth. Many believe that the 3D quality - and the negative print quality (rather than 'positive') image of such nature, could only be made with an incredible amount of energy but within an infinitesimally short space of time. I have no doubt in my mind, that this is the image of the body of Christ recorded in time at the moment it transcended into Light and passed directly through the cloth.

Many of course, will scream out that the shroud is fake, a forgery completed in the 13th century, but without one scrap of evidence to support such a claim. Over the decades millions of dollars have been offered to anyone who can prove the shroud is a forgery, but thus far there have been no takers.

To quote 'Come Alive Ministries';

> All hypotheses put forward to challenge the radiocarbon dating of the length of linen cloth bearing the negative image of a crucified man, have been scientifically refuted, including the medieval repair hypothesis, the bio-contamination hypothesis and the carbon monoxide hypothesis. Furthermore, a variety of methods have been proposed for the formation of the image, but the actual method used has not yet been conclusively identified.

Personally, I find it impossible to believe that a thirteenth century mastermind, had the ability and technology to create a forgery that cannot be shown to be a forgery with today's modern technology. Which only leaves one option, the Shroud of Turin is genuine, but because it only dates back to between 1260 and 1390 AD, this would suggest that Jesus lived roughly 1,000 years later than claimed.

Which would mean the Western Church was still in its infancy in 1000 AD, and hence much of history was to be rewritten to create the illusion that it was nearly a thousand years old. Even much of the supposed first millennium history of the early western church, which was written by its own members is fraudulent, and was documented for its own benefit.

To this very day the majority of Catholics, including Pope Francis, still believe that the apostle Peter was the first Pope, and the rock upon which the church of Rome was founded. From this initial deception, developed the unbroken succession of the popes, each claiming the divine right to occupy "the throne of saint Peter," the fictitious first Bishop of Rome. One massive problem here, for Peter was never in Rome. Nor did Peter establish a church in Rome, nor did he become Bishop of Rome, nor did he meet Jesus in Rome, nor did he create a line of succession by the laying of hands to future Bishops of Rome. The first was Pope Linus, a Gnostic named after Linus, the son of Apollo aka Apollyon/Abaddon ('Destroyer') of

Revelation 9:11.

As foretold by Jesus, Jerusalem aka Babylon fell in 70 AD, yet men waited until the eleventh century to form the Knights Templar, the Cathars, etc. and go after the Holy Land by force. Why the 1000 year gap? Then we have the Patricians for example, who were noble family members of the Roman Republic, and who, it is said, disappeared between 0-100 AD, and appeared again in the 11th or 12th century in Europe, so exactly 1,000 years later. Again, why the thousand year gap?

Those who hold with the past fulfilment of prophecy, will claim the thousand year gap was the millennial reign of Jesus Christ, yet it turns out that there wasn't more than a 10-12 year gap, and Fomenko proves it using astronomy. Which is not to say the millennial reign has not yet occurred, but rather that one thousand years have been covered up, or deleted from the timeline. Either way, this has been accomplished for the sole reason of hiding the reality that the prophesied thousand years has already been fulfilled.

Beyond sending Western Rome 1000 years back however, there is no conclusive evidence yet for a recently added 1,000 years. When first starting out to investigate the official historical time-line, it really doesn't take too long, before one begins to realize they've entered a vast and sprawling, web of deceit. For much of the early history of the first millennium is either based on guesswork, or in some cases, even forged documentation. In fact it's reached the point, whereby some investigative historians are now asking such questions as, how fake is Roman Antiquity? and how real is Julius Caesar?

Writes editor-in-chief and publisher, Ron Unz, in the 'Unz Review, An Alternative Media Selection';

> What about the Augustan History (Historia Augusta), a Roman chronicle that Edward Gibbon trusted entirely for writing his *Decline and Fall of the Roman Empire*? It has since been exposed as the work of an impostor who has masked his fraud by inventing sources from scratch. However, for some vague reason, it is assumed that the forger lived in the fifth century, which is supposed to make his forgery worthwhile anyway. In reality, some of its stories sound like cryptic satire of Renaissance Moors, others like Christian calumny of pre-Christian religion. How likely is it, for example, that the hero Antinous, worshipped throughout the Mediterranean Basin as an avatar of Osiris, was

the gay lover (eromenos) of Hadrian, as told in Augustan History? Such questions of plausibility are simply ignored by professional historians. But they jump to the face of any lay reader unimpressed by scholarly consensus. For instance, just reading the summary of Suetonius' *Lives of the Twelve Caesars* on the Wikipedia page should suffice to raise very strong suspicions, not only of fraud, but of mockery, for we are obviously dealing here with biographies of great imagination, but of no historical value whatsoever.

Officially the city of Pompeii was lost until 1748, and whatever they claim was dug out in 1599, was not linked to Pompeii at the time. Yet due to some highly questionable "fakish" evidence, there is some quite compelling evidence, that Pompeii suffered its fate in 1631, which makes our official history 1,552 years off.

writes one of the admins at "stolen history";

> Indeed, it appears that the first millennium has effectively been padded-out, so as to expand the events of the 8th to 10th centuries, so that they encompass the entire millennium. This has been accomplished through the phantom duplication and mirroring of historical events.

Gifted historian, mathematician and researcher Gunnar Heinsohn, is a professor emeritus at the University of Bremen, Germany. He focuses on hard archaeological evidence, and insists that stratigraphy (layers created by man) is the most important criterion for dating archaeological finds. He shows that, time and again, stratigraphy contradicts history, and that archaeologists should have logically forced historians into a paradigm shift.

"Unfortunately", says Heinsohn;

"In order to be consistent with a pre-fabricated chronology, archaeologists unknowingly betray their own craft."

> When they dig up the same artefacts or building structures in different parts of the world, they assign them to different periods in order to satisfy historians. And when they find, in the same place and layer, mixtures of artefacts that they have already attributed to different periods, they explain it away with the ludicrous *"heirloom theory,"* or call them *"art collections"*.

Heinsohn proposes that as much as 700 years are missing from early Roman and Jewish history, stating;

"Nowhere in Jerusalem has been found even a single stratigraphy with continuous settlement layers from 1 to 930 AD. Jerusalem's excavation sites, just like their Roman counterparts, must be content with only c. 230 years of building layers between 1 and 930 AD."

In an article titled *Jerusalem's First Millennium AD: 1000 years long or only 300?* (October 2022; 2nd edition) Heinsohn writes;

> In the city of Rome, archaeology shows, no new residential quarters, roads, latrines and water pipes were built between the 230s and 930s AD. All churches dated to these 700 years also use the style and construction technology of the period before 230 AD. These puzzling facts may be ignored, but only if the missing 700 years of hard evidence show up in the archaeology of regions that are considered to be even more eternal than the Eternal City itself. However, even the Hebrew City of the Patriarchs, Hebron, suffers from about 700 years without settlement layers in the first millennium. Similarly, the people of Samaria-Sebaste build no new residential quarters between the 3rd and 10th centuries. [....]

Can Jerusalem, at least, fill the missing 700 years? Of course, say the historians, who date ancient archaeology with Anno Domini chronology. However, these scholars never explore or explain the origins of AD dating. Though they always firmly believe it, they never ask who introduced this chronological system, or when and where it originated.

First published in 1991, *The Phantom Time Hypothesis* is a historical conspiracy asserted by the Bavarian-born historical revisionist, Heribert Illig. It suggests a conspiracy by the Holy Roman Emperor Otto III, Pope Sylvester II, and possibly the Byzantine Emperor Constantine VII, to fabricate the Anno Domini dating system retroactively. This tinkering with the time-line was done in order to place them at the special year of AD 1000, and to rewrite history, in order to legitimize Otto's claim to the Holy Roman Empire. Illig believed that this fabrication was achieved through the alteration, misrepresentation and forgery of documentary and physical evidence.

According to this scenario, the entire Carolingian period, including the figure of Charlemagne, is a fabrication, with a "phantom time" of 297 years (AD 614–911) added to the Early Middle Ages. Illig concludes that the AD era had counted roughly three centuries which never even existed. The main problem with Charlemagne is with architecture. His Palatine Chapel in Aachen, Germany, exhibits a technological advance of 200 years, with for example arched aisles not seen before the eleventh century. On the contrary, Charlemagne's residence in Ingelheim, Germany, was built in the Roman style of the second century, with materials supposedly recycled from the second century.

Both Heribert Illig, and the German scholar, Hans-Ulrich Niemitz challenge such absurdities and conclude that Charlemagne is a mythical predecessor invented 919-1024 by the Ottonian emperors to legitimate their imperial claims. All Carolingians of the eighth and ninth centuries and their wars are also fictitious, and the timespan of roughly 600-900 AD, is a phantom era.

In 2008, Steve Mitchell, a British amateur archaeologist, argued that the English monk Bede, who was the first to use the AD system of Dionysius Exiguus for historical purposes in his *Ecclesiastical History of the English People* (completed, according to the author, in AD 731) may have made an error with the date which has resulted in a corresponding error in the AD system we use today. Mitchell noted how it appeared from Bede's history, that almost nothing of note had happened in England between the reigns of the Roman emperors, Marcian and Maurice, whose accession dates, according to Bede, were AD 449 and AD 582, a span of 133 years.

From here, and on the basis of perceived archaeological and historical gaps, Mitchell began to develop arguments that the 250-year-long Early Anglo-Saxon Period (which encompassed the reigns of Marcian and Maurice) may have been artificially extended by up to 200 years.

In 2013, Gunnar Heinsohn argued for a much greater shortening of the first millennium. In Heinsohn's view, the artificial stretching of the first millennium was not a consequence of the deliberate invention of false histories, but of the chaos caused by a major catastrophic event. According to Heinsohn, a number of minor events which are believed to have occurred in different parts of Europe during the 230s, the 530s and the 930s, were manifestations of a single huge catastrophic event which brought an end to civilised life throughout Europe.

In this scenario, the activities of the emperors regarded as ruling from Rome between AD 1-230 and those ruling from further east between AD 290-520, as well as the activities of rulers in northeastern Europe between AD 701-930, were all taking place at the same time. This triplication of the history of a single 230-year period would in itself result in a false extension of the timescale amounting to 460 years, and, considering the situation as a whole, around 700 years of history, from the third to the tenth centuries, would already have been completed before the date when it was supposed to have started.

Between the years 535 and 536, a series of major climatic events did indeed take place, and not just in Europe, that could rightly be described as a single world-wide cataclysm with catastrophic consequences. Numerous accounts from all over the world from that period describe the sun as getting dimmer and losing its light. Many also described it as having a bluish colour. The effects were also observed with the moon, which is recorded to have lost some of its brightness. The reduction of the light resulted in the reduction of heat, no rain, and a very long winter which resulted in crop failures and for birds and other wildlife to perish. Famine and plagues struck many areas and there were a huge number of deaths. The catastrophic event struck Korea, the Americas, Europe, Africa, and Australia. While written records do not exist for all countries, archaeological and geological data revealed evidence of the climatic changes. Studies done on the trunks of trees, for example, showed that 536 AD had been the coldest in 1,500 years.

This may well have been the time of the mud-flood, evidence for which can be found across most of the earth, and which buried many towns and cities, and wiped out entire populations. However, there are so many discrepancies with regard to the accuracy of the timeline, it's quite possible that this series of cataclysmic events actually took place at the close of the first millennium, rather than half the way through it? In fact, Heinsohn's research, along with that of others, presents the evidence of a worldwide cataclysm in the tenth century that totally redefines the first millennium, reuniting history with archaeology, geology, geography and mythology.

Gunnar Heinsohn is not the first, and certainly won't be the last historian to question the official chronology. Nor is he the first to propose that due to the vast amount of inconsistencies and anomalies in the official historical record, a new chronology is required. While other authors have written on new chronology, it is most commonly associated with, Anatoly Fomenko, and the concept is most fully explained in his book, *History: Fiction or Science?* originally published in Russian. Every theory it contains, no matter how unorthodox, is backed by solid scientific data.

What if someone told you that there isn't a single piece of firm written evidence or artefact that can be reliably, independently and irrefutably dated to before the eleventh century? Well, that is exactly what Anatoly Fomenko is saying! Furthermore, he claims that many historical events do not correspond mathematically with the dates they are supposed to have occurred on. He states that *all* of ancient history (including that of Greece, Rome, and Egypt) is simply a rewriting of events that occurred in the Middle Ages and that Chinese and Arab history are fabrications of the seventeenth and eighteenth century Jesuits.

Fomenko only mentions shifts of events, not a calendar change. More precisely, Fomenko discovered three important chronological shifts, of about 333 years, 1053 years and 1800 years. According to Fomenko's claims, the written history of humankind goes only as far back as AD 800, there is almost no information about events between AD 800–1000, and most known historical events took place in AD 1000–1500. He also presents a reasonable argument, that world history prior to 1600 AD has been widely falsified to suit the interests of a number of different conspirators including the Vatican, the Holy Roman Empire, and the Russian House of Romanov, all working together to obscure the "true" history of the world.

Along with his associate, the Russian mathematician Gleb Nosovsky, Fomenko has produced tens of thousands of pages of painstaking research in support of his "New Chronology." One major discovery of Fomenko and Nosovsky is that our conventional history is full of doublets, produced by the arbitrary end-to-end alignment of chronicles that tell the self-same events, but are "written by different people, from different viewpoints, in different languages, with the same characters under different names and nicknames."

I recall once listening to a lecture on YouTube by an astrologer, whose name now escapes me, who talked about a group of Russian scientists, including mathematicians, historians, astronomers, astrologers and others, who had also looked at astrological charts and descriptions of various battles, as well as natal charts of various famous historical figures, and that in these accounts they found overlapping pieces of information, causing them to suspect that i.e. Hero A and Hero B or Ruler A and Ruler B were most likely then one and the same person.

In which case there's a high probability, that various famous historical figures may *not* have been different people at all, but due to oral histories may have been given different names in different regions. Rather than try to paraphrase the following, I will quote directly from the website Stolen History.

> Whole periods have been thus duplicated. For example, drawing from the previous work of Russian Nikolai Mozorov (1854-1946), Anatoly Fomenko and Nosovsky show a striking parallel between the sequences of Pompey/Caesar/Octavian and of Diocletian/Constantius/Constantine, leading to the conclusion that the Western Roman Empire is, to some extent, a phantom duplicate of the Eastern Roman Empire. According to Fomenko and Nosovsky, the capital of the one and only Roman Empire was founded on the Bosporus some 330 years before the foundation of its colony in the Latium. Starting from the age of the crusades, Roman clerics, followed by Italian humanists, produced an inverted chronological sequence, using the real history of Constantinople as the model for their fake earlier history of Italian Rome. A great confusion ensued, as "many mediaeval documents confuse the two Romes: in Italy and on the Bosporus," both being commonly called Rome or "the City".
>
> A likely scenario is that the prototype for Titus Livy's History was about Constantinople, the original capital of the "Romans". The original Livy, Fomenko conjectures, was writing around the tenth century about Constantinople, so he was not far off the mark when he placed the foundation of the City (urbs condita) some seven centuries before his time. But as it was rewritten by Petrarch and reinterpreted by later humanists, a chronological chasm of roughly one thousand year was introduced between the foundation of the two "Romes" (from 753 BC to 330 AD).

The new chronology also contains a reconstruction, an alternative chronology, radically shorter than the standard historical timeline, because all ancient history is "folded" onto the time period known as the Middle Ages. Fomenko argues that the events of antiquity generally attributed to the civilizations of the Roman empire, ancient Greece and ancient Egypt, actually occurred during the Middle Ages, more than a thousand years later.

Even the Russian-Jewish catastrophist, Immanuel Velikovsky, who preceded Fomenko by 30 years, stated the chronology of history can be off by a much as a staggering 1600 years. He described this in great detail in his *"Ages in Chaos Series" (Vol. I – III)* and also proposed a revised chronology for ancient Egypt, Greece, Israel, and other cultures of the ancient Near East.

As noted earlier, when setting out to investigate the historical time-line, it soon becomes apparent that something is suspiciously wrong with the official record. Trying to determine which parts of history, or historical figures are genuine and which parts are fraudulent, or at best distorted, goes way and above and far beyond the definition of complexity. Even during history lessons back in my schooldays, it seemed there was little known about the early Anglo-Saxons, but plenty of information about the Roman era in Britain, and then all of a sudden, history jumped forward to the Norman invasion of 1066. Beyond which there was very little once again, until the 15th and 16th centuries when we get to Walter Raleigh, Copernicus and Columbus etc. Are there a number of centuries of history unaccounted for?

It would be far too easy to sit back and criticize folk from centuries past, who first fell for the time-line deception. For the majority most likely didn't even have a paper calendar hanging from their kitchen wall. Let alone a reminder of the precise minute, hour, day, month and year, on a mobile device sitting in their pocket. Even the wrist-watch wasn't invented until the nineteenth century, and then only worn by the elite.

Calendars

Published in 2009, and written on the basis of retro-calculations of eclipses and other astronomical phenomena, author Zoltán Hunnivari claimed that AD 960 was the same year as AD 1160, and almost two centuries of history have been fabricated to fill the space between these two dates. According to Hunnivari in *From Harun Al-Rashid up to the Times of Saladin;*

"The revision to the Christian Calendar was made by Pope Innocent III in AD 1016, with that year becoming AD 1206 at a stroke".

Writes Hunnivari (p. 87)

"The resetting of the calendar did not cause any difficulties since the Christian calendar before was used in only a very narrow circle of the Western Church."

If Hunnivari is correct with his estimations, and a phantom two hundred years were added to the historical timeline "at a stroke", and to suit the personal interest of Pope Innocent III, this would bring the whole Roman papal succession into question. For Pope Innocent was considered one of the most powerful and influential of the medieval popes. He exerted a wide influence over the Christian states of Europe, claiming supremacy over all of Europe's kings. This field of influence however, according to Hunnivari, was wielded by the Pope, a full two centuries earlier than we're told.

The Gregorian calendar in use today, did not exist before October 15, 1582. Gregorian dates before that are proleptic, that is, using the Gregorian rules to reckon backward from October 15, 1582. The Gregorian Calendar we use today was first introduced by Pope Gregory XIII in 1582, and amidst a most peculiar run of events, which we will return to later.

Almost two centuries later, on September 2, 1752, the Gregorian Calendar was adopted in England, and the country skipped ahead 11 days. According to Encyclopedia Britannica, the current discrepancy between the Julian and Gregorian calendars is 13 days, which will become 14 days in 2100.

There are documents from the early middle ages that are dated 987 and when we refer to such documents we say they were written in 987. Could that mean there are days that would be missing between 987 and 1582 that were never calculated or accounted for between the two calendar systems? Quite frankly, I've no idea. Some however, have suggested the discrepancy amounts to hundreds of years, or possibly even a thousand.

Because none can go back in time to check what really happened, we can only speculate, and it has been proposed that folk who went to sleep on Sunday, October 4th , 582 AD, woke up on Monday, October 18th, 1582 AD. They were not aware that an extra *one thousand years* had been added to their calendars because they didn't have access to calendars. Their source of the date and time was the Church of Rome. Hence, they were led to believe that the Julian date of Sunday, October 4th, 582 AD, was followed by Friday, October 15th, 582 AD, on the new Gregorian calendar. Today, we believe that the Julian date of Thursday, October 4th, 582 AD, was followed by Friday, October 15th, 1582 AD, on the new Gregorian calendar with no change in weekday continuity.

Easter

It was originally feasible for the entire Christian Church to receive the date of Easter each year through an annual announcement made by the Pope. For according to Wikipedia, as a moveable feast, the date is determined each year through a complex astronomical calculation to ensure that Easter is celebrated on the first Sunday after the Paschal full moon, which is the first full moon on or after 21 March, a fixed approximation of the March equinox. Determining this date in advance requires a correlation between the lunar months and the solar year, while also accounting for the month, date, and weekday of the Julian or Gregorian calendar.

Writes Qmeta at stolen history.net;

> In order to maintain the proper day of the week for Easter when jumping from year 582 to 1582, ten days needed to be added. Easter of the following year, 583, was April 20th, while Easter of 1583 fell on April 17[th.] The question the Church must have asked itself is, "How far out of sync would the Julian calendar be if we kept it another 1,000 years, until 1582?"

> The correct answer evidently, would have been 'thirteen days', but if they added that many days then in the following year (1583), Easter would have fallen on a Wednesday. In order to keep Easter on a Sunday, they added only ten days. Today, we see this as an error of judgement, rather than the genius that it actually is.

Why Genius? Apart from the fact that it wouldn't have aroused any suspicion amongst the majority of folk, it kept the emphasis on Good Friday and Easter Sunday, when everyone knows it's impossible to cram the three days and the three nights when the lifeless body of Jesus lay in the tomb, between the two days. Even for many Christians, this anomaly has remained a bone of contention for centuries.

Jesus was adamant that his lifeless body would remain in the tomb for three nights and three days, and he would rise from the dead on the third day.

Matthew 12:40. For as Jonas was three days and three nights in the whale's belly; so shall the Son of man be three days and three nights in the heart of the earth.

Luke 24:7. Saying, The Son of man must be delivered into the hands of sinful men, and be crucified, and the *third* day rise again.

All four Gospels state that, on the evening of the Crucifixion, Joseph of Arimathea asked Pilate for the body of Jesus, and, after Pilate granted his request, he wrapped it in a linen cloth and laid it in a tomb.

Matthew 27:57. When the *even* was come, there came a rich man of Arimathaea, named Joseph, who also himself was Jesus' disciple: V.59. And when Joseph had taken the body, he wrapped it in a clean linen cloth.....

In all parts of the world a day and night is 24 hours, and 3x24=72. Matthew, Mark, Luke and John stand in agreement. Jesus was buried in the evening, Wednesday evening to be precise. However one might try to juggle the numbers, three days and three nights, or 72 hours *later* can never equate to a morning, but can only possibly be an evening. Why is it generally taught that the Lord rose from the dead in the early morning hours?

On the *first* day of the Jewish week, in the early hours of *Sunday* morning, the tomb was found to be empty, because Jesus had risen from the dead the previous evening.

Mark 16:2. And very *early* in the morning the *first* day of the week, they came unto the sepulchre at the rising of the sun.

Matthew 28:6. He is not here: for he is risen, as he said. Come, see the place where the Lord lay.

The Jews recognize Saturday as the Sabbath, the seventh day of the week. In most Gentile countries however, Saturday is considered the Sixth Day, and is the only day of the week that retained its Roman origin in English. Saturday=Saturn's or Satan's Day.

From a Jewish perspective Jesus rose from the dead on the seventh day, toward the close of the Jewish Sabbath. From a Gentile perspective, having defeated him who held the power of death, Jesus rose back to life on Saturn's or Satan's Day.

As noted by one of of the moderators at the website. Stolen History;

> If no one added 1,000 years to the calendar, another possibility is that the Julian calendar itself was just created out of thin air and imposed on the previous calendars. So the church at one point simply said "Jesus died xxx years ago, and that's why we live in the year xxx", and people believed it. But this could only happen once the memories of the biblical times were already gone. And if the events of the Bible happened 500-1000 years ago, the church could have only introduced the new dating system

sometime after- between 1500 and 1600, for example. Then some time later they realized that the Julian calendar had several issues and introduced an updated version - The Gregorian calendar. This probably happened within a few generations.

The Gregorian Calendar is of itself an enigma and somewhat confusing. For whilst the first seven months are named from pagan gods and pagan festivals, the remainder of the year is out of sync. Some believe there is an occult significance to this, namely the pagan false gods of old bring confusion to the entire year. *January* is named for the Roman god Janus, the protector of gates and doorways. Janus is depicted with two faces, one looking into the past, the other into the future. *February* is named from the Latin word *februa*,"to cleanse," and Februalia, was a festival of purification and atonement that took place during this period.

March is named for the Roman god of war, Mars. This was the time of year to resume military campaigns that had been interrupted by winter. March was also a time of many festivals, presumably in preparation for the campaigning season. *April* is named from the Latin word *aperio*, "to open (bud)," because plants begin to grow in this month. In essence, this month was viewed as spring's renewal. *May* is named for the Roman goddess Maia, who was considered a nurturer and an earth goddess. **June** is named for the Roman goddess Juno, patroness of marriage and the well-being of women. *July* is named to honour the Roman dictator Julius Caesar (100 B.C.– 44 B.C.) who was considered a god or demi-god. *August* is named to honour the first Roman emperor Augustus Caesar (63 B.C.– A.D. 14) who many also considered a god or demi-god. *September* (which means seventh) is the ninth month of the year, *October* (which means eighth) is the tenth month, *November* (which means ninth) is the eleventh month and *December* (which means tenth) is the twelfth month of the year.

Jonathan Cahn, who has been fooling Christian Zionist for years, has recently published his latest book, 'Return of the Gods', which has become a best-seller. In it, he proposes that the pagan gods of ancient Rome etc. are very real entities that have operated in history, and are clearly operating in the tragic developments of modern day society. Although I've not read this book personally, I believe he is right about this, and have watched a 20 minute video in which he talks about the subject matter.

Cahn states that records of past events reveal that there was a time when the kingdoms all over the world collapsed, and all the powers of their gods no longer had any power. It seems that Cahn, who is both a futurist and dispensationalist, puts this loss of power down to the spread of the gospel. But I think it far more likely that man's real enemy, the principalities and powers, lost their strongholds and power over the nations when Jesus Christ cast Satan into the abyss, the bottomless pit for a thousand years. And it is this period of time which has been largely falsified and covered up. We tend not to question the "official" historical narrative because we grossly underestimate the deceptive nature of the ancient principalities and the powers which war against us.

An argument against the change from Julian to Gregorian calendar being accompanied by an added 1,000 years is that some countries still had the Julian calender until the 20th Century, and the inhabitants would have remembered the added years. Unless of course the hundreds of thousands of folk back in the nineteenth century, who were declared insane by their respective governments, and committed to spend the rest of their life's in a Lunatic Asylum, were actually the folk who recognized and spoke out against the tinkering with the calendar?

We looked at this world-wide phenomena in my previous book, and noted how no realistic and justifiable explanation is given for the thousands of lunatic asylums which appeared on the scene across Europe, Russia, Australia, North America and Canada during the 1800s. Reason and logic demand there must have been a determining factor behind this massive world-wide outbreak of supposed severe mental health issues. For if not, then individual governments must have been working together, committing multitudes of folk to spending the rest of their lives in lunatic asylums for political reasons. Furthermore, this act of locking away hundreds of thousands, or possibly millions of adults, was the most likely reason for the millions of orphans who seem to have suddenly appeared, as if out thin air. And predominantly in those nations with the greatest number of recently opened lunatic asylums. Which might also explain the existence of the early photographs which reveal towns and cities being virtually empty.

Either way, and however the controllers managed to pull it all off, this calendar change was only part of the timeline deception.

Coins

The fact that even in Christian Europe there are no AD-dated coins before 1234 AD is sheepishly passed over. Furthermore, there seems to be no definitive answer as to why numerous old coins and other artefacts have a Non-numeric character included in the date. I have been looking at a range of old English coins from the Georgian era. Up until 1771 the coins have the prefix i or J instead of the 1, but it appears that everything after 1787 has a number 1. There are *other* artefacts, including documents, buildings, mile-stones, grave stones, and items of wooden furniture, which have the letter i or j preceding the year that can be found on the Internet. From the moment the letter j is presumed to be the number 1, one thousand years has been added to the date of that coin etc. An old coin which is date-stamped I 621 for example, is passed off as being 1621. Many believe that the letter i or j preceding the numerical year, denote the millennial reign of Jesus or Iēsous. For Jesus said in *Matthew 26:11;*"The poor you will always have with you", which would indicate there would be a monetary system in place during the Millennial Reign.

Time loop?

Immanuel Velikovsky argued that electromagnetic effects play an important role in celestial mechanics, whilst in more recent times, historical revisionist, Michelle Gibson, proposes that an artificial time-loop was created between the years 1492 and 1942, with the mid-point being the year 1717. Whilst on the face of it, this might sound completely absurd, Michelle's research into precise dates and matching historical characters and events is quite meticulous, and she goes into great detail.

In a recent presentation she proposes that a rift in space-time resulting in a 3 dimensional time loop, was caused by the Philadelphia Experiment carried out by the US Navy, on October 28, 1943. The goal was to create an electromagnetically-charged invisibility cloak, to make ships invisible to enemy radar, but the result exceeded all expectations. The USS Eldridge was wrapped in steel cables with high voltage energy produced by large generators running through them which produced an extremely powerful electromagnetic field. The Naval destroyer completely disappeared, not only from the radar screens but also from our reality. The ship materialized once again hundreds of miles from Philadelphia at the military base in Norfolk. Witness reports claim that all of a sudden, the Eldridge materialized in the waters around Norfolk. It was seen for only moments, then suddenly it was sitting right back in the water where it started with a crazed, insane crew on board. Legend holds that some of the sailors were literally fused with the steel components of the ship when it rematerialized in Philadelphia.

Although the U.S. Navy maintains that no such experiment was ever conducted, many eyewitness have claimed the Philadelphia, and similar types of experiment did indeed take place.

This might sound a little far fetched, but I suspect that behind all the confusion over our true timeline, supernatural powers have been at work. For Daniel the prophet warned of a person, which honoured the God of forces, and thought to *change times* and *laws*. *(Daniel 7:25.)* An inference to the seven Noahide Laws maybe?

I think, at this point, it is impossible to ever pin down a firm timeline, for to achieve this we would probably need whatever hidden archives are stashed away in the Vatican Vaults, or the palaces, mansions and temples etc. of the controllers, that are kept hidden from the uninitiated. Yet the consensus of opinion offered by multiple researchers and alternative historians appears to be, that a phantom seven hundred to one thousand years have been added to the historical timeline. As previously mentioned, this doesn't necessarily mean that we are *not* living in 2022, but that a fictitious thousand years have been added, to replace the millennial reign of Christ.

This includes what we've been taught about the Middle Ages, much of which is utter nonsense. Gallant knights on horseback in full body armour rescuing fair maidens is merely a fantasy, a back-dated hoax to account for a period of roughly 500 years. Mark Twain aka Samuel Clemens, left a trail of clues to indicate this in his 1889 satirical novel, *A Connecticut Yankee in King Arthur's Court.*

In the book, a Yankee engineer from Connecticut named Hank Morgan receives a severe blow to the head, and is somehow transported in time and space to England during the reign of King Arthur. After some initial confusion and his capture by one of Arthur's knights, Hank realizes that he is actually in the past, and he uses his knowledge to make people believe that he is a powerful magician. He becomes a rival of Merlin, who appears to be little more than a fraud, and gains the trust of King Arthur. Hank attempts to modernize the past in order to make people's lives better.

Twain wrote the book as a burlesque overview of romantic notions of chivalry, after being inspired by a dream in which he was a knight himself, severely inconvenienced by the weight and cumbersome nature of his armour. Which if thought about, is quite ridiculous. Re-enacting medieval battle-scenes for an hour or so is one thing, but a day spent by a metal-clad knight dehydrating in his own body sweat is another. There is also a possibility that Samuel Clemens himself, played the role of the nineteenth US President, and high-ranking Freemason, Rutherford B. Hayes. As suggested by an 84% facial similarity meter. Which proves nothing of course, apart from the uncanny similarity between the two.

Some believe that a phantom 700 years were added to to the timeline when the millennial reign ended in 1070 AD, making Satan's release coincident with July 4, 1776, his Independence Day, the year both the Illuminati and America were founded.

Others believe the millennial reign ended in 1692, when a series of earthquakes occurred in England, Holland, Flandern, France, Germany, Zealand and most parts of Europe. The same year an earthquake caused soil liquefaction in Jamaica, when Port Royal sank into the ground, and was over-swept by the sea.

During the main shock the sand was said to have formed waves. Fissures repeatedly opened and closed crushing many people. After the shaking stopped the sand again solidified, trapping many victims. Liguanea (present day Kingston) and the Spanish town of St Jago fared little better, and the majority of houses were destroyed.

According to Robert Renny in his 'An History of Jamaica' (1807): "All the wharves sunk at once, and in the space of two minutes, nine-tenths of the city of Port Royal were covered with water, which was raised to such a height, that it entered the uppermost rooms of the few houses which were left standing. The tops of the highest houses were visible in the water and surrounded by the masts of vessels, which had been sunk along with them."

the text at the top of this image reads; "Within two minutes the town was sunk underground and 2,000 souls perished."

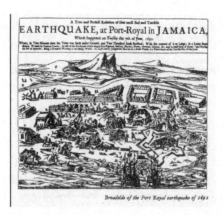

Broadside of the Port Royal earthquake of 1692

What if the timeline we have been taught about in school, actually starts in the mid 1800s with a new false historic narrative superimposed onto the old world infrastructure? One which brought cruelty, great suffering, degradation and division to humanity? When tying the threads together, or joining the dots, a fast growing number of folk who are prepared to think outside of the box, have reached the inevitable conclusion, that yes, sadly, this has been the case. We have all been deceived big time. And I'm not talking just about the moon landing, 9/11, and the ongoing covid scam etc.

The last days for this world in general will not be a repetition of the horrific tribulation years suffered at the end of the age for Israel, or at least, not to the same degree of intensity. For Jesus assured us of this in *Matthew 24:21*. "For then shall be great tribulation, such as was not since the beginning of the world to this time, no, ***nor ever shall be***".

As we approach the end of the ages, the world will become more corrupt, more delusional, and every form of ungodliness will abound. Generally speaking, men will become increasingly lovers of self, and power, and of money, until the point of opening themselves up to the strong delusion. Which means to adopt a false sense of reality. A delusion sent by God himself, not as a punishment per se, but as a reward for the heart of man. For a time will come when men will desire to believe the Lie, rather than to believe the Truth. And for this ***cause***, God will send strong delusion. *(2 Thessalonians 2:11.)*

Over the decades paedophiles have infiltrated into all levels of western government, especially in the US and the UK. It has become so all-pervasive today because once these degenerates get into the very highest levels of government, then they are in a position to appoint others of like mind into all other important positions in the establishment. Here in the UK, the Government has desperately tried to keep the lid on the true scale of ritual child abuse and rampant paedophilia perpetrated by the rich and the powerful, often at the very heart of the British Establishment. Even the late 'Iron Lady' Margaret Thatcher was responsible for covering up the sordid exploits of government ministers, by choosing to ignore former Tory activist Anthony Gilberthorpe, who named countless MPs who were partaking in paedophilic activities.

In the mid 90's B.B.C. 'Crimewatch' presenter Jill Dando, tried to get her B.B.C bosses to investigate a VIP paedophile ring linked to the B.B.C. Government, and Royalty. What happened? On 26 April 1999 she was shot dead on the front doorstep of her home in Fulham, London. The 'scapegoat', an innocent man by the name Barry George, was convicted and imprisoned for 8 years and denied compensation when he was eventually released. Her killer is still at large, for where the state becomes involved in a crime, then the police who are run by the state will never be allowed to solve it.

But it would seem that to address the matter is strictly Taboo, as there's a deliberate conspiracy of silence. For no President, Prime Minister, or leader of any major government has ever made any serious investigation into what surely amounts to the most heinous of crimes against humanity.

Media coverage gives us the impression that the investigations are honest and genuine, and on occasion they even name names, and throw the public a bone in the form of a Scapegoat. Yet time and again the investigation into paedophile rings by the likes of the Metropolitan Police are deliberately hampered by paedophiles who hold positions of power within the very establishment under investigation.

As a nation, how did we ever allow ourselves to get into such a state? Primarily, by turning our back on God and expelling him from our entire education system.

Hidden Land

In *1534*, Jesuits under Ignatius Loyola and Roman Catholic missionary, Francis Xavier, took their first blasphemous oaths on the 'Feast Day of Lucifer' (August15th) in a ceremony held in the crypt of the Martyrium of St. Denis, in Paris. The final period of Loyola's life was spent in Rome or its vicinity, where in 1539 he founded the 'Society of Jesus', of which he became Superior-General. The Superior-General is now known as 'the Black Pope,' and what most folk fail to realise is, that by having financially indebted the Catholic Church, Illuminated Jesuits have controlled the Vatican and the White Pope with a Jesuit Black Pope, for over 400 years. The current Black Pope, Arturo Sosa, who controls Francis the White Pope, is alleged to be the most powerful man in the world.

In *1543*, and at the request of Pope Leo X, Polish astronomer Nicolaus Copernicus, a member of the 'Third Order of St. Dominic', proposed that the Sun is at the centre of the Solar System, in which case the earth and the planets must be moving around it. Really? King David says earth is *stablished* (fixed) in Psalm 93:1 and his son Solomon does as well in the Book of Ecclesiastes.

Up until the Jesuit Order was created, the most common school of thought in regards to cosmology was that the Earth was flat and round, as had been the teachings for 5,000 years. Once the Jesuits gained power around the world, they instilled the globe earth and the heliocentric theory into the education system of the western world, step by step by step, until after just a few generations, everyone on Earth KNEW the Earth was spinning whilst travelling around the Sun at incredible speeds. In fact, it could be said that the Jesuits became the guardians of orthodox theoretical science; 'the tongue of the Chaldeans.' *(Daniel:4)*

In*1546*, the Roman Catholic Council of Trent, which officially recognized several books of the Apocrypha, listed the first and the second book of Esdras, as part of the biblical canon. Indeed, both books of Esdras were included in the original 1611 King James Bible because the translators included the Apocrypha between the Testaments. Believing it not to be the inspired word of God, they eparated these books from the text of Scripture by marking it with the word "Apocrypha". Some scholars believe that 2 Esdras, which contains six Messianic references, was written shortly after the AD 70 destruction of the temple in Jerusalem during the reign of Emperor Domitian (AD 81—96). We will return to the second book of Esdras later.

In *1569*, the Flemish geographer and cartographer Gerardus Mercator, produced the Mercator World Map, which became the standard map projection for navigation because it is unique in representing north as up and south as down everywhere, while preserving local directions and shapes.

In *1577*, Mercator penned a letter to the Welsh Druid occultist, John Dee, who was the Rosicrucian mentor of Francis Bacon and mentor and court astrologer to Queen Elizabeth I, the daughter of Anne Boleyn, who some claim was a Druid Witch. Dee believed he and the Queen were 'Merchants of Light' spiritually descended from Hermes Trismegistus aka Thoth, the god venerated since the days of Abraham by the Sabians. He also claimed to receive spirit messages from angelic contacts, and due to his psychic powers, John Dee was known as 'the magical architect of the British Empire'. Dee is also renowned as being Britain's greatest master-spy, upon whom, Ian Fleming based his 007 character, James Bond.

In *1580,* Francis Drake returned to England having supposedly circumnavigated the Earth.

In *1582*, the Gregorian Calendar was introduced by Pope Gregory XIII.

Mercator's letter, dated 1577, mentions the "inventio fortunatae", as well as the hidden land of King Arthur, Mount Meru and the centre of the Earth being the North Pole. The letter details several expeditions and their observations at and near the pole, including the height of Mount Meru, the indrawing seas, and the surrounding mountainous islands.

The reference to the hidden lands of King Arthur is very telling, for the similarities between the legendary figure with his 12 knights of the round table, and Jesus Christ and the 12 apostles is quite striking. It is quite likely in fact, that all the mythology surrounding King Arthur, Camelot and Avalon, is partly based upon the millennial kingdom, when the kings and priests of Jesus Christ reigned on the earth. Whereas the Arthurian legend itself is fantasy.

Sure, the circumstantial evidence strongly suggests he was based on a real warlord not long after the end of Roman Britain. Many of the people mentioned in the earliest Arthurian stories are real people known to have lived in Cornwall and South Wales at that time. The problem is that "Arthur" is almost certainly just a nickname and we don't know what his real name was.

There may be some truth after all, in William Blake's stirring hymn of 1804?

"And did those feet in ancient time walk upon England's mountains green?And was the holy Lamb of God on England's pleasant pastures seen".

Whilst there is no clear identification with a particular geophysical location, Mount Meru is considered to be the centre of the physical, metaphysical and spiritual universe. The "indrawing seas" are in reference to a great whirlpool where the individual seas meet, and from where a great number of ships never returned, allegedly resulting in the loss of thousands of lives. The 'Inventio Fortunata' ('Discovery of the Fortunate Islands', is a lost book written by an unnamed monk from Oxford, England, who had travelled to the far north in the mid-fourteenth century, and recorded his experience. He duly presented the finished work to King Edward III, from which point, the Inventio Fortunata seems to have mysteriously disappeared.

A certain Dutchman however, one Jacobus Cnoyen, summarized *Inventio Fortunata* in his own book, *Itinerarium*, as it was related to him in 1364 in Norway, by a Franciscan monk who had met the author. It contains a description of the North Pole as a large magnetic island (the Rupes Nigra) surrounded by a giant whirlpool and four continents. The central magnetic mountain being so powerful that it pulled the nails right from the explorer's boats. The enclosing whirlpool and four directional rivers bordering the mountain, were said to change every 6 hours, thus creating the tides. Strangely enough, although recorded in the annals of history, Cnoyen's book, *Itinerarium,* also disappeared.

In his letter dated 1577, Mercator described the North Pole as follows:

> In the midst of the four countries is a Whirlpool, into which there empty these four Indrawing Seas which divide the North. And the

water rushes round and descends into the Earth just as if one were pouring it through a filter funnel. It is four degrees wide on every side of the Pole, that is to say eight degrees altogether. Except that right under the Pole there lies a bare Rock in the midst of the Sea. Its circumference is almost 33 French miles, and it is all of magnetic Stone.

Mercator's projection map, which can be viewed online, shows the North Pole as a large circular landmass, completely surrounded by ocean, with all Earth's continents laying beyond. Much like the description in Genesis of the original Eden, this vast island contains a central body of presumably, fresh water, from which 4 major rivers flow into the surrounding ocean. At the precise centre of the central body of water, stands Rupes Nigra, a large magnetic mountain, from which radiate ley-lines in each and every direction. Like many of the other early old world maps, each individual ley-line is clearly marked running across both land and water.

Is it possible that this large magnetic mountain was the primary location from where free electromagnetic energy was extracted from the Aether back in the old world, as discussed in my previous book?

However, Mercator did not explain how he constructed or arrived at the map projection. Being a Freemason, or controlled opposition of the 'hidden hand', Mercator would have revealed the truth, but only a partial truth.

Orontius Finnaeus, another big name in cartography from the same era, also includes Mount Meru on his projection. With very much the same dimensions and layout, it shows a central peak surrounded by water and beyond that four islands separated by four rivers. So what about these magnetic traits? Map historian Chet Van Duzer of Berkley University has this to say about Mercator's understanding of the North pole:

> At the center of the map, and right at the Pole, stands a huge black mountain; this mountain was made of lodestone, and was the source of the earth's magnetic field. The central mountain is surrounded by open water, and then further out by four large islands that form a ring around the Pole. The largest of these islands perhaps 700 by 1100 miles, and they all have high mountains along their southern rims. These islands are separated by four large inward-flowing rivers, which are aligned as if to the four points of the compass– though of course there is no north, east, or west at the North Pole: every direction from this center is

south. Mercator's notes inform us that the waters of the oceans are carried northward to the Pole through these rivers with great force, such that no wind could make a ship sail against the current. The waters then disappear into an enormous whirlpool beneath the mountain at the Pole, and are absorbed into the bowels of the earth. Mercator also tells us that four-foot tall Pygmies inhabit the island closest to Europe.

So what was going on here? Is this a real place now covered over by thousands of acres of frozen ice sheets which we're told are up to 3–4m (9.8–13.1ft) thick ? Not so long ago people seemed to know of its existence and had quite accurate charts to show this as well.

Known as "phantom islands", old maps from all over the world show islands which no longer exist, yet were reported by sailors from ages past. Who are we to say, that the jolly old 'Jack Tars' must have had too much rum and had been hallucinating? when the Scriptures say;

Revelation 6:14. And the heaven departed as a scroll when it is rolled together; and every mountain and *island* were moved out of their places.

What they will never reveal however, is that Polaris sits directly above the magnetic North Pole, and the entire star-system slowly revolves high above and around the circular, stationary, and relatively flat earth. Many believe the majestic phenomena known as the Northern Lights, is actually a shimmering reflection of the rainbow surrounding the glorious throne of God "in the sides of the north" above the firmament.

Returning briefly to the second book of Esdras (RSV), where in chapter 7 verses 3-9, the writer is informed by an angel that;

There is a sea set in a wide expanse so that it is broad and vast, but it has an entrance set in a narrow place, so that it is like a river. If any one, then, wishes to reach the sea, to look at it or to navigate it, how can he come to the broad part unless he passes through the narrow part? Another example: There is a city built and set on a plain, and it is full of all good things; but the entrance to it is narrow and set in a precipitous place, so that there is fire on the right hand and deep water on the left; and there is only one path lying between them, that is, between the fire and the water, so that only one man can walk upon that path. If now that city is given to a man for an inheritance, how will the heir receive his inheritance unless he passes through the danger set before him?

Then in chapter 7 verse 26, the angel informs Esdras;

For behold, the time will come, when the signs which I have foretold to you will come to pass, that the *city* which now is *not* seen shall ***appear***, and the *land* which now is ***hidden*** shall be disclosed.

This now unseen city which will appear, I suspect, is in reference to the New Jerusalem which comes down from heaven, and prepared as a bride for her husband. *(Revelation 21:2.)* This occurs beyond the final judgement however, and in the new heavens and new earth. On the other hand, there is most likely a hidden location somewhere on this earth, which is referred to in *Revelation 20:9* as 'the beloved city' and 'the camp of the saints'.

Mercator's letter of 1577, in my view, is all part of the controllers "hidden lands" agenda, where some, but only partial truths are revealed. Four centuries would pass, before the hidden land agenda really kicked off in earnest again. This time, with the 33 degree Freemason, Admiral Richard E. Byrd at the helm. Unlike the books of old, such as '*The Inventio Fortunata*' and Jacobus Cnoyen's *Itinerarium,* which both mysteriously disappeared, *Admiral Byrd's Secret Diary* mysteriously appeared on the scene, around 70 years after his death.

Byrd's legacy was twofold in my opinion, in the sense of promoting both the hollow-earth theory, as well as the theory of physical continuity. For a hollow earth suggests our place of residence is upon a massive spinning globe, whereas physical continuity suggests that earth exists upon a continuous horizontal plane. In other words, if one were to travel beyond the southerly extremities of the known earth, one would continue outwards at the same level, and into the great unknown. On the other hand, if one were to travel beyond the presumed north pole, one would continue through an opening in the surface and enter an inner world, within the earth itself.

For this is exactly what the admiral, or the fraudsters who wrote it, claim in Admiral Byrd's Secret Diary, which opens with;

> I must write this diary in secrecy and obscurity. It concerns my Arctic flight of the nineteenth day of February in the year of Nineteen and Forty Seven.

The diary closes with a final entry made on 30/12/56:

> These last few years elapsed since 1947 have not been kind. I now make my final entry in this singular diary. In closing, I must state that I have faithfully kept this matter secret as directed all

these years. It has been completely against my values of moral right. Now, I seem to sense the long night coming on and this secret will not die with me, but as all truth shall, it will triumph and so it shall.

This can be the only hope for mankind. I have seen the truth and it has quickened my spirit and has set me free! I have done my duty toward the monstrous military industrial complex. Now, the long night begins to approach, but there shall be no end. Just as the long night of the Arctic ends, the brilliant sunshine of Truth shall come again....and those who are of darkness shall fall in it's Light. FOR I HAVE SEEN THAT LAND BEYOND THE POLE, THAT CENTER OF THE GREAT UNKNOWN.

Between the first and the last entries, the entire diary consists of a series of flight logs which record both air-speed and altitude as the admiral travels towards the north pole. Initially all is well as they fly over vast areas of ice and snow, until both the "Magnetic and Gyro compasses begin to gyrate and wobble", and they are "unable to hold their heading by instrumentation."

Byrd records how it's as though an external force is now flying the plane, and guiding them into an uncharted area with forests growing on the mountain slopes, and streams running through green valleys which shouldn't be there. Then lo and behold, he spots a mammoth-like creature in the valley below. If that weren't enough excitement for one day, he now witnesses several disc-like flying craft, a group of tall, blonde-haired men, and a beautiful, underground crystal city, where his plane lands remotely. Byrd is welcomed by an esoteric master and records how he is greeted in his diary;

"We have let you enter here because you are of noble character and well-known on the Surface World, Admiral." Surface World, I half-gasp under my breath! "Yes," the Master replies with a smile, `you are in the domain of the Arianni, the Inner World of the Earth. We shall not long delay your mission, and you will be safely escorted back to the surface and for a distance beyond. But now, Admiral, I shall tell you why you have been summoned here.

Byrd is know informed by the esoteric master, how he and his people are deeply concerned for the safety of the human race which has now entered the atomic age, and is told;

"Your race has now reached the point of no return, for there are those among you who would destroy your very world rather than relinquish their power as they know it. Your recent war was only a prelude of what is yet to come for your race. We here see it more clearly with each hour..do you say I am mistaken?"

At this point, and whether or not the diary is genuine is in one sense irrelevant, for Byrd's reply is truly astounding.

"No," I answer, "it happened once before, the dark ages came and they lasted for more than five hundred years."

like I say, whether or not Byrd's Secret Diary is genuine is irrelevant, for what did the author mean when saying "it happened once before?" What happened once before? When did it happen? and why imply that the dark ages which followed lasted over 500 years? Was he referring to the Dark Ages as we know them to be, which had phenomenal architecture, but virtually no history?

Either way, the Admiral is commissioned with both informing the US Government of the inner world and its inhabitants, and warning the authorities of the esoteric Master's concerns.

On March 11, 1947, Byrd claims to have attended a staff meeting at the Pentagon, where he informed the President about his experience, and relayed the concerns he received from the esoteric master. And how on behalf of humanity, he was under strict orders to remain silent in regards to all that he had learnt.

So, whether or not Admiral Byrd's Secret Diary is genuine or a forgery, and regardless of an inner world within the earth, the burning question remains. Why include the statement; "It happened once before, the dark ages came and they lasted for more than five hundred years?"

The previous year on 26 August 1946, the Secretary of the US Navy, James Forrestal, organized a naval task force to Antarctica. While American newspapers reported the operation to be just a mapping expedition, its actual military character sticks out like the proverbial sore thumb.

Led by Admiral Byrd's command ship, the ice-breaker 'Northwind', 'Operation Highjump' comprised of an aircraft carrier, twelve warships, a submarine, over twenty air-planes and helicopters, as well as a crew of over four thousand men. Why so soon after the war would the US Military expend so many resources at risk of great loss to explore such a harsh region as Antarctica? This question which baffled the Press at the time, is one that still remains unanswered. It was initially spun as a 'scientific operation' and although Byrd himself said just before their departure on December 2, 1946: *"the purposes of the operation are primarily of a military nature,"* he refrained from divulging any further information.

To this day, the true purpose of the secretive US armed forces expeditions during the 1940's and 50's to Antarctica remains a mystery, and one can only speculate as to what may have been discovered. Is it possible that the US Government (and others) have knowledge of, and possible access to land, sea and ice, from beyond Antarctica? Is it possible that in one sense, they've had no other option than lie, each told in order to defend and maintain the lies we've been indoctrinated with since childhood?

For since a very young age we have all been indoctrinated by the gospel according to NASA, and have grown up believing the Earth to be a giant spinning ball travelling around the Sun. Hence subconsciously believing Earth to be travelling within the firmament which God calls Heaven.

The concept of a Globe earth, even a stationary one presents a seemingly insurmountable problem. A ball remains a ball regardless of its size, and we all inwardly know it's impossible for a vessel to sail up the outer surface of a ball. How do the curved oceans stay attached to the earth? How can rivers possibly flow for hundreds of miles uphill? Why don't objects and people drop off the bottom of the ball, and plummet head-first into the heavens, which amazingly still remain above them? Ridiculous questions on one level, I know, yet perfectly reasonable on another. For science is supposed to be based on observation and experimentation, and to accept an unproven theory, such as gravity, to be a proven fact, is not only fundamentally wrong, it is also quite ludicrous. Where is the evidence that earth is a globe? Where is the evidence for a spinning and rapidly travelling earth? Where is the evidence for a curved expanse of surface water?

From the time the Agency was established, and while NASA have lied shamelessly to rob the American tax-payer and keep the world's public entertained, the real space missions have been carried out in secret by the US Air Force, but primarily by the US Naval Space Command. Which then begs the question why the Navy should have a vested interest in a region beyond the known boundaries of the habitable earth, if there is no water?

Will NASA one day announce the discovery of the long-lost Atlantis? Remember NASA Shuttle names? Enterprise, Columbia, Challenger, Discovery, Atlantis, and Endeavour. Challenger and Columbia were destroyed in mission accidents in 1986 and 2003 respectively.

Our Endeavour is the Discovery of Atlantis, using Columbia to eliminate Enterprising Challengers.

Consider the words of Yale Professor and Donald Trump Science Adviser, David Gelernter;

> The Apollo landings are the biggest fraud in mankind's history, worse than the global Warning nonsense. NASA is well aware travel beyond the Van Allen Radiation Belts is impossible; how can we manage to organize a Mission to Mars when we never went to the Moon?

Antarctica

John G. Hagner is best known as the founder of the Hollywood Stuntmen's Hall Of Fame. In 1946-47 however, Hagner served as a seaman aboard the USS aircraft carrier the 'Philippine Sea' during Operation Highjump.

In his book 'Antarctica: A Personal Experience', John G. Hagner writes;

> A new discovery was made by the Admiral. From the air he saw, photographed and recorded exciting sightings of luxurious green valleys, brown mountains of shimmering beauty and lush vegetation abounding over hundreds of square miles of flat land. It was determined that this area was completely shut off from the driving blizzards that are so plentiful at various times of the winter months. Mountain ranges that reached thousands of feet into the skies were responsible for this incredible phenomenon. Temperatures were warmer, including the water temperature.

Have you ever heard of lush vegetation, luxurious green valleys and shimmering brown mountains in Antarctica? Of course not, for such a scenario cannot possibly exist on the earth that we've all been led to believe is a globe.

An article appeared in the 'National Geographic Magazine', Vol.92, Number 4 (October 1947) titled. 'Our Navy Explores Antarctica', in which Admiral Byrd refers several times to the 'Great unknown' and the 'Mystery Land beyond The Pole'.

A mystery land beyond the Pole? How can that possibly be? Byrd apparently answered that question on December 8, 1954,when he appeared in an episode of the American TV series 'Longines Chronoscope' that ran on CBS Television from 1951–1955.

During the interview conducted by Larry LeSueur and Kenneth Crawford,(on YouTube), when asked whether there was still anywhere left on the earth to explore, Byrd casually but emphatically replied:

> Strangely enough, there is left in the world today, an area as big as the United States, that's never been seen by a human being.

And that's beyond the pole, on the other side of the South Pole.

In hindsight he probably should not have made such an outrageous statement, for at this point, the presenter quickly steers Byrd away from the subject, even resorting to the suggestion that frozen food companies should consider setting up storage facilities in Antarctica. In fact, the highly respected Admiral had made an impossible statement. There is no room for a vast unseen and unexplored area of land on the globe-earth model.

There's no disputing the fact that Byrd was a level-headed and seasoned military man through and through, and one of the greatest polar explorers of modern times. From all accounts, he was highly respected as a most courageous and honourable man, and certainly one of integrity. Would it not be incomprehensible for a man of such calibre to make these enigmatic statements, if referring to any known territory? It's one thing to dismiss unknown land as a fantasy, but it's not so easy to dismiss Byrd as a lying charlatan.

I'm no expert and each must draw their own conclusion. But having watched the interview a number of times and having listened intently to his tone of speech, while hanging upon every word he says, and having scrutinized his facial expressions and body language to the best of my ability, I can only conclude that the Admiral was telling the truth. Which at the time I might add, was an extremely hard pill to swallow.

For this vast land area, if indeed it exists, cannot possibly be shown on any current map of the earth designed for educational purposes or commercial use. For all are based on the globe-model. There is no room left on the globe for land the size of the USA beyond the South Pole. But since according to Byrd, it does exist, we can only conclude that today's maps are incorrect, incomplete and do not represent a true picture. This unknown land could only possibly exist, if it were located beyond the recognized boundaries of the earth, and if the earth itself is relatively flat and exists on an extensive horizontal plane.

In his eye-opening book 'Worlds Beyond The Poles' (1959) Amadeo F Giannini records how this hitherto unseen connecting land which lies beyond Antarctica, was first discovered on 12th December 1928 during a Rockefeller-funded expedition led by Captain George Hubert Wilkens and Rear Admiral Richard E. Byrd. News of this astounding discovery was promptly suppressed by the US

Government, and apart from Byrd's comments when interviewed in 1954, (which he likely should never have made) and a brief radio announcement made a couple of years later in January 1956, the world's public have never been informed.

The radio announcement at this time (January 13, 1956) said:

> On January 13, members of the United States expedition penetrated a land extent of 2,300 miles beyond the South Pole. The flight was made by Rear Admiral George Dufek of the United States Navy Air Unit.

Amadeo Giannini records how this remarkable 2,300 mile flight beyond the South Pole, followed a continual course over land, sea and ice. Yet the radio announcement made on January 13, 1956, seems to have fallen on deaf ears.

After returning from his Antarctic expedition on March 13, 1956, Byrd remarked:

"The present expedition has opened up a vast new land."

Other statements attributed to Admiral Richard E. Byrd include;

"I'd like to see that land beyond the Pole. That area beyond the Pole is the Centre of the Great Unknown." "That enchanted Continent in the Sky, Land of Everlasting Mystery."

The centre of the great unknown? A continent in the sky? Was he hallucinating? Did he lose the plot? Or was he referring to the unknown land the size of the United States of America which he claimed to exist beyond the South Pole? A land situated above and beyond the perpendicular cliff of ice rising 200 feet above the sea? Necessitating an operation aptly named 'High Jump' to reach it maybe?

Richard Byrd passed away in his sleep on 11March 1957. The following year NASA was established on 29 July 1958. The Antarctica Treaty' was signed in Washington D.C. in 1959, since which time the entire area of supposedly frozen wasteland has been heavily guarded by the Military.

The treaty remains in force indefinitely, and as of June 2021 fifty countries, comprising around two thirds of the world's population, have acceded to it. No government controls Antarctica, therefore the continent is effectively locked-down, and more like a 'no-man's land' from a traditional and legal perspective. Nations cannot even agree over Syria, yet for 60 years the Antarctica Treaty remains unbroken? That's completely illogical for it defies the very nature of man!

Someone might say; "There's nothing untoward going on in Antarctica. My cousin works there as a research scientist."

Yes, I'm sure he does, but the 'known' continent covers 14 million km sq and there are rigidly enforced restrictions as to where your cousin can or cannot go. All expeditions to Antarctica south of 60°S must obtain permission from the national Antarctic operator or the relevant government department. Until recently yachts arriving without permission were tolerated, but this evidently, is no longer the case.

Joe Public can take a sightseeing trip to Antarctica by cruise ship or plane, but Joe Public is denied all access to the restricted areas of Antarctica. Most cruises to the continent visit the Antarctic Peninsula, which stretches toward South America. Few airlines fly between cities having a circular route over Antarctica. Direct flights between South Africa and New Zealand would overfly Antarctica for example, but no airline has scheduled such flights for 'security reasons'. And by the way, it's not possible to travel over a presumed pole point, and arrive on the other side of the earth, as proposed by the globe earth model. The earth can only be circumnavigated by travelling westward for example, until one returns to their starting point,

There's a video on You-Tube where Pan Am claim to have flown a plane over the North Pole. But it's a very misleading claim, because when you check out the flight path, it's nothing more than a trans-Atlantic flight from London to Seattle via the Arctic Circle. Effectively the plane flew in a northerly direction around the presumed North Pole, and returned in a southerly direction over Canada. In other words the flight was from East to West by way of a detour around the presumed North Pole.

If Admiral Byrd is to be believed however, one thing is certain, the powers that be, along with our prestigious world leaders, are fully aware that the Earth is not a globe in the sense we are led to believe.

Well, what do you know? In 1972 NASA presented the 'Blue Marble' to the world, a globe in all its glory which included the entire south polar ice cap.

The "blue marble" is a figment of the imagination which even NASA admit is fake. Nevertheless, they would have us all believe that we live within the firmament which God calls Heaven, and which he specifically formed to contain the celestial bodies. Furthermore they would have us believe that Earth is a giant spinning ball, zooming around the central sun. it is all a pack of lies, which is confirmed by the word of God. For the Bible describes the earth as being motionless, circular and spread out flat, and existing beneath the firmament which God calls Heaven, and not within it.

The Ark of Gabriel

Though historically unconfirmed, the story goes that the Ark of Gabriel is a box containing a series of end-time messages, allegedly written by angels called 'Watchers' and given to the followers of Muhammad to be opened at the end of the age. Like a Dan Brown novel, the messages were hidden in the Hira Cave near Mecca, where Muslims believe the Angel Gabriel revealed the Quran to Muhammad on Laylat al-Qadr (the 'Night of Power.')

There is never a shortage of fakers and de-bunkers, and in a world gone mad, uploaded disinformation is a tool frequently used, especially by the CIA and other government agencies, to confuse and muddy the waters. On his website, 'What Does It Mean', CIA DIS-Information asset David Booth aka Sorcha Faal states;

> Western governments and their intelligence services actively campaign against the information found in these reports so as not to alarm their citizens about THE MANY CATASTROPHIC EARTH CHANGES AND EVENTS TO COME, a stance that the Sisters of Sorcha Faal strongly disagrees with in believing that it is every human beings right to know the truth.

The name, 'Sorcha Faal', comes from the ancient Gaelic language of Ireland, the 'Emerald Isle', and has the meaning of:'She who brings Light to the dark and barren place.' A Luciferian word play on Genesis 1:2-3. For Sorcha Faal refers to the light of Lucifer, not to the light of God.

Osama bin Laden was falsely blamed for 9/11/2001. On 9/11/ 2015, a crane owned by Osama bin Laden's family construction firm, toppled over during excavation work at the Grand Mosque in Mecca. 111 people were killed and a further 394 injured. Two weeks later, during the Hajj annual pilgrimage in Mecca (September 24, 2015)

4,000 Muslims were killed during a mass human stampede. The death toll was originally significantly underplayed by Saudi authorities.

According to CIA DIS-information asset David Booth (aka Sorcha Faal) however, the falling crane incident and the human stampede tragedy, were both cover stories concocted by the Saudi authorities. The alleged culprit on both occasions, he among others claim, was the 'Ark of Gabriel'.

The excavation work at the Mosque is alleged to have unearthed an ancient artefact known as Gabriel's Ark, which produced a plasma emission, resulting in the death/injury of the 505 victims on 9/11/2015. Another plasma emission occurred two weeks later during the Hajj, which resulted in the deaths of a further 4,000 Muslims. The Custodian of the Islamic Mosque, reportedly contacted Patriarch Kirill, an alleged paedophile and the head of the powerful Russian Orthodox Church, who in turn contacted the alleged paedophile, Pope Francis. On hearing the news, Russian President Vladimir Putin reportedly dispatched the naval research vessel 'Admiral Vladimisky' to collect the ark from the Saudi port of Jeddah (the gateway to Mecca) and transport it to the Antarctic.

Strangely enough, some of this is actually True. The Antarctica-bound Admiral Vladimirsky left Northwest Russia's Kronstadt on what was termed a "unique research expedition" on November 6, 2015, to arrive at the port at Jeddah on December 16. The reason for its call there has not been officially explained, with Russian media merely reporting the venture as a "business visit" and as "carrying on its campaign according to the plan". The unprecedented mission being undertaken by the Admiral Vladimisky research vessel, was the Federation's first Antarctica expedition in 30 years.

It is also strangely true, that for the first time in history since the Great Schism of 1054 which divided the Christian church East from West, that the heads of the powerful Russian Orthodox Church and the Church of Rome met together on February 12, 2016. The highly secretive three hour meeting between Pope Francis and Russian Patriarch Kirill was held in a VIP lounge at José Martí International Airport near Havana, Cuba. The purpose of the meeting according to the official version, was to ensure the Japanese and Korean armed forces aligned with the Russian, US and European military alliance.

Nothing happens in politics by chance however, and the following week on February 18, Patriarch Kirill visited a Russian outpost in Antarctica, reportedly to see the penguins. Kirill was photographed blessing the icy waters, and is alleged to have blessed the Ark of Gabriel during a service held at the Russian Orthodox 'Church of the Life Giving Trinity'; the only church in Antarctica.

Again, nothing happens in politics by chance, and later that year on November 9, U.S. Secretary of State and Brotherhood of Death member, John Kerry, landed in Antarctica, during the peak of the U.S. Presidential Election. The question many American citizens asked at the time; why would the serving Secretary of State leave the U.S. at such a critical time just to observe global warming patterns in Antarctica? Stranger still was the December 1st medical evacuation of 33 Degree Freemason Buzz Aldrin, out of Antarctica, after a surprise visit there, apparently to become "the oldest person to reach the South Pole at the age of 86." On 7 Dec. 2016 Buzz Aldrin Tweeted, "We are all in danger; It is Evil itself." Shortly thereafter, Buzz Aldrin's tweet was deleted. But not before a number of keen-eyed viewers had taken a screen-shot.

The toppling crane and the human stampede incidents were blamed on Gabriel's Ark which was blessed by Pope Francis and Russian Orthodox Patriarch Kirill, before allegedly being taken to Antarctica by a Russian naval flotilla. A Pentagon spokesman said at the time that Kirill went to Antarctica "to extend Russian claims much like papal bulls that gave Spain much of the new world." However, there is almost certainly more to this than a simple claim on a military-protected area of frozen waste land.

Why all the secrecy? What's in Antarctica? Possibly dozens of scalar EM energy facilities capable of causing earthquakes in diverse places. Gabriel's Ark is a fake, and a possible future Scapegoat for the use of scalar EM weapons on a world-wide scale.

On the other hand, should genuine evidence actually exist, which can then be promoted in a manner whereby that evidence is misinterpreted or misconstrued, there would be no need to fake it. I refer to the possible discovery of genuine evidence, ancient artefacts which would appear to contradict the long-held beliefs of the three major monotheistic religions. Evidence for example, of a sophisticated society that once dwelt beyond the recognized boundaries of the earth. Consider how much of a game-changer a disclosure of such magnitude might be. And how much confusion it might cause for both the religious and the secular world alike. History as we know it today would need to be completely re-written.

The camp of the saints and the blessed city are evidently located on the earth somewhere. Is it possible they are located on a hidden land? The camp of the saints only appears once in the Bible, and in the same verse that uses the term "the breadth of the earth".

Breadth is an early 16th century English word related to broad; the measurement or distance from side to side of something; width. Synonyms listed by Merriam-Webster include distance, expansion, expanse, extent, field, length, plain, reach, sheet, spread, stretch and waste. None of which are terms one would generally apply to a sphere. According to Strongs New Testament Greek Dictionary 'breadth' translates from the Greek word platos (4114) meaning width:--breadth. Platos itself derives from Platus (4116) meaning;spread out "*flat*" ("plot"), i.e. broad:--wide. The word 'plate' (circular and flat) might spring to mind?

Revelation 20:9. And they went up on the **breadth** of the earth, and compassed the camp of the saints about, and the beloved city: and fire came down from God out of heaven, and devoured them.

Unless Those Days Were Shortened

Not only did Jesus say that the time of Jacob's trouble for Israel was worse than anything the world would ever experience again, he also said things would be so bad, that without Divine intervention in time, and for the sake of the chosen, humanity would have been wiped out.

Matthew 24:22. And except those days should be shortened, there should no flesh be saved: but for the elect's sake those days shall be shortened.

So what was really going on at the time? What might have caused the destruction of all flesh, had the days not been shortened? We know the armies ofRome and other nations came up against Israel/Jerusalem, but the Bible indicates that darker forces, powers *not* of this world, were operating in the background.

I've often heard Christians claim there can be no such thing as extraterrestrials, because if they truly existed, God would have told us so. Really? Let's be very clear, by Dictionary definition an extra-terrestrial is an entity not of this earth. From this correct perspective, the Bible is full of entities which fall into the category of extra-terrestrial.

The Bible tells of the hosts of heaven, of living creatures with wings and four faces, and wheels within wheels with rims full of eyes. It indicates that angels use a form of vehicle and tells of the chariots of God and the chariots of fire, without telling us what they are.

Ezekiel 1:14. And the living creatures ran and returned as the appearance of a flash of lightning.

Ezekiel 1:19. And when the living creatures went, the wheels went by them: and when the living creatures were lifted up from the earth, the wheels were lifted up.

This is not some type of Disney fantasy land, but the world beyond the veil, a world which is likely to be far more real than the reality we experience in our own physical world.

The Bible tells of the sons of God, the morning stars; it tells of the the rulers of darkness, the principalities and powers, the devils, 'the ancients', the watchers, the high ones, the mighty ones, the fierce ones; it tells of the fiery serpents, the locusts, the lion-like men and the horsemen, and all without informing us of who they actually are. 200 million entities along with their king, reside in the bottomless pit, whilst there are those who inhabit the heavenly or high places. That could mean anywhere from the Moon to Arcturus, from Orion to Pleiades, or even the 'Chambers of the South', as mentioned in Job 9:9.

According to 'Biblical Training Website', in Babylonian astronomy, because the celestial south pole is invisible from Babylonia, there is no South Pole corresponding to the North Pole, but instead a region called *Ea*. Job is supposedly applying the term 'chambers of the south' to the constellations of this region.

Ea (whose Sumerian equivalent was Enki) was the mischievous god of wisdom, magic and incantations, who since before the creation of man, resided in the watery depths underneath the earth, called the abzu. His wife Damgalnuna, his mother Nammu, and a variety of subservient creatures, such as the gatekeeper Lahmu, also dwelt in the abzu. In the Babylonian creation epic, Abzu (Apsû) is depicted as a deity and a lover to the primal diety Tiamat. She is the symbol of the chaos of primordial creation, who eventually gives birth to the first dragons, filling their bodies with 'venom' instead of blood. *(Credit:Wikipedia).*

Although I give no credence whatsoever to, or endorse these ancient mythologies, nevertheless they all have their roots, however distorted, in the opening chapters of Genesis. Literally Ab='Waters' Zu='Deep.' (waters of the deep.) Hence in mythology the Abzu is the name for the primeval sea in the void below the earth. These are 'the waters beneath the earth' *(Deuteronomy 5:8)* which equate to 'the deep' in *Genesis 1:2*, which relates to the abussos, the bottomless pit.

Is it just possible that the ancient world that perished, known as 'the world that then was', once existed (at least in part) beyond the boundaries of the circle of the earth? Whilst perhaps somewhat speculative, picture this. If the habitable earth and its oceans, is in the form of a vast circle, which in turn is established upon the floods, then what lies beyond? For everything beyond the outer extremities must be considered as hostile territory. Ground-Zero so to speak, the terrestrial 'surface' of the great deep, the abyss?

In his apocalyptic vision, the apostle John saw a 7-headed beast (kingdom) *arise* from out of the sea. Yet at the same time he was told by an angel that this beast will *ascend* from the abyss, the bottomless pit.

Revelation 13:1. And I stood upon the sand of the sea, and saw a beast rise up out of the sea, having seven heads and ten horns, and upon his horns ten crowns, and upon his heads the name of blasphemy.

Revelation 17:8. The beast that thou sawest *was*, and is *not*; and shall *ascend* out of the bottomless pit..........

Remember, "the world that then *was*", is also no longer, or is not, for it perished by deluge back in the heavens *of old*. *(2 Peter 3:5-6.)* So what and where is this sea? The Mediterranean with which John was familiar? The sea of Galilee, of which he was also aware?

Or could it be the waters surrounding the habitable earth, the great deep aka the Abzu, the bottomless pit? The waters which are *under* the earth? *(Exodus 20:4),* the floods upon which the habitable, circular, fixed and immovable earth is established? *(Psalms 24:2).*

This might explain how a fallen angel (star) is able to arrive from heaven and unlock the abussos here on earth. *(Revelation 9:1).* And how a time would come when billowing plumes of smoke rise from out of the bottomless pit. None in the world would have a clue where the smoke comes from, because its source originates from beyond the recognized extremities of the earth.

Revelation 9:1-2. And the fifth angel sounded, and I saw a star fall from heaven unto the *earth*: and to him was given the key of the bottomless pit. And he opened the bottomless pit; and there arose a smoke out of the pit, as the smoke of a great furnace; and the sun and the air were darkened by reason of the smoke of the pit.

Revelation 9:3. And there came out of the smoke locusts upon the earth: and unto them was given power, as the scorpions of the earth have power.

A far country

Moses warned the children of Israel, that if they were to forsake the Lord to serve other gods, they would be invaded by a nation from the far end of the earth, who spoke in an unknown language.

Deuteronomy 28:49. The LORD shall bring a nation against thee from far, from the end of the earth, *as swift* as the eagle flieth; a nation whose tongue thou shalt not understand;

And who are the kings of the north and the south? Human kings, one from each northern and southern extremity? Or otherworldly kings from 'the sides of the earth', from beyond the presumed northern and southern extremities?

Jeremiah 6:22. Thus saith the LORD, Behold, a people cometh from the **north** country, and a great nation shall be raised from the **sides of the earth.**

Daniel 11:40. And at the time of the end the king of the north shall come against [the king of the south] like a whirlwind, with chariots, and with horsemen, and with many ships; and he shall enter into the countries, and shall overflow and pass over.

Jeremiah foretold of the day when the earth shall mourn, and the heavens above will be darkened, yet he referred to those who come from a far country as 'watchers', a term used by Daniel for a particular group of angels. Hence, the 'far country' is not one of this earth. Confirmed by the prophet Isaiah, who informs us the far country is from the end of heaven.

Jeremiah 4:16. Make ye mention to the nations; behold, publish against Jerusalem, that **watchers** come from a far country...........

Daniel 4:13. I saw in the visions of my head upon my bed, and, behold, a **watcher** and an holy one came down from heaven;

Isaiah 13:5. They come from a far country, from the end of **heaven**, *even* the LORD, and the weapons of his indignation, to destroy the whole land.

The prophet Isaiah has much to say about the day of the LORD, the perilous times leading up to it, and the blessings which await the True Jewish remnant when it's all over. He tells how the remnant will see the king in his beauty in a far off land, which I believe refers to the millennial reign of Christ the King. The prophet goes on to describe a ferocious group of individuals, who will NOT be seen by the remnant, which suggests they would be witnessed by others.

Isaiah 33:17. Thine eyes shall see the king in his beauty: they shall behold the land that is very far off.

Isaiah 33:19. Thou shalt **not** see a fierce people [.......] a people of a deeper speech than thou canst perceive; of a stammering tongue, that thou canst not understand.

Who are this terrible crowd? Apart from their fierce character, not only is their vocal pitch so deep it's hard to make sense of, but they stammer when speaking. The Hebrew Dictionary defines 'law-ag' as to stammer in a derisory or mocking sense, as when ridiculing or imitating a foreigner.

The prophet Jeremiah also speaks of this same army of incoherent and mocking war-mongers. He claims them to be mighty men, an ancient nation from afar, and likens their vast arsenal of death to an eagerly awaiting tomb. The Hebrew word for 'mighty men' is gibbor which also translates as giant. *(Job 16:14)*. Isaiah also confirms that God will send an ancient nation, the gibbor—'the mighty ones'.

From *Jeremiah 5:15-16*. Lo, I will bring a nation upon you from far[.....] it is an *ancient* nation, a nation whose language thou knowest not, neither understandest what they say. Their quiver is as an open sepulchre, they are all mighty men. [gibbor]

Isaiah 13:3. I have commanded my sanctified ones, I have also called my mighty ones [gibbor]for mine anger, even them that rejoice in my highness.

Does this imply that the great tribulation suffered by Israel, or maybe even the entire earth, was undertaken by the armies of heaven? Who on earth are the ancient nation from afar, the fierce ones who cannot be understood or acknowledged, due to their deep vocal pitch, and mocking tongue?

Maybe the Scriptures concerning the last days for Israel, has been misunderstood in part, for according to Isaiah, 'who on earth?' is likely the wrong question to ask. The 'mighty ones' come not from some remote country at the end of the earth, but from a far country from the end of HEAVEN.

Isaiah 13:5. They come from a far country, from the end of *heaven*, even the LORD, and the weapons of his indignation, to destroy the whole land.

Joel tells us precisely who is in command of this truly formidable troop, because he declares them to be the army of the LORD.

Joel 2:11. And the LORD shall utter his voice before his army: for his camp is very great: for he is strong that executeth his word: for the day of the LORD is great and very terrible; and who can abide it?

But here's the thing, for although God's 'messengers' normally refer to human prophets or watchmen, Biblical accounts of angelic appearances indicate one of the chief tasks of these supernatural creatures is to deliver a message from God. When destruction came to Northern Africa, the messengers who arrived by ship were not sent as prophets to warn, nor as watchmen to sound the alarm, but sent for the sole purpose of causing great fear and pain.

Ezekiel 30:9. In that day shall messengers go forth from me in ships to make the careless Ethiopians afraid, and great pain shall come upon them, as in the day of Egypt: for, lo, it cometh.

What happened 'in the day of Egypt?

He cast upon them the fierceness of his anger, wrath, and indignation, and trouble, by sending evil angels among them (*Psalm 78:49.)*

Are these messengers sent by God, human? Or are they evil angels? It would appear to be the latter. Are 'the ships' these messengers are sent forth from God in, some form of inter-dimensional or supernatural craft that arrived in the skies and perceived to be alien space-craft? Many of the angels have a form of vehicle (the literal meaning of the Hebrew 'chariot') and there's even a hint that angel and vehicle operate as a single unit.

Psalms 68:17. The chariots of God are twenty thousand, even thousands of angels: the Lord is among them, as in Sinai, in the holy place.

The prophet Joel tells of a terrible but well organized army, who travel from over the mountain range with the destructive sound of flame and fire. Not restricted to street-level, when this unstoppable army invade the cities, they appear to be more animal-like than human, and run upon the walls and the rooftops. The prophet describes them in Joel 2:2, as;

"a great people and a strong; there hath not been ever the like, neither shall be any more after it, even to the years of many generations".

Joel 2:4-5. The appearance of them is as the appearance of horses; and as horsemen, so shall they run. Like the noise of chariots on the tops of mountains shall they leap, like the noise of a flame of fire that devoureth the stubble, as a strong people set in battle array.

Joel 2:9. They shall run to and fro in the city; they shall run upon the wall, they shall climb up upon the houses; they shall enter in at the windows like a thief.

The apostle John used similar imagery when recording his end-time vision, and like Joel before him, he also described how these terrifying entities have teeth like a lion. Around 1,000 years earlier, Samuel the prophet recorded an incident where two hybrids, the lion-like men of Moab, appeared on the scene, and were subsequently killed by a guy named Benaiah. *(2 Samuel 23:20).* Where did they come from? And more to the point, from where might this vast leonine army originate?

For this time it's not just a couple of odd strays, but an entire nation.

Could it be from 'the sides of the earth' as recorded by Jeremiah? and could that refer to lands beyond the South Pole, which extend into the celestial? First discovered by Admiral Richard Byrd, and which he described as that; "Enchanted continent in the sky."

John records how this great and terrible army, which cannot be wounded (according to Joel) is 200 million strong, and is presently awaiting release from out of the bottomless pit, with the intent to bring carnage to the earth, and to slaughter one third of the world's population with weapons of smoke, and of fire and brimstone.

Revelation 9:18. By these three was the third part of men killed, by the fire, and by the smoke, and by the brimstone, which issued out of their mouths.

From *Revelation 9:7-9.* And the shapes of the locusts were like unto horses prepared unto battle [.....] and their teeth were as the teeth of lions. [.....] And they had [.....] as it were breastplates of iron; and the sound of their wings was as the sound of chariots of many horses running to battle.

Joel 1:6. For a nation is come up upon my land, strong, and without number, whose teeth are the teeth of a lion, and he hath the cheek teeth of a great lion.

Revelation 9:16-18.. And the number of the army of the horsemen were two hundred thousand thousand: and I heard the number of them. And thus I saw the horses in the vision, and them that sat on them, having breastplates of fire, and of jacinth, and brimstone: and the heads of the horses were as the heads of lions; and out of their mouths issued fire and smoke and brimstone. By these three was the third part of men killed, by fire, smoke, and brimstone, which issued out of their mouths.

Whether or not the 200 million 'horsemen' and/or the 'locusts' are physical or spirit entities is perhaps debatable. But either way, because the apostle John goes to great lengths to describe this multitude of otherworldly beings in such graphic detail, it does beg the question why he would bother to do so if they would turn out to be invisible?

When the bottomless pit was opened, and its occupants flooded into the world, from a perspective on earth, it would surely appear as an invasion from outer space aka heaven or the firmament.

Genesis 1:8. And God called the firmament Heaven.

Revelation 12:7. And there was war in heaven: Michael and his angels fought against the dragon; and the dragon fought and his angels....

Revelation 12:9. And the great dragon was cast out, that old serpent, called the Devil, and Satan, which deceiveth the whole world: he was cast out into the earth, and his angels were cast out with him.

Revelation 9:1-3. And the fifth angel sounded, and I saw a star fall from heaven unto the earth: and to him was given the key of the bottomless pit. And he opened the bottomless pit; and there arose a smoke out of the pit,.....And there came out of the smoke locusts upon the earth: and unto them was given power, as the scorpions of the earth have power.

Locusts

Revelation 9:7-10 (paraphrased.) Each 'locust' is much like a war-horse, but a war-horse with wings, a crown of gold, and a metallic breastplate. Each has the power to inflict pain upon mankind for five months, by means of a sting at the end of a scorpion-like tail. Although each has hair like a woman, his face is that of a man, except for his teeth, which resemble the teeth of a lion.

In the Book of Revelation, John reveals the king of 'the locusts' by name, and does so in both the Hebrew and the Greek tongue. By so doing, the prophet not only shows that the 'king' of the abyss would be connected with both the Jews and the Gentiles, but also reveals his true identity. For in both languages Abbadon and Apollyon mean 'the Destroyer'.

Revelation 9:11. And they [the locusts] had a king over them, which is the angel of the bottomless pit, whose name in the Hebrew tongue is Abaddon, but in the Greek tongue hath his name Apollyon.

It would seem that rather than kill them outright, for a period of five months this brutal and terrible army of locusts will inflict great suffering and pain upon those without God's seal of protection. *(Revelation 9:4)*. Worse than anything envisioned by film director Ridley Scott, man would be tortured and terrified beyond belief. Little wonder then, that when the powers of heaven are shaken and the earth is invaded, mass heart-failure would inflict mankind.

Matthew 24:21. For then shall be great tribulation, such as was not since the beginning of the world to this time, no, nor ever shall be.

Isaiah 13:7. Therefore shall all hands be faint, and every man's heart shall melt:

Luke 21:26. Men's hearts failing them for fear, and for looking after those things which are coming on the earth: for the powers of heaven shall be shaken.

Yet these prophecies concerning the great tribulation and the second coming of Christ, were fulfilled when Jesus, followed by the armies of heaven returned in the clouds, just as he promised the first generation of believers. To claim or even suggest otherwise, would make Jesus guilty of misleading those he personally spoke to during his ministry years.

If the above understanding of what may have happened is more or less correct, it might also explain the accounts of flying chariots in the skies, and warfare described in almost nuclear terms, which is recorded in the ancient Sanskrit text, the Rig Veda.

The past-fulfilment of end-times prophecy , as is witnessed by the Scriptures, and was adhered to by many believers and theologians of the past, have been pushed aside, and futurism is now taught by most Pastors.

However, from a futurist perspective, many believe or at least suspect, that humanity will witness a faked alien invasion of Earth, via a series of terrifying holographic images projected in the heavens above, courtesy of NASA's highly secretive 'Blue Beam Project'. In principle, the deceivers will make use of the skies as a movie screen (on the sodium layer at about 60 miles) with laser-generating satellites and software already in place to run the sky show. With computer animation and sounds appearing to emanate from the very depths of space, astonished ardent followers of the various creeds will witness their own returned messiah in convincing lifelike reality.

Much of this is conjecture of course, but however things may or may not turn out to be, please realize these people who are falsifying prophecy which has already been fulfilled, have planned a grand stage show to herald the arrival of their Messiah.

The United Nations Space Alien Ambassador, Mazlan Othman, (M. Othman) a Malaysian fake Muslim named after Mothman from the 2002 movie, 'The Mothman Prophecies', plans to use Beethoven's 'Song of Joy' as the anthem for the introduction of the new age one world religion.

Psychological preparations for such an event or one of a similar nature, have already been implemented with the film, '2001: A Space Odyssey', the 'Star Trek' series, 'Star Wars' and others, all of which deal with invasions from space and the coming together of all nations to repel the invaders.

Many are currently promoting a coming Great Awakening, a time of Enlightenment for humanity. The big question here is, which Light will humanity wake up to? The True Light, Jesus Christ? Or the Light of Lucifer aka Satan who can transform into an angel of light? *(2 Corinthians 11:14.*

Coronavirus and subsequent vaccines along with scalar E-M weapons and 5G are an all out assault on humanity by the enemy of souls, and designed for deception to bring war, strife, economic collapse, pestilence, famine, earthquakes and death just as Jesus warned in Matthew 24, Luke 21 and Mark 13. Yet all these prophecies were fulfilled more than 2,000 years ago, and everything going on in the world today, is to cause confusion over where we truly are in the Biblical time-line.

If you want protection ask Jesus Christ for it, for this is a spiritual battle no weapon formed by man can fight against.

Of Little Books and Seasons

I strongly suspect, that perhaps the early first century events that fulfilled the end-time prophecies for Israel, were types or shadows pointing to the ultimate fulfilment of these predictions again, but for the whole world in general, in the distant future? A dual prophecy in a sense, and one of the reasons for this line of thought is as follows.

Revelation 22:10. And he saith unto me, Seal *not* the sayings of the prophecy of this *book*: for the time is at hand.

Whilst John was told *not* to seal the words of prophecy of this *book*, for the time is at hand, he was also told to *seal* up some of the words he had heard, and furthermore, he was *not* even permitted to record them. These prophetic words which were *not* to be written down, were contained in a *little book*. Of course, we will never know this side of eternity, the unrecorded prophecies given to John. But we can certainly reason from the Scriptures, which just might provide us with a clue. For the mystery of God, as he'd previously declared to his servants and prophets, was finally *completed* at the thunderous voice of the seventh angel.

Revelation 10:7. But in the days of the voice of the seventh angel, when he shall begin to sound, the mystery of God should be finished, as he hath declared to his servants the prophets.

This angel, whose face was as it were, the sun, and his feet as pillars of fire, was most likely Jesus himself, who foretold that eventually there would no longer be such a thing as *time*. In other words, He predicted the very end of the Ages.

Revelation 10:2. And he had in his hand a little book open: and he set his right foot upon the sea, and *his* left *foot* on the earth,

Revelation 10:4. And when the seven thunders had uttered their voices, I *was about* to write: and I heard a voice from heaven saying unto me, *Seal up* those things which the seven thunders uttered, and write them *not*.

Revelation 10:5-6. And the angel which I saw stand upon the sea and upon the earth lifted up his hand to heaven, And sware by him that liveth for ever and ever, who created *heaven*, and the things that therein are, and the earth, and the things that therein are, and the sea, and the things which are therein, *that there should be time no longer:*

John is now told to take the little book from the hand of the angel and eat it. Which he done, describing how it was as sweet as honey whilst in his mouth, but when digested it turned bitter within him. Hence John describes his experience without divulging the contents of the Little Book. He is then told he must prophecy *again*, but this time, on a worldwide basis. In other words, whilst the mystery of God, as he had once declared to his servants and prophets, was now fully completed, the prophetic word was to be shared with the world in general. Sweet as honey because it was the word of God, but the harsh truth it revealed was a bitter pill to swallow?

Revelation 10:10-11. And I took the little book out of the angel's hand, and ate it up; and it was in my mouth sweet as honey: and as soon as I had eaten it, my belly was bitter. And he said unto me, Thou must prophesy *again* before many peoples, and nations, and tongues, and kings.

This, John did not personally accomplish, because courtesy of Nero the beast, he remained in exile until Jesus returned in the clouds. But we do know that over the decades prior to 70 AD, the first generation of Christians, preached the good news of salvation through Jesus Christ to many peoples and nations. And of course, the everlasting gospel is still shared and preached to this very day.

Yet it would appear, that within the Book of Revelations, there is another book, a little book of prophecy, that was never written down, and I am beginning to think that this unwritten prophecy within the "little' book" refers to the time frame known as "the little season. Which would explain why the Bible provides virtually no information regarding this unique period, and why God is graciously opening our spiritual eyes at this time.

For the truth concerning the Lord's second coming 2,000 plus years ago, has always been contained within the pages of the New Testament. But by and large we've missed it, and the Preterist or historicist view has been largely dismissed, as little more than a fringe movement within the larger Christian community.

Right now, we are fast approaching the End of the Ages, when there will *be time no longer.* Yet at the same time, methinks we can expect the second coming of Christ to be falsified, in order to convince folk that these prophecies, including the War of Armageddon and the fall of Babylon, have not yet been fulfilled. A third world war is certain to come, but don't fall for the deception. For it will not be the Biblical war at Armageddon *(Revelation 16:16),* which has already occurred and disguised in our history books as being the fall of Jerusalem and the fall of Rome. The coming world war will be that of Gog and Magog. *(Revelation 20:8.)*

As I see it, we are all the descendants of the first generation which were born into the time-period known as the Little Season. Who in turn, were descendants of those in mortal bodies who lived during the millennium. Who in turn were descendants of the relatively few mortals who survived the great tribulation and Armageddon. *(Isaiah 24:6.)* We are not in any way descendants of the kings and priests of God who reigned on the earth for a thousand years in their new glorified bodies. For like the angels of God in heaven, they were celibate. *(Matthew 22:30.)*

The Little Season

Many Christians have linked the Genesis account of the creation of the world in six days to a statement in 2 Peter, echoing Psalm 90, equating 1,000 years to a day, to mean the world as they knew it would end 6,000 years after the creation of Adam. We don't know the exact years from the creation until today, but we can get a rough estimate. This is what I was taught, and was told that the seventh day, the day of rest, equates to the seventh millennium or thousand year period, which in turn equates to the millennial reign of Christ. An understanding which I accepted at the time because it made some sort of sense. Except, what if the seventh day refers not to the millennium, as I was taught, but to the everlasting reign of righteousness in the new heavens and the new earth?

The age of Pisces heralded the birth of our King, so to speak, which would effectively mean His literal thousand year reign on earth, corresponded with the Fifth Day, or the fifth millennium since the Creation. 5 being the number of God's Grace. Meaning we are now fast approaching the end of the 6th day, or the end of the sixth millennium.

The term '"the thousand years" appears six times in the Book of Revelations, each in chapter 20, which also records how Satan must be loosed for "a little season." Hence, we have a tendency to compare the little season to the thousand years, when trying to figure out the length of time of the former. Using this comparison, we conclude that the little season can be no more than a possible 250 years, and maybe even far less.

Because many have proposed the little season began during the seventeen hundreds, it's hard to believe that after 300 plus years, we are still living in it. I also find it hard to believe that the little season actually began in the eighteenth century.

But what if the reason for the "thousand years" being mentioned six times in Revelations 20, is because the world, or age that began with Adam, will end after six millennia? From a perspective of 6,000 years, then the little season would likely be far longer than the approximate 250 years when comparing it to a thousand years. Even a period of 800 years for example, could rightly be considered a 'little season' in comparison to our entire 6,000 years timeline. If correct, it's quite possible that the little season began far earlier than we previously thought.

If we use the Biblical timeline, then Noah's flood occurred about 1656 years from creation, and Jesus was born 2,368 years or so after the flood in Noah's day, hence 4,024 years after the creation. Others have calculated the number to be 3,974 years, so let's say Jesus was born 4,000 years since the creation of Adam.

We know that Jerusalem aka Babylon fell around 40 years after Jesus' death and resurrection, but we cannot be certain when the millennial reign began, only that it would have been at some point after 70 AD, or a minimum of 4,070 years since Adam. Neither do we know when Satan was released from the bottomless pit. Was it immediately after the end of Christ's thousand year reign? Or was it some while later? We just don't know. If we assume that his release was immediate, this then occurred 5,070 years since Adam, which when deducted from the 6,000 year timeline, leaves an approximate 30 years.

Whilst this is all speculative, there is plenty of evidence to show that the standard timeline everyone believes we're currently in, is far from accurate, for it has been heavily manipulated. Anywhere from 700 to 1,000 years of world history, appears to be missing from the timeline.

Agenda 2030 has been set by the controllers for a reason. If we take into account that a possible 7-900 years has been tinkered with, could that reason be that by the year 2030, we have virtually reached the end of the 6,000 years that started with Adam?

An Astrological Age is considered to be from 2,000 to 2,160 years.

The celestial bodies are a divine time-piece given for signs, and for seasons, and for days, and years: (*Genesis 1:14*). Hence others say, 1656 years are recorded in Genesis from the creation of Adam to the flood. We know from astrological time keeping the spring equinox sunrise was in Taurus as the world emerged from the flood; soon after which the age of Aries began.

The first person born after the flood was Canaan, the cursed bloodline, and the most likely candidate for Sargon (*Isaiah 20:1*) who became the first legitimate king of the world with the title Sarru-kinno in Babel. In all likelihood his reign began at the Biblical age of countability and adulthood, which is 21, and coincident with the start of the age of Aries. 1656 years from Creation to Flood+2160 years Aries to Pisces+ 2160 years Pisces to Aquarius=5976 years. Now add the approximate 20 crossover years or so from Taurus to Aries, and we arrive at 5996 years since the foundation of the world.

Interestingly, Masons have their own dating system named from Lucifer; Anno Lucis ("in the Year of Light") which is used in Masonic ceremonial or commemorative proceedings, which is equivalent to the Gregorian year plus 4,000. For example, a date Anno Domini (AD) 2023 becomes Anno Lucis (AL) 6023.

This calendar era, which would designate 4001 BC as 'year zero', the year of creation, was adopted in the 18th century as a simplification of the Anno Mundi era dating system used in the Hebrew calendar. It therefore appears that Masons know full well, that the world that we live in, is literally at the threshold of the allotted 6,000 years.

The Golden Age

Please don't get me wrong here, for I'm not saying the world will end in 2030. But I am saying that for decades, and in their own subtle way, the controllers have been informing us that something catastrophic is coming our way. Warning the world of their diabolical plans in advance, is a requirement of Kabbalah, and the Illuminati have to take it very seriously because Satan is bound to this arrangement by God! Whether or not this is actually true is in a sense neither here nor there. They believe it, which at the end of the day, is all that really matters.

In 1641, Mother Shipton aka Ursula Southhill, a medium/witch was burned at the stake. She predicted wars, air-planes, earthquakes, fires, and half the world population dying just before the return of the 'Golden Age'. By this she meant the Golden Age of Saturn, which British secret service agent, occultist and black magician Aleister Crowley, referred to as the 'New Aeon of Horus'; a symbolic resetting of time to the golden pre-flood age. Theosophist, Freemason, Annie Besant, who died in 1933, predicted that Saturn (aka Satan) would reign in the age of Aquarius, which some believe started on March 20, 2020. This would have been coincident with the birth of Coronavirus, which literally means 'Crowned Serpent Venom'. Whereas COVID means Certificate Of Vaccination ID, and numerically the 19 equates to AI, artificial intelligence.

In 1957, the ascended master, Djwal Khul, (actually a demon) channelled book, 'Externalization of the Hierarchy' was published by Theosophist Alice Bailey. She/It predicted *2025* to be the "Great Assembly of the Hierarchy", the launch of the Aquarian civilization to emerge into manifestation. Modern-day Satanism (the Church of Satan) was born on Walpurgisnacht April 30, 1966, in the 'Black House', aka 'Hotel California' (made famous by the Eagles) in San Francisco. Church founder and author of the 'Satanic Bible', Anton LaVey, proclaimed 1966 as 'Anno Satanae' (Year One Satan). In 1968, Anton LaVey recorded Satanic Mass; the limited edition of the recording was released on Walpurgisnacht; April 30, 2019.

In 1968, the film Rosemary's Baby was released, depicting the birth of Antichrist. Rosemary is impregnated by Satan played by Anton

LaVey. American rock band,The Grateful Dead, released the song 'Darkstar', and Arthur Brown's 'Fire', featured the line "I am the God of hellfire". 'Sympathy for the Devil' was the opening track on the Rolling Stones 1968 album 'Beggar's Banquet', and the film 'Sympathy for the Devil' was released in France. The movie 'Planet of the Apes' was released and 'Hair' the Musical, about the 'Age of Aquarius' ensured London's West End was never the same again. In 1968, George W Bush (George Scherf Jr.)was nicknamed 'Gog' on his initiation into the Skull and Bones Society. In 1968 the first manned Apollo flight was completed and '2001: A Space Odyssey' was released.

Released in 2007, the concept album 'Year Zero' by rock band Nine Inch Nails, is a dystopian vision of the year 2022 when America dies and is reborn. Set in New York City, the movie Soylent Green portrays a bleak outlook for America with massive food shortages and riots starting in 2022. The movie was filmed in 1972, the same year the Club of Rome book 'Limits to Growth' was published predicting a 70% decline in the US population due to a huge drop in food production. .

Military organization Deagel uses statistics from Governments worldwide and also predicts a large and rapid decline in population, particularly in the developed nations beginning 2022-25.

Rockefeller clown, Jesuit Joe's 70% Vaccination goal for the US matches the 70% population drop predicted by Deagel and 'Limits to Growth'. Many Hindus believe the era of Kali Yuga will hit its zenith in *2025*, coincident with the drastic world population drops forecast in 'Limits to Growth' and by Deagel, along with Alice Bailey's predicted New Age manifestation.

As for Kamala Harris, she seems to have played an absolute blinder. On Inauguration Day, Harris played the role of the Whore of Babylon, wearing the same purple suit and pearl necklace worn by Lisa Simpson in the March 19, 2000 episode, 'Bart to the Future'. Kamala Harris is a Boule Society 'Noble Caste' (i.e. Aryan) Initiate, who shares her middle name Devi, with the Hindu goddess of sexual pleasure and ecstasy, who incarnates as the bloodthirsty goddess Kali in the Age of Kali Yuga.

On October 17, at the start of Navratri 2020, the 9 day festival dedicated to Durga the Hindu goddess of the universe, Kamala's niece Meena Harris, posted a Tweet with Kamala as Durga dispensing divine wrath upon the wicked. Durga is the principle aspect of the universal mother goddess Devi, which incarnates as the bloodthirsty Kali in the Age of Kali Yuga.

Many Hindus/New Agers regard this present age will end with Kali sweeping the battlefield of blood with her tongue in *2025*, followed by a return to the Golden Age aka the pre-flood Saturnian Age. *2025* being the year that military organization Deagel forecast a massive U.S. population drop of 70%.

In recent years the Saturnian symbology displayed in the grand opening ceremonies of the Olympic Games, has been little more than a spectacular show of Luciferian occult ritual, with a dose of Zionism thrown in for good measure. I refer in particular to London 2012. The 2012 London 'Zion' Olympics announcement made in 2005, came shortly after filming was wrapped up on 'Children of Men', a movie in which the UK has become a Police State. Set in the year 2027, and after 18 years of total human infertility worldwide, society is on the brink of collapse as humanity faces extinction. Until Kee is discovered, the only pregnant woman on Earth, who gives birth to a daughter and a baby's cry is heard for the first time in 18 years.

Protagonist Theo Faron, whose only child had died during an earlier Flu Pandemic, can be seen wearing a <u>London 2012 Olympic Shirt</u> throughout the movie. 2012 +18 ties in nicely with UN Agenda 2030. Coincidence? I think not.

The 2012 London Olympic opening ceremony featured the tree of knowledge of good and evil and Satan of course, a dead baby, the birth of coronavirus, dancing nurses, hospitals of death, the Phoenix rising, and a caricature of Boris Johnson (who was Mayor of London at the time) in a hospital bed suffering with coronavirus, 8 years prior to being allegedly admitted to hospital with coronavirus on Tartan Day, (April 6) 2020, the same day the Queen gave her coronavirus speech.

On February 11, **2017** the Jesuit director of the NIAID, Dr. Anthony Fauci addressed a forum held at Georgetown University on pandemic preparedness. With a smirk on his face, Fauci said;

"The Trump administration will not only be challenged by ongoing global health threats such as influenza and HIV, but also by a surprise infectious disease outbreak".

In 2020 the world bank issued a report of Covid-19 test kits exports by country back in **2017**.

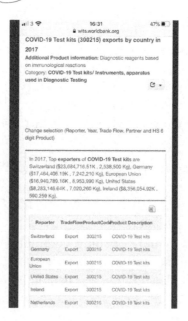

On March 20, 2020, US Secretary of State Mike Pompeo along with Donald Trump and Mike Pence, calls the coronavirus pandemic a 'Live Exercise' whilst live on CNN. Trump retorts "I wish you would have told us". "This is not about retribution," Pompeo explains "This matter is going forward — we are in a live exercise here to get this right." The following day, Mick Muvaney, Trump's Jesuit Chief of Staff calls Coronavirus a 'Hoax', and Mike Pompeo refuses to answer Jesuit representative Ted Lieu's repeated question; "Is Coronavirus a Hoax?"

On April 22, 2020, the Jesuit CDC Director Robert Redfield said; "The new challenge with Covid-19 is to convince everyone to get a Swine Flu Vaccine in the summer of 2020".

Meanwhile back in 2018, the BBC aired a documentary called 'Contagion! The BBC Four 'Pandemic', which disclosed the results of a citizen-science experiment: a simulation model of a pandemic influenza-like outbreak in the town of *Haslemere*, Surrey, UK.

On 28 February, 2020, the first confirmed UK case of Coronavirus was reported in *Haslemere*, the epicentre of the BBC's simulation model, would you believe? About as coincidental as the Bill Gates funded patent holder for Coronavirus, the Pirbright Institute, being just a few miles up the road from Haslemere, wouldn't you say?

In 2020 the World Bank website 'Covid-19 Strategic Preparedness and Response Program' reports the expected program closing date is March 31, *2025*.

On June 10, 2021, the Westminster City Council issued a Tender Notice to cover all of the 32 London boroughs and the city of London. The tender was for temporary body storage units in the event of excess deaths, with a specified contract end date of 21, June, *2025*.

The Shadow government, the controllers of the matrix, have long been showing us that 2022-2025 are the pivotal years for humanity. The world we know is rapidly collapsing into a totalitarian medical police state, where the ultimate goal is constant government surveillance of your location, your vaccine compliance, your medication compliance, your speech compliance and your total obedience to the medical police state regime that's killing you.

The Crimson Worm

Talmudic Rabbis open their Synagogues of Satan with the Vulcan Salute, a physical representation of the Hebrew letter Shin. Shin is symbolized by 3 nails commemorating the nails used to fasten Jesus to the tree amid the 2 crucified thieves. The 6 uplifted arms around Jesus' body formed the 7 branch candlestick Moses constructed for the tabernacle. The Pharisees knew this then and know this now.

Matthew 27:38. Then were there *two thieves* crucified with him, one on the right hand, and another on the left.

Deuteronomy 21:23. And if a man [….......] be put to death, and thou hang him on a *tree*: His body shall not remain all night upon the tree, but thou shalt in any wise bury him that day (for he that is hanged *is accursed* of God;)

Acts 13:29 And when they had fulfilled all that was written of him, they took him down from the *tree* and laid him in a sepulchre.

Galatians 3:13. Christ hath *redeemed us* from the *curse* of the *law*, being made a *curse* for *us*: for it is written, Cursed *is* every one that hangeth on a *tree*.

During his final hours, Jesus makes several allusions to Psalm 22, the most well known being; "My God, my God, why hast thou forsaken me?" These would be his last spoken words as flesh and blood, the only Aramaic (Syrian) words spoken, whilst hanging on the Tree.

Matthew 27:46. And about the ninth hour Jesus cried with a loud voice, saying, Eli, Eli, lama sabachthani? that is to say, My God, my God, why hast thou forsaken me?

In Psalm 22 Verse 6, the Psalmist says; "But I am a *worm*, and no man; a reproach of men, and despised of the people".

What did he mean by saying "I am a worm"?

The Hebrew word generally translated into English as worm is *'rimmah'*, which means a maggot, and appears a number of times in the Old Testament. In the New Testament, Herod ordered the 'Slaughter of Innocents' in a vain attempt to kill Jesus as a young child. He died of worms (maggots) just like his son Herod Antipas would, for rejecting Jesus Christ as King. *(Acts 12:23).*

In his Messianic Prophecy the Hebrew word used by the Psalmist for worm, is *to-law'* , which refers to a unique type of worm known as the 'Crimson Worm' or 'Scarlet Worm'. In fact *to-law'* is translated as crimson in Isaiah 1:18 and on six occasions elsewhere in Scripture as scarlet. Both scarlet and crimson are the colours of blood – deep red.

Image results for the Crimson Worm (*coccus ilicis*) show it to look more like a grub than a worm. When it is time for the female or mother crimson worm to have babies (which she does only one time in her life), she finds the trunk of a tree, stake, or stick. She then attaches her body to that wood and forms a hard crimson outer shell. She is so strongly and permanently attached to the wood that the shell can never be removed without tearing her body completely apart and killing her. She lays her eggs under her body and the protective shell.

When the eggs hatch, the baby worms stay under the shell. Not only does the mother's body give protection for her babies, but it also provides them with food. After a few days, the worms grow to the point that they are able to take care of themselves, and the mother dies. As the mother crimson worm dies, she oozes a crimson or scarlet red dye which not only stains the wood she is attached to, but also her young children. They are coloured scarlet red for the rest of their lives. After three days, the dead mother crimson worm's body loses its crimson colour and turns into a white wax which falls to the ground like snow. Sound familiar? It should!

Isaiah 1:18. Come now, and let us reason together, saith the LORD: though your sins be as **scarlet**, they shall be as **white** as snow; though they be red like crimson, they shall be as wool.

The scarlet red dye made from the crimson worm was used for the covering of the tabernacle, the robes of the chief priest and the temple veil that Jesus tore whilst nailed to the Tree. Psalm 22 foretells the suffering and death of Jesus Christ 1,000 years **before** he willingly shed his blood on the Tree. The Crimson Worm is a symbol of Jesus crucified on the Tree.

1 Pet 2:24 Who his own self bare our sins in his own body on the tree.

Colossians 1:14. In whom we have redemption through his blood, *even* the forgiveness of sins.

In order to establish the New Covenant in His Blood, Jesus exhaled his final breath as he cried out to the Father and gave up the Ghost whilst his blood was being shed on the Tree on Passover Eve, he was buried, and rose from the grave on the third day.

The **Old** Covenant, was a **physical** contract made with JEHOVAH *(Exodus 6:3)* written by holy men moved by the Holy Ghost which ended with the Crucifixion of the Testator. The **New** Covenant is the **last** offer of Covenant between God and Man; a **spiritual** contract made with JESUS *(Matthew 1:25)*, the same Testator JEHOVAH, made possible via the Holy Ghost.

The offer will only be on the table a short time longer. Do you want to be in Covenant with God? If so, I wouldn't leave it too long before sincerely asking Jesus for His help. Jesus died for yours and my sake.

Make no mistake, for whilst Jesus is Victor and in total control over all the affairs of this world, the god of this world (age) is the Great Dragon, that Old Serpent called the Devil, and Satan, which has deceived the entire world. *(Revelation 12:9)*. He is subservient to, hence works for Jesus Christ and he knows it. *(Matthew 4:7)*.

This world is effectively a spiritual Prison, and Satan the god of this world is effectively the Prison Warden who has blinded the minds of the unbelieving captives to the glorious truth and light of Jesus Christ who is the image of God. *(2 Corinthians 4:4)*. Jesus alone can remove the veil and set the captives free.

Luke 4:18. The Spirit of the Lord is upon me, because he hath anointed me to preach the gospel to the poor; he hath sent me to heal the brokenhearted, to preach deliverance to the **captives**, and recovering of sight to the blind, to set at liberty them that are bruised.

John 8:12. Then spake Jesus again unto them, saying, I am the **light** of the world: he that followeth me shall not walk in darkness, but shall have the **light** of life.

You can receive the Light of the Lord Jesus Christ or receive the light of Lucifer, but you cannot have both. You can receive the Peace of Jesus Christ or receive the false promise of peace offered by the coming Saturnian false Christ. But you cannot have both. Jesus Christ is man's only sure and steadfast hope.

If you have never accepted Jesus Christ as Saviour, but have come to believe His reality and the approaching end of the age, and want to accept His Free Gift of Eternal Life, you can do so now, in the privacy of your home. No qualifications in theology are required, but you must believe from the very heart of your being. And if you struggle to do so, then Jesus loves it when we ask, and is always willing to help us with any unbelief.

Mark 9:24. And straightway the father of the child cried out, and said with tears, Lord, I believe; help thou mine ***unbelief.***

Once you truly believe and accept Him as Saviour, you are spiritually Born Again, and are as assured of Heaven as if you were already there.

Choose your Saviour wisely.

Printed in Great Britain
by Amazon

26130320R00116